BOONE COUN
2040 9101 101 278 5

D1491047

Hundred Miles to Nowhere

An Unlikely Love Story

WITHDRAWN

"Big city girl marries a small town guy—that story. But never more engagingly told than in *Hundred Miles to Nowhere*. It's full of humor, heart, and in the end proves that love always wins. Women will love this book, and I did, too."

—Will Weaver, author of *Sweet Land* and *The Last Hunter: An American Family Album*

"An absolutely stunning debut. Brilliant, breathtaking and hopeful. Korenne is the ideal storyteller: part enchantress, part dogged reporter, wise, studious, generous. Her book is a superbly crafted journey into the unexpected riches of the rural American wilderness, and of the heart."

—Josh Axelrad, author of the memoir *Repeat Until Rich: A Professional Card Counter's Chronicle of the Blackjack Wars*

"I'm a romantic, but even I would have given poor odds to a romance between a man and a woman with different religions, different careers, different interests and—most important—different relationships to the Minnesota wilderness. But no matter that one's a native outdoorsman, the other a transplanted Jewish Philadelphian/New Yorker singer-songwriter! *Hundred Miles to Nowhere* makes you believe in the power of love, and of literature."

—Mark Oppenheimer, author of *Wisenheimer: A Childhood Subject to Debate*

BOONE COUNTY PUBLIC LIBRARY
BURLINGTON, KY 41005
www.bcpl.org

SEP 13 2017

" Korenne's memoir chronicles her odyssey from New York to New York Mills with lush texture, exquisite description, and engaging storytelling. With unflinching candor, Korenne leads us on a thoroughly enjoyable romp through her two worlds."

—Jerry Mevissen, author of *Good Shepherd*

"Elisa Korenne has written an action-packed, heart-driven page turner. Each line is crafted with the focus and care of the song lyrics for which she has become known. You will want to slowly savor the reading of it, enjoying the rich nuances of Korenne's words and brilliant storytelling. *Hundred Miles to Nowhere* is a narrative tale of self-discovery in which preconceived notions of identity are turned sideways, and we eventually arrive at a place where we come to believe that with a little patience and humility, love truly is enough!"

—Joe Jencks, international touring performer,
songwriter, entertainer, educator, and
co-founder of musical group Brother Sun.

Hundred Miles to Nowhere

An Unlikely Love Story

By

Elisa Korenne

North Star Press of St. Cloud, Inc.
St. Cloud, Minnesota

Copyright © 2017 Elisa Korenne
Cover art © Chip Borkenhagen/Riverplace Press
All lyrics © 2000–2017 Elisa Korenne

All rights reserved.

ISBN: 978-1-68201-064-8 (paperback)
ISBN: 978-1-68201-080-8 (ebook)

First edition: June 2017

Printed in the United States of America.

Published by:
North Star Press
19485 Estes Road
Clearwater, MN 55320
www.northstarpress.com

Author's Note:
This is a work of creative nonfiction. I have modified some details to better tell my story and to protect the privacy of some of the people involved. In some cases, I have adjusted the timeline of events; in others I have made two people into one. Some names and identifying details have been changed. The conversations in this book were written to evoke the feeling and meaning of what was said and do not represent word-for-word transcripts. Otherwise, I have tried to honor the truth of my experience and present every event as accurately as my memory allows.

For my sons, Z. and J.,
whose journeys into being—to my ongoing joy—paralleled the creation of this book.
This is your origin story.

Table of Contents

I recited and followed this song-of-the-places-in-between as a map.

– Rory Stewart, *The Places in Between*

It's a hundred miles to nowhere
And nowhere's where I've been
Can't seem to get to somewhere
Though I keep trying

– Elisa Korenne,
"100 Miles to Nowhere"

Prologue

Sometimes, surrounded by the endless Minnesota sky, I believe I have come home. Other times, I am sure moving from New York City to rural Minnesota was a mistake.

It is morning, and I walk the half mile down my gravel driveway, humming a melody that may one day grow up to be a song. Pastures unfold in every direction, separated by copses of aspen and pine, oak and maple. Like most autumn mornings while burgundy leaves linger on the oaks, I take Meadow for a walk. Really, the yellow lab is my excuse to walk myself. Every morning when I start my walk, I hope that, this time, motion will help me outpace my melancholy.

A breeze pulls the warmth from my body, stealing the last skin-sense of Chris next to me in bed. He was the reason I moved here, the beacon that drew me away from the concrete sea of city.

I am no longer sure he is enough to keep me here.

Regrets have escaped their trap again, and I am glad I am alone while they stalk me. Away from Chris, I stop pretending everything is okay.

I unravel a tangle of earphones and select a recent "This American Life" podcast, placing one earphone in my ear and letting the other dangle free. In my right ear, behind Ira Glass's nasal drawl, I hear the background noise of New York City traffic. In my left ear, the chuckle-call of sandhill cranes. I cannot tune out one ear in favor of the other, just as I can no longer be only one version of myself.

I stand at the intersection of two lives.

In my old life in New York City, I woke to a world alive with activity. Trucks grumbled at idle underneath my window, and the air was thick with diesel and the scent of cumin from the Mexican restaurant across the street. The only sky was a thin slice at the top of my window.

In Minnesota, the sky has its own topography. Over a monotony of flat landscape, the sky is filled with crags and altitude, mountains and valleys, color and elevation. Today's sky is an expanse of soft gray blankets. A pink sun shines through a small opening to the east, a crack of morning light beneath cosmic bed sheets. The air is thick with the promise of rain, and I inhale earth, pine, and sweetgrass, hoping the scents might cultivate the barren terrain inside me.

In New York City, I walked a purposeful vector to the subway, along the way accommodating crowds of pedestrians in a practiced dance. Over the course of four blocks I passed eight restaurants, four boutiques, a laundromat, a Dominican bodega, a gourmet grocery, and a Korean deli.

Meadow and I have walked the equivalent of four Brooklyn blocks and passed nobody. We are not even halfway down my driveway. The driveway bends sixty degrees toward the road, and I can no longer see my house, just fields lined by clumps of thorny mountain ash.

To the north, a rotting wood-plank deer stand is poised like a macabre Tinker Toy on stilts. The empty rectangle of its window stares at me, an unlidded eye where hunters rest their rifles and sight their prey. I am the deer before the hunter shoots. I long to run, but I don't know which would be worse: standing as still as I can, hoping to blend into my surroundings, or bolting back to where I came from.

Part I

The Watering Place

December 2005–January 2007

1

Accepted

Forget what you've seen, this is a new dream
Trust me, I truly believe
It's our biggest chance yet, so step up and place your bet
– "The Next Big Thing"

December 2005
Brooklyn, New York City

The first thing I learned about Minnesota was that it wasn't where I thought it was. That was Missouri. Minnesota was between Wisconsin, Iowa, North Dakota, and the Canadian border.

With a New Yorker's myopic view of my own country, this information didn't help me much.

But I was a veteran traveler, and I knew how to prepare for a trip to a new place. I borrowed every book on Minnesota I could find in the New York City public library system. A pile of ten dog-eared travel guides teetered above lyric sheets on my desk, each in turn explaining to me that Minnesota had over ten thousand lakes, the people of Minnesota were as nice as they were reputed to be, and the one thing a visitor to Minnesota must do is go canoe camping in the Boundary Waters Canoe Area Wilderness.

I had never before considered Minnesota as a place to visit, let alone live. I hadn't believed the invitation from the New York Mills

Cultural Center until my neighbor Jane pulled the letter from my sweaty hand and confirmed it.

"You did it! I told you you could get into an artist residency." Her hip canted to hold her front door open; the rock music from her speakers thumped into the cement-block hallway separating our apartments. "You even got a stipend."

"I did?" I swiped at the letter. At my mailbox in the narrow vestibule at the entrance to our building, I hadn't gotten past "Congratulations."

Jane pushed the door further open with her hip, letting me into her haven of modernist furniture and books of poetry. The architecture of her apartment was identical to mine, one floor below, but her sleek minimalism was poles apart from my maze of mismatched thrift-store furniture and musical instruments.

Jane pulled an atlas from her bookshelf and flipped to the Minnesota page. She traced her finger to a tiny dot in the northwest quadrant of the state. "New York Mills. In Otter Tail County," she said.

"Otter Tail County," I repeated softly, heart thumping along to Jane's rock music. The rhythm traveled to my feet and shook my hands, and soon I hummed and wriggled my hips as the meaning of the letter sank in.

I had been invited to be a resident artist for one month in a small town in Minnesota. I was going to be able to work on my songwriting in a county called Otter Tail. Otter Tail. A name that evoked wildlife, farmland, trees.

My glee at leaving the city felt like a betrayal. Eight years after moving here, I was still trying to make the city into my first real home. By the time I applied to visit New York Mills, I had lived in New York City twice as long as I had lived anywhere else in my life. After six elementary schools, four states, and five countries, I had come here to settle down. I had traveled across six continents for school, work, and play, and finally found myself drawn here: the place where I would establish my roots.

It had been a relief to finally settle in one place. To live in an apartment I wouldn't have to pack up for a while. To be so familiar with my street that my body knew how many steps it took to get to the laundromat, the grocery store, the sandwich shop.

Where I would settle had never been in doubt. All my life, New York City had been my true north. No matter where I traveled, my internal compass always pointed to the skyscrapers and boundless energy of the city. I had been born here. My parents had met here. My relatives lived here. Most of the people I had known from high school in Pennsylvania and Yale University in Connecticut had found themselves pulled to the city like metal shavings to a magnet. Throughout my travels, I always knew I'd return. But eight years into my city life, I still felt like I was looking in from the outside.

I was sure an artistic trip to a far-away place would cure this unfortunate illusion. Visiting a world as different from New York as Otter Tail County would prove through contrast—I was sure—how much I belonged here. I would return home from the middle of nowhere and remember why I had chosen New York City.

Jane stepped into my makeshift dance floor between her Ikea couch and the bookshelf. "Hey, I gotta get back to writing," she said. She returned my letter. Her door shut behind me with a steel *clank* and I was trapped again in the dim, cement-block hallway.

Jane was a successful poet. She had won awards for her writing and spent most of her days working on her next book. She was the one who had introduced me to artist residencies—places that gave artists time and space to create. It sounded like bliss to me, a singer-songwriter constantly trying to juggle the freelance consulting I did to pay my rent with the obligations of booking gigs, writing songs, recording, and managing an ever-changing roster of side-musicians.

I walked across the landing, slower now, past the apartment where the faded man with mild eyes lived. He was the symbol of all I didn't want to be: a person still living alone in a tiny one-bedroom apartment in the thick of middle age, never having made it, never having seen the world, let alone changed it.

I intended my life to be different. I would make a name for myself as a singer-songwriter. My Smith Street apartment was a jumping-off place where I would gather myself and bloom before planting myself in a larger garden.

But I hadn't gotten far. In fact, some days I was sure I had moved backward. For the love of songwriting, I had given up a promising international development career. Once upon a time, when I had started an international nonprofit, I found myself talking to heads of Fortune 500 companies in corporate board rooms. Now, I struggled to play two or three fifty-dollar gigs a week. With my first acceptance to an artist residency, I was finally heading somewhere.

The New York Mills Cultural Center had listened to my edgy and elegant acoustic and rock music and liked it enough to invite me to write songs for the entire month of May. One whole month away from the daily routine of subway tunnels, honking traffic, and concrete horizons. I had been awarded fifteen hundred dollars for being a songwriter, plus time and lodging to live and write for a month.

I was going to the prairie to be an artist. I would gain artistic credibility and return to New York to relaunch my life.

I called up an image of myself playing guitar in the midst of an amber wheat field. My stifled laugh sounded like a gunshot in the closed hallway. Guitars looked a lot better backstage at CBGBs than they did in a field.

I hugged my acceptance letter to my chest and scrambled down the linoleum-covered stairs to my apartment, my cozy nest of solace, my retreat from the noise and motion of the city. A velour L-shaped couch took up most of the main room. The exposed brick wall was covered with souvenirs from my travels: two marionettes from Thailand, a wool blanket from Bolivia, a carved fertility statue from Ghana. My wheeled Ikea desk was jammed into the corner between dresser and stove, until work required me to pull it into the center of my living room.

I swiped my arm across the desk to clear a space in the center, shifting a mishmash of half-written songs, guitar picks, and a costume necklace. I placed the acceptance letter carefully on the surface and stepped back to see how it looked in my apartment.

It looked good.

Maybe this artist residency in Minnesota was the antidote to my dissatisfaction. Maybe I would find what I was looking for in Minnesota.

I didn't know what that was, but I knew I hadn't found it in New York City.

The next day I hopped out of bed and padded barefoot to the desk. The letter was still there. "Congratulations." "Sincerely, Lynn Kasma, Executive Director of the New York Mills Cultural Center." It still looked good.

2

Bothered in Brooklyn

If one day we're supposed to meet
Then you're someplace now doing something I can't see
Sometimes I try to imagine you
And what you're doing while I wait here for you
– "I Don't Yet Know You"

January–April 2006
New York City

There was no time to linger in admiration of my acceptance letter. The residency was in May, and now I had to earn money to support my music habit. Today's consulting work included a client meeting with the director of a nonprofit. She expected me to deliver a report on how recently released convicts could achieve self-actualization. My personal life didn't make me an expert, so I had some research to do.

After putting the final touches on my report, I dressed in business casual and took the subway into Manhattan to the nonprofit's Wall Street office. The meeting went long, and by the time I exited the building, the sidewalks were crowded with people in suits.

With a freelancer's luxury of scheduling, it was rare for me to be on the subway at rush hour; I usually tried to avoid the crush. Every molded plastic seat was filled. I wedged myself between standing passengers. I balanced, clutching the steel grip-pole, tugging and pulling against the train's motion as it rocked and stuttered a halting path to Brooklyn. Somewhere under the East River, a seat opened. I whisked into it before another person could take it.

Sitting, I could comfortably watch the other commuters, ranks of motley New Yorkers, bodies touching, eyes averted. Some read, others listened to earphones. While my neighbor napped, head bobbing sideways till it touched my shoulder and snapped up, I stared out the subway window at the flat black non-view of tunnel walls. I imagined green pastures and wide spaces, and wondered, yet again, whether life would be better in the countryside.

I pulled my *New Yorker* magazine out of my purse. As I tucked magazine between elbow and thigh, I spotted a familiar face in the front of the car. It was Jodi, whom I had known since our mothers met while walking us in strollers on the streets of Queens. Once upon a time, Jodi and I had written scraggly mirror-print letters on teddy-bear stationery between my home in New Zealand and hers in Staten Island. Today we lived four blocks apart in Brooklyn. Me, an aspiring songwriter. She, a big-shot journalist. Me, alone. She, with her new husband, Ron.

Jodi sat; Ron stood over her, sheltering as an oak tree. Both were reading: Ron the *Times*, Jodi a book. They bobbed and swayed in unison, an unseen bond yoking their forms together. Their quiet communion was acid on a raw wound. Jodi and Ron read separately, but they were together, even in repose. Surrounded by the crowd, the two made one.

In the gap between their mutual belonging and my solitude, desire cut through me like a blade: I wanted what they had. Maybe this was the belonging I had been looking for in New York City, in my career. Maybe home was not a place, or a destination, but a connection to another person.

They hadn't seen me. I dropped my gaze to my magazine and exhaled with relief.

I should have said hello. I should have waved. I was too far away for conversation, but I could have given up my seat and gone to them, walking my hands across the subway poles like monkey bars. It had been weeks, maybe months since I'd seen Jodi. There was always something to catch up on.

But I couldn't move. I couldn't wave. I could barely look at them.

I had dated. I had dated a lot. I met guys at parties. I met them online. Nothing had worked out. Finding love was not something I could control. It was safer to place my bets on another type of fulfillment, and I was putting all my chips on my music career.

I trudged from the subway. Too tired to cook dinner, I picked up take-out at the Chinese counter with the bulletproof glass. Curled up on my couch, I picked at fried dumplings. I took a bath in my grime-ringed bathtub and soothed myself with a half slice of heavily frosted chocolate cake from the bakery down the street. The purple flowers on my Calvin Klein sheets looked muted and sad in the tube of light from my reading lamp. Sleep was interrupted by intermittent road noise till the diesel roar of rush hour jumpstarted my morning.

On a music-focused day a few weeks later, after a morning of songwriting and returning emails to potential venues, I allowed myself to indulge in planning my Minnesota adventures. All the guidebooks said canoe camping in Minnesota was not to be missed. I started by calling a list of outfitters near the Boundary Waters. I asked each one whether they might have a group trip available for me to join in May. By the time the third outfitter said no, I asked why. "May is too early in the season for most people up here," they said. "It's too cold."

From deep in my memory, I recalled freshman year in college, when one of my friends in Theater 101 used to tell hair-raising stories of delivering newspapers by bicycle during a Minnesota winter. He claimed his eyelashes iced together, and sometimes his eyes would even freeze open. I was convinced he was exaggerating for dramatic effect. Now I began to wonder if maybe he hadn't been.

The outfitter continued. "If you could get a group together yourself, we'd be happy to offer you a private guide."

I signed off and decided to advertise for canoe tripmates on Minneapolis Craigslist, the Internet bulletin board.

Sitting at my wheeled desk in my brick-walled living room, I read three email responses to my Craigslist post. One was from a manic-depressive woman hoping the outdoors would cure her mania. Two were from young-sounding men who thought a canoe trip would make a great date.

I gave up on Craigslist and dialed the number for Lynn Kasma, executive director of the New York Mills Cultural Center. Her voice trilled with enthusiasm to hear from an upcoming visiting artist. After introductions, I leaned the phone against my shoulder and tugged at a pulled thread in my pants. "Is there any chance you might know someone who could help me organize a canoe-camping trip to the Boundary Waters? It's too early in the season for the canoe outfitters."

Lynn laughed from deep in her belly. "I know the perfect guy for you." A siren began to wail outside my window. "Chris Klein is one of our board members. He's an experienced outdoorsman, a triathlete, works in his family's insurance business, and is an all-around good guy. He'll be happy to take you canoeing. I think you'll like him; he's got a sparkle to him."

She gave me his contact information, and I set down the phone. The siren's pitch dropped as it moved away from my building.

My hand was still on the phone receiver when the fantasies began. Chris was a tall, muscular man with a sharp jawline and a week's worth of backwoods stubble. He was the silent type, a mountain man, only inclined to speak when he had something to say. He was a man strong enough to carry two backpacks and row across oceans. Maybe Chris would be my chance at what I saw between Jodi and Ron on the subway.

I broke off my daydream. *You haven't even spoken to the man yet. He could be married. He could be an axe murderer.*

Then I remembered I wasn't looking for love in the Midwest; I was trying to go on a canoe-camping trip. I emailed him.

A couple of weeks went by, and I didn't hear from Chris. My series of daydreams spawned spin-offs, Chris's face always a blur. In the first fantasy, Chris hammered a tent stake into the ground then stepped back to admire his work. The camera of my mind panned wide to show him silhouetted on a steep mountain slope in boreal wilderness. In another daydream, a solitary Chris stood on a rocky shore with a spear made out of a tree branch, surveying the glassy surface of a lake.

Two weeks later, I still hadn't heard from Chris. During one otherwise unproductive day when I was supposed to be creating a program plan for a technology nonprofit but was instead noodling on my guitar, I called Chris at his office.

"Klein Insurance." The woman's Minnesota accent scraped my ears.

"Hello. Is Chris Klein available?"

Typing sounds and distant conversation filled in the woman's long pause. "I don't think so. Who's calling?" The "oo" sound of "who" came out of the woman's nose.

My normal speech felt rushed compared to hers. "This-is-Elisa-Korenne-I'm-the-upcoming-visiting-artist-trying-to-get-in-touch-with-Chris-about-a-canoe-trip."

The pause felt longer than a red light. "Who did you say?"

"Elisa Korenne." I slowed down to match the woman's pace. "Please tell him this is regarding the visiting artist."

"Okay, dear. I'll tell him."

I dug my fingers into my temples and scrunched up my eyes until the sounds of the traffic outside my windows came into focus and then receded into background noise.

I needed to know more about this man.

I typed "Christopher Klein" into Google. A long list of entries about Christopher Kleins filled my screen, not one of them from New York Mills. I narrowed my search to Minnesota. I changed the spelling of Chris's name. No luck. I searched the social networking website Friendster. Nothing. MySpace. Nothing again. LinkedIn? He wasn't anywhere.

The next day, I returned from a gig to discover a message on my answering machine. "Hallooooo . . . this is Christopher Klein calling you back." A cheerful masculine baritone surfed the diatonic scale, relishing every wave and curl of each long flat nasal vowel. I stopped breathing for a second. "It's a bee-you-tiful day here in west-central Minnesota," he said in the practiced swagger of a radio DJ. "I'm looking forward to talking to you." I squinted in disbelief and pressed repeat. "Hallooooo . . ." His accent was the one from the movie *Fargo* I had thought was an exaggerated punchline.

I dumped my messenger bag on the desk and plopped down on the couch, jostling my two curled-up cats. They stretched, disgruntled. I patted each of their heads and called my friend Maggie. She answered with her usual gleeful, "Hiiiii-eee!"

"Maggie—you are not going to believe this guy I'm supposed to go on a camping trip with!" I put my feet on the armrest and scooped the nearest cat into my lap.

"Did you Google him?"

"Yes. I couldn't find him."

"What about Friendster?"

"Mags, this guy is not on Friendster."

"Everyone's on Friendster! Maybe you spelled his name wrong."

"No, Mags, really. Listen to his message." I held the phone to the answering machine. "Hallooooo . . ." The message was even more alien on the third listen. I put the phone to my ear. "Well?"

Maggie's laughter bubbled into my earpiece. "This guy is definitely *not* on Friendster! Wow, I've never heard an accent like that. I thought that accent was made up for the movie *Fargo*."

"I know!" I yelled into the phone.

After agreeing that the only way I was going to learn more about Chris was by talking to him, we ended our call. A bit breathless, I dialed the home number Chris had left on my machine.

"Halloo," the baritone voice came at me live and in real time. I sat up straighter on the couch.

"Hi, this is Elisa Korenne, the upcoming artist-in-residence."

"Well, hullo there. How are you this fine evening?"

"Um, fine . . . thanks. Did Lynn Kasma tell you I was looking for someone to go camping with?"

"She did."

A beat. I picked at a cuticle. It was still his turn to speak. He didn't. "Oh, good," I said. I waited a few more milliseconds, the couch edge digging into my legs. "Would that be something you might be able to help me with?"

"Sure," he paused. "Except the Boundary Waters . . .well, that's a bit far away from here."

"How far?"

"About six hours' drive."

I hadn't realized Minnesota was that big. Chris continued. "It's been a busy time for me at work, so I was thinking it might be easier if we stuck a bit closer to New York Mills. There's a river about an hour away that's a beautiful paddle ride. It's called . . ." I wasn't sure, but it sounded like he said "Curling River." "It'll take about three days, and there are some great camping spots along the way. I'll find some people to go with us."

It wasn't the Boundary Waters, but it was canoe camping in Minnesota. We set the date for the first weekend in May.

When we got off the phone, I logged into MapQuest to learn more about the river that would be the site of my mighty canoe-camping adventure. According to the Internet, there was no Curling River in the entire state of Minnesota.

3

Being the Artist

Teeth too big for her mouth
Biting off a fair amount
All her insides are out
– "About"

May
New York Mills

Between January and April, I relished the breaks to my daily routine when I could book gigs along my route to Minnesota and shop for outdoor gear for the canoe-camping trip. A week before my scheduled arrival in New York Mills, I packed my Honda Civic with all the musical equipment I would need for writing and performing, left a check for the cat-sitter, and turned west onto the Brooklyn-Queens Expressway. Performances with musicians and friends dotted my route. Local papers across the country told readers Elisa Korenne was coming to play Pittsburgh, Chicago, Iowa City, Minneapolis. On the stretches of road between gigs I wondered what would I do with four continuous weeks of songwriting. What would I do in a place where I knew nobody and my only occupation was filling the blank pages of my notebooks? My only break in the expanse of songwriting ahead of me was a three-day canoe-camping trip led by man I'd never met.

New York Mills was a three-and-a-half-hour drive across wide open spaces from Minneapolis. There were no other cars in sight. The thin strip of asphalt on which I drove was merely an interruption to fields and trees, more fields and more trees. There were no tall buildings to shield me from the sky, no people to watch to distract me from myself.

When a sign announced the exit for New York Mills, I coasted off the highway onto wet streets that reflected the sky in long puddles. Modest clapboard houses lined a wide road to the center of town. An old brick building on the railroad tracks had the words "New York Mills Creamery" molded into concrete above the entrance.

There were no traffic lights, just a stop sign with a flashing yellow light. The two main streets were wide enough for cars to park diagonally along both sides and empty of all the things I associated with a settlement of people. No string of pretty little boutiques. No pizza place. No sandwich shop. I couldn't imagine how people lived, and what they did, in a town with such sparse amenities.

Beyond the few buildings and under the low-hanging clouds, a water tower was painted black on white with the silhouette of Rodin's "Thinker" perched on a tractor. The Minnesota guidebooks had mentioned that New York Mills hosted the annual Great American Think Off philosophy competition. Maybe that was what people did here.

Across the intersection, a tiny park nestled along the railroad tracks with a picnic shelter. The wooden sign at the entrance read "Central Park." I almost laughed out loud. New York Mills had a sense of humor—here was an appropriately sized central park for a much, much tinier New York.

I followed the directions Lynn had given me across the railroad tracks and pulled into the dirt driveway of a gold cottage with red shutters. This would be the place I would call home for the next four weeks. Lynn, a generously proportioned woman with chin-length wheat-colored hair, stood waiting for me in the driveway. She enveloped me in a hug and led me through the back door making small talk about my trip. She swept her arms around the clean and airy kitchen. "Welcome to your new home."

I dropped a small suitcase on the black-and-white linoleum floor. The cottage was twice the size of my apartment in Brooklyn. It smelled of wood, lemon, and a hint of finger paint.

The kitchen opened into a living room where another door offered a peek into a bedroom with diaphanous white curtains and a queen-sized bed.

Lynn handed me an orientation packet and keys. "Everything you need to know should be here. Feel free to call me if you need anything. Oh, and no need to lock your doors. It's completely safe around here." I weighed the keys in my hand. Lynn invited me to lunch the following day, spread her lips in a naughty grin and said, "Don't do anything I wouldn't do." Her voice disintegrated into peals of laughter out the back door.

I walked to the middle of the living room and stretched my arms out as far as they could go. I had this place for four whole weeks. Four weeks to write songs. With no other obligations. The nervous tension I had been cultivating for the last week spilled out of me. A tingle started near my solar plexus and spread to my limbs. I jumped into the air, arms and legs reaching outward. "Wee hoo!" I yelled. The sound reverberated between walls, floor, and ceiling. This space was waiting to be filled with song. I sang a scale. The white walls reflected the notes back to me. I almost skipped as I relayed suitcases and gear from car to cottage.

My head was bent over a suitcase when I heard a sharp knock on the door. I started—who would be coming to visit me here? A woman with wild brown curls stuck her head in the kitchen in a cloud of turpentine and underarm sweat. She thrust a beribboned basket full of candy at me. "Happy May Day!" she said. "I'm Pam!"

A vintage skirt snagged on my watch. Before I could say anything, Pam was speaking again. "The kids and I made May Day baskets today." She shoved the basket toward me, talking as if we were already well-acquainted. "Say, I'm on the way to the church but if you would like to come over, you can anytime. Artists always come over to watch television. I'm an artist, too. My husband's the doctor. Gary. We live a few miles out of town. Come by anytime. We'll be watching *Project Runway* tomorrow night. You should come. Good to meet you. Say, gotta go. My number's on the bulletin board inside. Call anytime. Bye!"

The screen door slammed behind her, and all that was left of Pam was the hint of her sweat in the air and the May Day basket swinging limply from my wrist.

I leaned against the doorjamb, discombobulated, feeling like Alice after she fell into Wonderland. The New York Mills world seemed to have different rules than the ones I knew. I tried to mold the clay of my discomfort into yet another sturdy argument for why New York City was the right place for me. I couldn't help but acknowledge, though, that no one had ever stopped by to drop off a May Day basket, or any other neighborly gift, during my years in New York City.

A pang of hunger pulled me out of my reverie. It was time to stock the cupboards. I picked up two sets of keys, car and cottage, and reviewed the map to the supermarket. I stepped out the door and lifted the key to the lock. I hesitated. I was in the country now. I could leave the door unlocked. I tucked the key in my pocket.

Two steps toward my car, a bungee-like pull sent me back to the door. I twisted the cottage key in the lock till the tumblers thudded.

The grocery's produce aisle contained five globes of iceberg lettuce, some pink tomatoes, and a few bags of apples. Definitely no brown rice. I stopped at the car mechanic shop next to the Creamery to discuss the repair of my Civic's undercarriage, which had been broken by a wayward hubcap on an Iowa road. Unlike any service experience I had ever had, the mechanic was able to look at my car immediately.

While I waited, I decided I probably ought to meet Chris before I went into the wilderness for three days with him. That way there would be time to cancel the trip if he turned out to be an axe murderer.

When I returned to the cottage with my repaired car, I called him. He answered with a radio-voiced "Hello." I suggested we meet before the weekend. He suggested dessert the following night.

I went to bed wondering what Chris looked like.

I had a productive morning of guitar and vocal exercises before Lynn pulled up to the house to take me to lunch. She drove a beat-up Toyota sedan with a large crack across the windshield. The roads to the restaurant went straight over long stretches of country till they curved suddenly to make way for a lake. Twice, Lynn slowed for huge tractors wider than the lane, one so high up off the pavement a car could have driven right underneath it.

At a table overlooking a golf course, a woman of about sixty waited for us. She had sparkling eyes and dark hair cut into a page-boy. "Lina is from New York City, too," Lynn said. "She moved here ages ago."

My lips parted in surprise. *Who would* choose *to move* here*?*

Lina's whiskey-colored eyes crinkled around the edges. "I've been here about thirty years, now." She leaned back into her chair. She was rounder than most New Yorkers, but her eyes, dark and fiery, could have belonged to my city.

She explained she had come to be closer to nature. She had followed the Back to the Land movement west and fell in love with the area. Her first husband had left, but she stayed and married a local man named Jerome.

I sipped water and felt its coolness travel to my center. I tried to imagine trading warehouse parties under the Manhattan Bridge for farmland in Otter Tail County, Minnesota. I couldn't.

"You know," Lina tilted her head at me as if she knew what I was thinking. "I'm not the first to leave New York for this area. The town was named New York Mills because it was founded in 1884 by a New York businessman who came here to build lumber mills."

And he stayed? I choked on my next swallow of water.

After lunch, Lynn dropped me off at the cottage. I sat down and lifted my acoustic guitar. It was unnaturally quiet. I couldn't hear trucks idling outside the windows, or the distant sounds of people. My leg twitched. After the camaraderie and conversation of lunch, I felt alone, isolated, a solitary being in the middle of emptiness. Even the vibrations of the guitar strings couldn't fill up the void.

I put the guitar in its stand and grabbed the keys. Maybe I'd feel better—and could get some writing done—at a coffee shop with a few people around.

The coffee shop was in the old brick creamery. Framed prints of cows hung on yellow walls and milk cans filled the corners of a large space with too few tables. A stuffed Holstein cow stared wide-eyed at me from a plastic chair. The man behind the counter was tall and gaunt, with white hair and beard sandwiching a squinty glare. "You the new artist?" he demanded.

I almost dropped my handbag. "Uh, yes."

"What kind of art do you do?" he barked.

I glanced down to make sure I wasn't wearing a kick-me sign that said I AM THE ARTIST. "I'm a singer-songwriter." I straightened my bag strap. "How did you know?"

He raised a pair of pale eyebrows and held my gaze for a long second before answering. "It's obvious."

I extended a hand over the cash register."I'm Elisa. What's your name?"

"Jack," he grunted, keeping his hand to himself. "What'll you have?"

I put my hand in my pocket. "What brand of chai do you serve here?"

Jack grinned."City girl, aren't ya?" He bent down and there was the creak and whoosh of a fridge door. "Oregon Chai." I ordered it. "Where you from?"

"New York City."

"Figures. It'll be right out."

I sat down at one of the pale wooden tables and took out my notebook. The entrance bells on the front door rang, and Dan the mechanic entered and walked directly to my table. "Hello," he said, voice soft. "I may have left a bolt loose in your Civic. I saw your car, and I thought I'd let you know."

My lower jaw hinged to the side as I took in what was happening: a mechanic had sought me out, in the town coffee shop, to provide extra service.

I stared. Dan waited. "Oh, um, you need my keys?" Dan nodded. I reached into my purse. My key chain was a minimalist sculpture of brass crafted in Israel. Besides my car key, it held the keys to my Brooklyn apartment. It was my main link to my Brooklyn life. My hand tightened, metal carving grooves into flesh. I unclenched the keys into Dan's open hand.

From the window, I watched Dan pull out of the parking lot in my car, feeling like he was taking one of my limbs with him. I could still feel the imprint of keys in my palm, but when I glanced down all I could see was the arc of my lifeline diverging in two craggy paths. I picked up my pen and returned to my notebook.

Twenty minutes later, when Dan handed me my keys, a volume of air I hadn't realized I'd been holding in my lungs whooshed out of me. "Thanks," I said.

"Youbetcha."

I heard footsteps and Jack's voice behind me.

"So, you're going canoeing this weekend, eh?"

I craned my neck to look at him. "How do you know that?"

Jack was already walking to the counter. "Word gets around."

My first time out on my own in New York Mills felt more personal than any experience I'd had in New York City.

4

Dessert

Flirt with me
But not enough
Make me hungry
For what I didn't want
– "Flirt with Me"

May

A fist rapped at the back door to the cottage. My heart leaped into my throat. The mysterious Chris Klein was here for our pre-camping outing, my opportunity to assess his likelihood for axe murder. My voice wavered on "Come in." He stuck his head inside, so it canted horizontally and floated, strangely disembodied, in the door-frame. "Hello," he called in a friendly growl.

I jumped from my chair. He straightened and entered the kitchen, full-bodied. Small details made themselves plain all at once. His wide smile showed a missing molar. His blue-collared shirt was buttoned almost to the top. His loose khakis rode up at his knees.

This wasn't the tall, sharp-jawed mountain-man of my dreams.

"Hello." I reached out my hand for a handshake. *Not a chance*, bleeped my automatic, internal, male-in-vicinity radar readout. A list of reasons Chris was not my dream man chittered in a mental printout. *Too heavy. Too short. Too uncouth.* Four months of romantic daydreams disappeared in a cartoon puff. "Good to meet you," I tried to ignore the sinking feeling in my stomach. "How are you?"

"Snappy, scrappy, and happy." Chris did a little business with his hands that involved pointing his index fingers at me one at a time in syncopated, choreographed rhythm.

Not your type, my mate-detector bleated, louder.

"Where are we going?" I asked, voice too chipper.

Chris's hands relaxed from their finger-guns. He wasn't much taller than me. He smoothed short, thinning brown hair and his round face crinkled into a smile. "The Station House in Perham, the next town over, is a nice place with decent desserts." He led me out to the dirt driveway and held open the passenger door of a silver Buick LeSabre. "It's cheap to fix, and the senior citizens think it looks professional," he said with a wink. I smoothed my A-lined skirt and slid into the car.

Arriving in Perham after ten minutes of stilted small talk, I opened the car door, and the smell from outside pushed back at me: meaty, heavy, and musky, dumpster crossed with butcher. I coughed and breathed in again cautiously. "What is that smell?"

Chris's brow furrowed, then relaxed, as if the smell was so commonplace it took him a moment to notice. "Dog food." I followed his gaze away from the parking lot to a bright blue factory. "Perham has three main industries: dog food, potato chips, and candy. It always smells like something here."

Just my luck I'd come when it smelled like dog food. I pulled a lock of my long brown hair in front of my nose and inhaled through it until we were inside the Station House. The waitress greeted Chris by name. I crossed my legs tightly as I sat in the vinyl booth. When the waitress left with our menus, I wrapped my cardigan closer around me. I had no more excuses to avoid his gaze. Surprisingly, Chris's eyes were a kaleidescope of color, at once blue-gray, brown, and green.

"The Cultural Center lent your CD to me," he said. "I really enjoyed it. How long have you been making music?"

I settled into the bench seat. "Well, I've always sung, but I've been writing songs and performing solo for about five years."

"What did you do before that?"

"International development nonprofit." I tilted my head to the side, a bit sheepishly. "I co-founded an international technology organization called Geekcorps."

"You started a nonprofit?"

The waitress arrived with our desserts, giving me time to gather my thoughts into the elevator speech I used to describe Geekcorps. I had been working in a nonprofit after getting my master's degree in international development, around the same time as dot-coms were taking off. I noticed the organization wasn't taking advantage of the development potential of the Internet. A friend of a friend had sold his dot-com, and he was thinking about the same thing from the technology perspective. We got to talking and started Geekcorps—Peace Corps for geeks. It took high-tech workers to small businesses in the developing world, with the intention of strengthening local economies. It had been subsumed into a larger nonprofit before I left.

I took a forkful of chocolate cake.

"Why'd you leave?"

Dark sweetness glued my tongue to my teeth. His interest felt genuine, the searching way he looked at me almost intimate. Unlike most of the guys I met in New York, this one actually wanted to hear my answers to his questions. "I discovered songwriting. And I realized I couldn't devote myself to both international development and music. I was happier when I was creating, so I chose music. How about you? How did you get into insurance?"

Chris dipped spoon into ice cream. "I never planned to get into insurance." He lifted spoon to mouth and took time to swallow before continuing, as if he were trying to decide how much he wanted to tell me, how much I wanted to know. His decision made, he rested his spoon in his dish and started to talk. "I was flailing around in college, and my father called me one day to ask what I was doing with my life.

He invited me to come help him in his business." His cheek twitched. "I said no. I swore I'd never go back to the town where I grew up. So I went and hiked the Appalachian Trail, and—"

"The AT?"

I led Chris into a conversational detour. His outdoor adventures spawned more questions from me, leading to stories of bears, waking up in the middle of the night to flooded tents, carrying his hiking partner and both backpacks to safety when his friend sprained his ankle, and collecting boxes of supplies from small-town post offices up and down the East Coast. "When I got back, my dad called me and asked me again to come work for him. He said it was the last time he was going to ask. I didn't have any better ideas." Chris shrugged, leaned back in his chair, and spread his arms. "Thirteen years later, I'm still here." His speech ended, Chris dropped his eyes to the table. An expression that hovered between pride and shame played on his face.

My posture had relaxed into the shape of the vinyl booth seat. I had been so engaged in Chris's stories and our shared laughter I had forgotten to be uncomfortable. I jabbed a forkful of cake into my mouth and a tine clinked on my teeth, slipped, and stabbed my tongue. I had also forgotten my original reason for meeting Chris this evening: to make sure he wasn't an axe murderer.

As if he were reading my mind, Chris spoke. "So, Pam and Gary Robinson are willing to come with us for the day on Saturday, but I couldn't get anyone else to commit to camping."

My stomach dropped through the faded carpet tiles of the restaurant floor. The whole point of all of this was to go canoe camping, not on a canoe daytrip. But—two days before our planned outing—if I still wanted to go camping, then that would mean camping with Chris. In the wilderness. Alone.

He tapped his spoon on his dish. "I was thinking that, if you like, we could go for the day so you would have a group."

The waitress wiped down the table next to us, and I smelled the foul, moldy scent of old dishrag. A daytrip, or camping with someone I barely knew. My urge to adventure sparred with the city-bred wariness that had kept me safe over eight years of late-night city wanderings. Chris seemed normal, but what did an hour at a public restaurant tell me about what he would be like in the late-night isolation of a wilderness campground?

I reviewed the last hour. Chris opened the car door for me, delivered me to a nice restaurant and initiated the most engaging conversation I had had in a long time. I felt no sense of danger or foreboding. Chris was as nice as ice cream in July.

I said, "No," so firmly that his eyes widened in surprise. "I want to go camping. I'm in Minnesota, and the guidebooks tell me that in Minnesota you must go canoe camping." I heard my Type A-ness and grinned self-deprecatingly. "Therefore, I must go canoe camping." Chris squinted at me, doubtfully. "Really, I'd like to. Let's do the whole three days."

"Are you sure? I don't want you to feel uncomfortable."

"I'm sure."

Chris nodded slowly. "Okay. Want some ice cream?"

I had just agreed to spend two nights in the wilderness with this guy. Alone. "Sure." I reached my fork over and raked its tines through the slurry of half-melted ice cream. Melted drips fell through the gaps in the fork onto my cupped palm. The ice cream was slippery in my mouth. "Wanna try my cake?"

He reached across the table with his spoon, and I felt the slightest bit unsafe, intruded upon. The waitress dropped a black plastic check wallet on the table. Chris swiped it up before my hand could reach it. "Artists don't pay," he said.

The soft yellow lamp above the booth seemed to flicker. He had called me an artist. Not a freelance consultant with a music habit. Here, with Chris, I wasn't another over-educated thirty-something who was trying to make it in the arts while keeping a day job. It occurred to me that in Chris's company I didn't feel the constant need to prove myself. In his eyes, I was already the person I wanted to be.

We left our empty dishes on the table. The conversation in the car felt unforced, our pauses easy and unfettered.

When Chris pulled into the driveway at the cottage, I leaned the car door open, and felt a new pull connecting me to this unfamiliar man. "See you Friday," I said.

"Looking forward to it," he answered.

I unlocked the back door. Chris's headlights made two bright discs on the garage as he waited to make sure I was safely inside. I flipped on the porch light and watched his headlights flash an arc across the neighbor's house and into the street.

In the fresh absence of Chris's company, I felt strangely vulnerable, like I was walking alone on city streets in the wee hours of the morning, my footfalls echoing against shut-eyed buildings.

The last time I'd felt this exposed, I'd been naked in the middle of Manhattan's Federal Plaza among a crowd modeling for "The Naked Photographer."

Stanley Tunick took photos of crowds of naked people arranged artfully in public spaces. Only the edgiest people in the city even knew about him, and he was looking for volunteer models in Manhattan. All my roommate Michelle and I had to do was show up early on Saturday morning at a meeting spot within walking distance from our financial-district apartment. And take off our clothes. In public.

"What do you wear to a naked photoshoot?" I had asked Michelle the night before.

Her laugh was a bark, short and harsh. "Not much?"

The morning of the shoot, a breeze scattered litter across the plaza, lifting the scent of garbage from the street. The minutes ticked through my body. The photographer rose from the corner of the plaza and set up his camera.

I was about to be naked.

Michelle and I shed our clothing with everyone else. Shirts, pants, underwear, bras; up, down, left, right. A stampede of people bared strips of skin to cool air, then emerged from the cocoons of their clothing like tender flesh-colored butterflies, damp and fragile-looking. The slapping of bare feet on pavement made a sound like applause.

My bra loosened with a hook-and-eye pop. The parts of my body that were usually clothed felt cold in the open air. My thighs rubbed together with the strange sensation of my own skin touching itself. I didn't look down: If I didn't see myself naked, then no one else could.

We lay down in the middle of the plaza, bare skin kissing cold concrete, hard and smooth along the length of my body. The pavement smelled of metal and cigarette butts. My skin tingled, bare to the city around me.

Exposed, among a crowd of people I didn't know, I felt freer than I ever had before.

I heard a series of clicks. The amplifier spoke, "We're done. Everybody get dressed." The naked mass of horizontal people rose to vertical, transforming from peaceful tableau into storm of humanity.

Clothed again, I felt renewed, the dust of the streets smooth as talcum powder on my thighs. I had come to the edge of a cliff I hadn't realized was there and jumped off. I had been naked in front of strangers and had an internationally known photographer take my picture on the streets of New York. I had been exposed. I had been me without cover. I had lived, if only for a few minutes, as me, undisguised, unshielded. I had been seen. And it felt good.

I wondered what camping with Chris would feel like.

5

Tandem

You've come to dance with danger
Which is it? Fight or flight?
– "Hunger"

May

Chris's car rumbled up the driveway to pick me up for our camping trip. My stomach bobbed like it was already on the canoe. I zipped up my backpack and the zipper caught the skin of my palm, stinging.

Not only had I spent little time in the wilderness, I was about to be in the wilderness with someone I had only met once. I was about to be away from cell phones and the Internet and civilization for three days with someone I barely knew, someone who could very well—despite vetting him over cake and ice cream—be an axe murderer.

My pulse picked up, and I willed myself to calm down as I walked to the door. I gave myself a silent talking-to: *You want to explore the Minnesota outdoors. Chris is a very nice person, an outdoorsman, and a board member of the Cultural Center. It would look bad if something happened to a visiting artist on his watch. There is nothing to worry about.*

I pasted a friendly smile on my face, hoping it was a suitable expression for greeting a relative stranger with whom I was about to spend three days camping.

The Chris who floated through the door seemed taller than the one I had met a few days before. Triathlon-defined muscles on his chest and arms made attractive ridges in the fabric of his T-shirt. A snippet of my mountain-man fantasy played on my mental movie projector. This time the man had Chris's face.

"Whoa," he said. "Nice gear."

"Thanks," I said, proudly. I turned to hide the flood of warmth in my cheeks. In the city, men who came to my door to take me out—was this a date?—were less earnestly complimentary.

Chris lifted my heavy pack without apparent effort. I scrambled to shove my small travel guitar over my shoulder and followed him to the car, this time a dark-blue Isuzu Trooper with mud-spattered dents and dings.

"Is this yours, too?"

Chris stowed my bags in the back. "Yep." Through the interior of the vehicle, Chris's voice sounded like it was coming from underwater. "One for work, and one for play."

Our two doors shut, closing us in together. He started the car and we resumed our easy conversation from two nights before. The trip was beginning.

About an hour later, Chris pulled off a gravel road onto a sweeping property overlooking the Crow Wing River that, once upon a time in an urban apartment, I'd thought was called Curling.

Racks of canoes and plastic drums spewing bouquets of paddles lined the parking area of the canoe-rental place. The owner and Chris talked about the weather and the state of crops for twenty minutes as I tugged impatiently at raw cuticles with my teeth. How long did it take to rent a canoe? In New York City, I would have been onto the next canoe-rental place already. Then I realized there probably was no next canoe-rental place around here. I chewed the inside of my cheek.

The owner disappeared. "Are we leaving soon?" I asked.

"Don't worry." He placed a hand on my shoulder. "We have enough time."

My cuticle was bleeding by the time the owner reappeared and led us into a twenty-two-person van pulling two twelve-canoe trailers and drove us over neglected gravel roads to a bridge over the river. When the van parked on top of a bridge, my teeth were chiming from the bumps. I arranged my daypack and guitar bag on my back. The men had already maneuvered a canoe off the trailer and into the water.

This was it.

The van disappeared in a clatter of wheels on gravel. My heart hopped like a toad in my throat. I was alone in the wilderness with a man I barely knew.

My feet dug into the shore. From here, I could always walk along the road back to civilization. Once I got into the canoe, there would be no way out.

Chris held the lip of the canoe and waited.

I set my right foot in the boat and balanced, one foot sturdy on land and one foot bobbing with the gentle flow of the river. Water made a musical tinkle against the metal hull. I wanted to be the kind of person who would go on this adventure. I lifted my back foot from shore. The craft bobbed as it took my weight. The metal seat felt cool against my bottom. Small dots of water soaked through my pants to my skin, small tingles of possibility.

Chris pushed the canoe away from shore and jumped in with one graceful motion. We glided into the river. "You don't need to paddle so hard." Chris's voice was sure and steady behind me. "The current will do most of the work."

My cheeks pricked with heat. I was supposed to be the competent one. I was sure I had paddled a canoe before, at summer camp maybe. But I had never known it required skill. I turned to watch Chris behind me, each stroke slow, efficient, effortless. I tried to tune my body to his rhythm. In New York, I could smoothly navigate with guitar, amplifier, and gear up and down multiple flights of subway stairs. On the river, I battled water with each loud, splashing push. My arms ached. I laid my paddle on the hull of the canoe and leaned back for a break.

The sky melted into a symphony of color. Below, reeds undulated with the water, vivid in late afternoon light. The water tinkled with Chris's paddle strokes. I smelled watercress, and its sharp green tang burned away my remaining discomfort. I had no more worry about paddling. No concerns about being away from home or brooding about my restlessness in New York City. Right now, my world was as small and big as the river.

There was a quiet *kerplunk* to my right, and a naked tail wriggled into the water. "Muskrat," Chris whispered. A pile of sticks rose like a haystack from the water, and I twirled my entire body around to watch two beavers *plink* into the water in one motion. A bald eagle sailed silently above us. A wood duck quacked behind an inlet hidden by strands of wild rice. My ever-present and judging internal monologue was silent.

We listened to the flute-like chorus that Chris explained were frogs, and the weight of my daily concerns poured from me like water from a watering can. Chris's presence was a palpable thing behind me. I breathed in the smell of old campfires. Intimacy pooled in the shadows between us.

"Here's the campground." A wave of foreboding battered through me. The river's ease spilled away. We were about to spend the night together. "Paddle hard to the left and run the canoe up on the rocks." I pushed with the paddle, and the metal scrape of keel against rock vibrated up my spine. "Let's find ourselves a campsite." Chris leaped out and headed into the trees. I gingerly stepped over the edge of the canoe and hesitated, one foot at the transition point where the water lapped the shore, the other foot hooked on the lip. Chilled water lapped into my sandal.

"Don't worry, our stuff will be fine here. It's not New York City."

I wasn't worried about my stuff.

I stepped ashore, committing to land, and the night. Chris wound his way down a narrow path through trees, dusk mingling beneath them. I followed. We selected a large riverside campsite and doubled back to the canoe to relay the gear.

I was really doing this.

Chris set up one tent with practiced, efficient motions. In under a minute, he jumped to his feet alongside a fully formed tent. "That's yours. Now we gather wood."

The second tent was still in a bundle on the table. My hands made fists in my pockets. "Aren't you putting up the second tent?"

Chris paused and squinted at the sky, darkening now, Venus glimmering through the branches. "Naw. Minnesota nights are beautiful. I'm sleeping outside."

I relaxed my hands. I could do this. This was going to be okay. One step at a time. Now all I had to do was help collect wood. I turned from the picnic table and plucked a few twigs off the soft ground around the fire pit. When I had a handful, I proudly laid my sticks by the fire grate and waited for Chris's praise. I heard nothing but frogs and insects. I looked around.

Chris was gone.

A vein in my neck jumped. Something screeched in the dark, and then something else rustled behind a thicket of thorny brush. Panic snaked up between my shoulder blades. Being alone with Chris in the wilderness was not as threatening as being alone *without* Chris.

A scraping sound jerked my head toward the thicket again, the sound of tree branches flinging back into position. Through winter-wilted vines, a flashlight flooded my eyes with brightness. Behind the beam, Chris dragged half of a tree behind him.

I had collected a nosegay of twigs. Chris had felled a tree.

"Guess we needed a little more wood than this," I said sheepishly, gesturing to my paltry pile of sticks. Chris didn't answer. Muscles flexed under his T-shirt. He dumped the tree by the fire pit and wiped his hands on his pants. As Chris broke thick branches from each other, I returned to the wilder boundaries of the campsite to redeem myself. By the time I'd collected an armload of sticks, Chris had arranged broken pieces of tree in neat piles by size. He lit a pyramid of twigs in the fire pit. A bright orange centerpiece flickered into life in a nimbus of orange tendrils. I warmed shaking fingers near the flames. My front prickled with heat.

Even during trips abroad, I had never felt so far away from New York City.

We cooked dinner over the fire. Chris stirring the pot and assigned me sous-chef tasks of chopping vegetables, demonstrating how to use the raw wood of the picnic table as a cutting board. It seemed unsanitary, but when Chris handed me a cracker with white cheddar and raw garlic he had sliced on the table, I put it in my mouth without question and let the sharpness and smoothness meld on my tongue.

We talked about the people I had met and the work he was doing. After an afternoon spent propelling myself on a wild river, our modest dinner was as satisfying as a meal at the Four Seasons.

By the time we were roasting the marshmallows for s'mores, I had forgotten my anxieties, and we joked freely about the merits of my slow browning versus his quick, fiery blackening.

When we finished licking s'mores off our fingers, we reclined in folding chairs.

"Would you sing me a song?" Chris asked.

I pulled out the guitar and dove into "If I Had a Hammer," an old folk song I figured Chris would know. I wasn't surprised when his baritone flowed into mine. He had a nice voice, deep and full. When the song was over, I muted the last chord from my guitar strings.

"How about a song from your CD?" he asked.

I blinked. It was always strange to play my music for individuals. The smaller the audience, the harder the crowd. Chris looked at me expectantly. I strummed the first few chords to "Marrow," my voice breaking a bit on the first line. Chris joined in, loudly and lustily, on the chorus. I stopped playing.

"You know this?"

"Sure. Lynn gave me a copy of your CD, remember. Keep playing!"

I was glad the dimness of the night hid my shy smile. I started the song where I'd left off, and our voices streamed together.

When my yawns came too frequently for me to keep singing, I stood up. "You sure you'll be okay sleeping outside?" The pause hung in the fire smoke between us. Why had I said that? Did it sound like I was inviting him into my tent?

"Sure. It's beautiful out. But if it starts raining, I'm coming in!"

My legs stiffened halfway to standing.

Once, when I'd traveled alone to Petra, Jordan, I had attracted the attention of the young male hotel keep with a master key to my room. He flirted with me, then blatantly hit on me, and when I refused him, he insulted me. By the time I climbed the stairs to my room, I was scared. He could enter my room whenever he wanted. I shoved the night table in front of the door. It wouldn't keep the door shut, but the sound of it scraping across the floor would alert me to any ingress. In the middle of the night, I woke, sure I heard the door jiggle in its frame. I spent the rest of the night with the covers pulled tight around me, too hot to sleep, too scared to move.

Here, there was no furniture to drag in front of the tent flap.

6

Tuning In

Will you be my favorite, and tease me when you come to call
Slide down the banister just to prove you won't fall
Will you change the length of your stride to stroll beside me
Then stand on the corner and hold me tight

– "Favorite"

May

I woke up sweating. The sleeping bag had wrapped itself around me in the night, tight as river reeds around a paddle. Consciousness arrived in fits and starts. I stretched my toes into the bottom of the sleeping bag and reached each hand out to the corners of the tent. I had made it through the night in a tent in the Minnesota wilderness. A wisp of down from the sleeping bag floated in sunbeams streaming through holes in the tent weave. I was alone. I jerked to wakefulness, not sure if I felt disappointed or relieved.

The branches between the tent and the sun performed a shadow puppet show on the tent roof. Mad line drawings unfolded like comics, and the river tinkled in accompaniment. I unzipped the tent flap. A few feet away from where I had laid my head, sparkles of sunlight reflected off water. Birds chattered. Trees were dressed scantily in delicate early spring cover, dew-clad leaves beginning to unfurl from buds.

I had rested better than I had in months—birdsong was more satisfying to wake to than diesel trucks coughing and stuttering under my window.

I turned to the section of ground where Chris had bedded down the night before. All that was left of him was flattened grass.

I pursed my lips and surveyed the campsite. His sleeping bag was rolled up on the picnic table. "Chris?" I called into the trees. There was no answer. He must have walked up the path to the pit toilet. I eased myself to the shore to listen to the river's music and wait for him to return.

A few minutes later, Chris jogged into camp in running shorts, panting and dripping with sweat. I asked the obvious. "Did you go for a run?"

"Yep. Four miles." Chris pulled an apple out of the food bag and made wet crunching sounds. A day's worth of canoeing seemed like exercise enough to me. "Pam and Gary said they'd show up in about half an hour. We should pack up." He smiled at me. There was no trace of awkwardness or tension, as if we hadn't spent the night only a few feet apart.

Waking up with a guy usually felt a lot more uncomfortable.

Chris stowed the kitchen supplies into his large pack, and I realized it was more than comfort. I felt cared for. I was in the wilderness with a guy I barely knew, and I couldn't remember ever feeling so safe. I could grow to like this feeling of being taken care of.

A bird chittered at me from a branch above. What was I thinking? I couldn't afford to think about Chris that way. I wasn't planning to move to some tiny town in the middle of nowhere.

With a final shove, Chris made my room for the night disappear into a red sack. I tried to do the same with my thoughts.

While he filled the water bag at the pump, I sat at the edge of the river, toes swinging into the water. Human voices reverberated through the trees, out of place among the gentle sounds of river and trees. The voices resolved into an ongoing stream of a woman's voice punctuated by the occasional male grunt.

Pam and Gary Robinson were here with their canoe.

I hefted my day bag and turned to face our companions. Chris shouted a greeting. With their arrival, he seemed further away than he had moments before.

We paddled in two canoes, Pam and Gary in one, Chris and I in the other. My muscles stretched and sang as they mirrored Chris's strokes.

When we came upon three dozen painted turtles sunning themselves on a fallen log, they slipped off en masse, orange-splattered shells disappearing into brown water with barely a ripple.

I wondered how much of a ripple this trip would make in my life.

With Pam and Gary around, yesterday's ease between Chris and me came into stark relief. Despite cooking dinner together, our shared songs around the fire the night before, and the easy rapport with him that morning, Chris now felt more like the stranger he was.

I could feel him behind me, a tingle in the small of my back. I turned around to catch his eye, to try and renew whatever had connected us the night before. His smile was stiff, and he was soon staring at the water in front of us again, reading the rocks underneath from the ripples on the surface.

I wondered what he read in me.

After lunch, Pam fossicked for found materials for her sculptures. Her fingers—distorted and bleached underwater—sorted through handfuls of pebbles. I walked into the river. Water flowed between my toes. The slow pace, the smell of the earth, the flow of the river satisfied something deep inside me, something I hadn't even realized was longing to be fed.

From her bag of river finds, Pam removed a few rocks, rocks that looked for all I could see like every other rock in the river, and showed me how she was going to arrange them in sculpture. In Pam's hands, the most unlikely pairs of objects transformed, magically, into works of art.

When afternoon started to fade to evening, Pam and Gary pulled onto shore. With hearty goodbyes and invitations for dinner when we got back, they disappeared into the trees toward their parked car. When Pam's voice melted into the sounds of birdsong and rustling leaves, the relative silence felt empty. The space between Chris and me empty, too. I climbed into the canoe, more gracefully than I had the day before. Chris pushed us from the bank. The silence between us crackled like radio static. I didn't know how to bridge the gap, what to say, how to tune into him.

A fish jumped, and we both spoke at once, then stopped and laughed. The muscles in my neck relaxed. We were back. Whatever "we" was. This ease between us familiar and strange at the same time. An unseen link, like the one I had seen between Jodi and Ron on the subway.

I roamed my memory. No, I had never felt this easy with anyone before. Not the people I grew up with. Not the people I went to college with. Not my friends from New York City. What was it about Chris? He was so far away from anything in my experience, and yet . . . and yet.

We arrived at the campground dock. I knew what to do this time, and we worked in tandem, the process of bringing canoe to land and our gear to the campsite now quicker and more efficient.

Chris pulled the tent bag from his oversized Duluth pack.

"Are you sleeping outside again tonight?" I asked.

"Yep."

"I think I'll sleep outside, too." I lifted up my sleeping bag and threw it onto the leaf litter by the fire pit.

Chris grinned and returned the tent to his backpack.

A few car doors slammed across the river. A car radio started blasting country music from tinny speakers. The backbeat of country rock distorted as it shifted over the water, like an image in a funhouse mirror.

"Local teenagers," said Chris, dejected. "Sounds like they'll be here for a while."

I groaned in the direction of the noise.

"I'm sorry. You leave New York City to find peace and quiet in the wilderness, and then this." Chris's nose wrinkled.

"It's not your fault."

"Well, I did convince you not to go to the Boundary Waters."

"True."

I looked at Chris, then in the direction of the bass line coming at us through the twilight. I walked a few steps toward the water. A twangy singer's voice echoed along the banks of the river. I took a deep breath, gathered all my New York City brashness, and yelled, "Could you turn it down?" The tail end of my voice echoed against the slope across the water.

Chris's head tilted to the side as he looked at me, half-awed, half-embarrassed. "I can't believe you did that."

I grinned at him. "Had to try." Another car door slammed. The song changed to one sung by a man. "I don't think they can hear us," I said.

The country music accompanied us through dinner, sounding louder once we lay down to sleep. Leaves shifted under my sleeping bag, and their sweet dampness wafted around me. Chris lay his sleeping bag parallel to mine, a modest six feet away. I closed my eyes and willed myself to sleep against the thumping twanging sounds from across the river.

I could feel Chris's presence through the thick night air between us. I could almost feel his body's warmth. Three car doors slammed in a row; the sound of the music dissipated as the cars drove away. I sighed audibly.

"That took long enough." Chris's voice bubbled up from the darkness.

We laughed together, our mirth melding with the soft lapping of water against the shore.

I fell asleep replaying Chris's laughter in my head.

7

Gone Fishin'

Crack! Crunch! Feel it slide
– "Andy the Lightbulb Eater"

May

The next morning, we lingered over a breakfast of granola and powdered milk, neither of us seeming to want to begin the leg of the river that meant the end of our trip.

Normally, after forty-eight hours with anyone, I would have been screaming for a reprieve. But there was something about Chris that made me want more. Every obstacle—the stretch of rapids that almost flipped us, the miniature sandbar I managed to ground us on when I volunteered to take the rear canoe steering position—was another opportunity to delay the end of our excursion.

Inevitably, we arrived at the canoe rental. The trip was over. We dragged our canoe on shore and shuttled the gear to the Isuzu waiting for us in the parking lot. The sky had clouded over, and the soft gray light seemed as wistful as I felt.

"I'm sorry you didn't get to fish," I said, my heart already feeling the upcoming drain of Chris's company as I placed his unused fishing rods into the trunk. He shoved the cooler to the side to make room for my guitar and leaned a hand on the Trooper to stare at the river for so long I wondered if he had heard me.

"It's fine that I didn't fish," he said thoughtfully, "but I thought you might want to. Considering you never have, and that you want to try everything in Minnesota."

A thrill swam up from my middle and flooded my heart. "I would love a flyfishing lesson."

"What are you up to this afternoon?" Chris grinned at me wickedly, knowing I had left my day wide open to accommodate our canoe trip. "I know just the place."

In the middle of the state park parking lot, Chris handed me the spare pair of fishing waders we had picked up from his garage. His well-worn waders tickled the skin of my leg with a thrill of intimacy.

I tightened the buckles on the overall-like bib. The too-big booties were deflated balloons at the ends of my feet. I fastened my sandals over them, and long fabric toes stuck out like clown feet. I took a few tentative steps. My feet crunched. It must be the Velcro on the sandals. Something buzzed, and I flicked my eyes to see a ladybug split her red shell in half, extend her wings, and take off in flight.

Chris handed me a fishing rod and led me to the water. His manner was suddenly gruff as he demonstrated the proper technique for a basic fly fishing cast. As instructor, his voice was deeper and more remote. I compared this version of Chris to the gentler version I had seen by the campfire. I wondered if I had imagined it, or whether there were untapped depths to this man.

"Pretend your arm is a clock. Now position the rod at ten o'clock and then two o'clock. Ten, two. Ten, two." Chris's fly rod shaped the stroke, his hand tracing the arc of a clock face. His thin filament of line careened after the rod, drawing fleur-de-lises in the air.

I tried to make my rod move as elegantly as Chris's. It seemed important for me to prove to him I could do this, to show him how well I could take on country skills.

Ten, two. Ten, two. I let the line go and it lolled in the air. My loops crossed, tangled and drooped.

"You let it go too early. Once you've gone back and forth a few times, when the line has good momentum, then let it go." He gathered up loops of loose line in his right hand, and I thought I heard disappointment in his voice. "You want your fly to gently touch the water, barely glance the surface. You're trying to imitate how a real fly would land." Chris demonstrated again. His line moved like a dancer: precise, controlled. It glided through the air in descending helixes and placed the fly on the water with no splash, only a tiny circular ripple giving away its position.

I slapped at a tickle on my arm. Another ladybug. I flicked the small hard body off my skin and moved my rod the way Chris did. Why couldn't I do this? There didn't seem to be much to it, no reason I couldn't get the hang of it. My line zig-zagged through the air, snarling up. My fly slapped the water and went under.

"Keep practicing." His voice was flat. He walked twenty paces away and started casting with his back towards me.

I had been dismissed. I swatted at another ladybug. The insect's hard shell glanced off my hand. On my third and fourth tries, I let the line go too early. On my fifth and sixth tries, I let the line go too late. On my seventh try, the fly careened straight down toward my face. I yelped and ducked.

Chris turned his head, eyebrows raised in a question.

"I'm fine," I said, a little too quickly. The water made flushing sounds around me.

Chris returned to filament and fly.

I slammed my next cast into the water. Ten tries. Twelve. I couldn't make my line float like Chris's.

Whatever. I was leaving in a couple of weeks anyway. No reason for me to try and prove myself to some random guy living in the middle of nowhere. So we had a good time canoeing. That didn't mean anything. I reeled up my line and waded to the nearest shore for a break, rod slumped in defeat.

The land, thick with reeds, jutted out of the water. I sat, flattening grass. My feet dangled in water. A halo of reeds floated above me, fuzzy tips moving strands of my hair like ghostly fingers.

In the middle of the lake, Chris stood, the vision of a solitary fisherman. His line flowed through the air. The unexpected closeness that had grown between us was as distant as the canoe we had left on the river. Water lapped against my calves, and the ensuing ripples floated to the other side of the lake. Dampness soaked through the seam in the waders at my left thigh. Great. He'd lent me busted waders. Now my pants would be wet.

Chris dropped his rod and scanned the lake to find me. He waded toward me and, without a word, sat down, making the long stalks of grass shuffle in unison above our heads. Clouds tumbled in slow motion across the sky. Chris inhaled with a sound louder than the breeze. "Got tired of casting?"

The cloud-dragon above me was now a roaring wildcat. "Yes." Chris nodded, and his gaze traced a matching set of clouds reflected on the surface of the lake. "I'm not sure fly fishing is for me."

Chris snapped to standing. His waders shushed through the water to the path. I batted away a couple of red-and-black blurs and followed him.

Well, that's over. Clearly I'd failed his test, too.

I perched on the lip of the SUV's back door and unhooked the bib straps of the waders. I unrolled them from the top to find a few ladybugs dotting my shirt. Wet fabric bunched in my hands. A few more ladybugs wriggled near my waistband. I brushed them off. With each new inch of now-damp pant leg, more ladybugs. I gagged at the proximity of so many insects to my skin and moved faster. Fabric pooled around my ankles. The calves of my gray pants were crawling red and black. I recalled the crunching sounds under my feet before we started fishing, and I wanted to squirm out of my skin. The waders were home to a colony of ladybugs. I had been standing in a ladybug nest for the last hour.

I made a sound just short of a shriek. "What the hell? Damn it!" The folded toes of the waders wouldn't untwist from my sandal straps.

Chris watched me leap and jump and kick, his expression frozen in confused observation. I shoved one foot into pavement and doubled over the other. I wrestled nylon and canvas, pulling, shoving, desperate to escape the once-attractive insects, now grisly and terrifying en masse.

I hopped, hip banging into the side of the car, right foot crunching more ladybugs, then I lost my balance. Chris's face melted into mirth, sudden full laughter escaping in convulsions. Steadying myself with the car door, I yelled, "You put me in a ladybug nest!"

Chris kept laughing. Hard.

My bootie let loose with a tearing sound, and the last bit of fabric fell into a pool on the pavement. I brushed orange streaks into pants, belly, arms. Sheets of ladybugs fell from my body.

Chris was folded over, laughing so hard now he didn't make any sound.

I tore off my socks, encrusted with ladybug carcasses. I checked myself, front and back.

Chris's eyes blinked bright with tears, his breath catching in silent guffaws. He wiped tears from his cheeks, hiccuping words out between giggles. "Why don't we (hiccup) fish in a (hiccup) place where you don't have to wear waders?"

I glared at Chris as I brushed down my pants, hard, with a grease-stained towel. I stormed off toward the lake to wash.

What had I been thinking? This guy was a jerk.

"I'm sorry. I'm sorry. It was just funny," he called across the parking lot. His words bounced against the surface of the water before they melted into giggles.

Clearly, not boyfriend material. I Velcroed now-clean wet sandals onto my feet.

Chris tried mightily to stifle his giggles. I got in the car and slammed the door extra hard.

8

City Girl in the Country

If I jumped off the mountaintop
Gravity would make me drop
There wouldn't be any more to lose

When I get back to the mountaintop
I'll twirl around like a spinning top
Until my heart's been born anew
– "Mountaintop"

May

To make up for laughing at me, Chris took me out to a lakeside barbecue restaurant. Over dinner, our conversation unhitched again, and we almost regained the ease we had found on the river. When he dropped me off at the artist cottage, he tried to hold my gaze. "So, what are you doing Tuesday night?"

I demurred. I had a gig. He promised he would come. I wasn't sure how I felt about that.

The next morning, I had work to do: songwriting, and the business that comes with it. After a morning of free-writing, I drove off to find the post office so I could mail publicity materials to venues where I would be performing the following month. The New York Mills post office was in a small brick building, its lobby checkered with brass post office boxes.

"You must be the new artist." A dainty, well-groomed man looked me up and down from behind the counter where he was sorting packages by size.

I hugged my stack of manila envelopes more tightly to my chest. "How does everyone know?"

"Not hard to tell, around here." His voice was nasal and gravelly at the same time. "What kind of art do you do?"

"I'm a singer-songwriter." I let my eyes glance away from the intensity of his gaze to rest on the wall-to-wall shelving unit of package-filled cubby holes.

"I'm Duane, the postmaster. Most people call me Buzzer." He cut the string tying together a pile of letters.

"Nice to meet you."

I placed my packages on the scale, and Buzzer ignored them. He leaned forward against the counter. "Are you going to be singing at the school for your community service?"

"No, I'll be performing gigs in the area instead."

"Oh, that's too bad. We always love it when the artists come to the school."

An envelope slipped from my stack. I caught it and set it right. "I'd love to do something for the school, but I . . ."

Buzzer bent over to reach under the counter and stood up with a cordless phone. He put the phone to his ear and held up his index finger. "Hi, Ruth. Yes, I have the artist here, she's a singer . . . Sure . . . She's not scheduled at the school . . . Hold on . . ." Buzzer handed the phone to me. "My wife, Ruth, teaches sixth grade. She'd like to talk to you."

I reached my hand out shakily and took the phone, my brows furrowed. "Hello?"

Within a minute, thanks to the New York Mills postmaster-cum-booking agent, I was scheduled to teach songwriting at the elementary school the following week. I handed the phone to Buzzer.

"Nine dollars and forty-six cents. So you're going to be teaching at the school now, huh?" His face lit up with sly glee.

"Do you act as booking agent for all the visiting artists, Buzzer?"

He winked at me. "Only the ones I like."

I left still trying to reconcile the overlap between post office, arts organization, and school.

I drove twelve miles through farmland to Perham, where Lynn had said I'd find cute stores to entertain me for an afternoon off. I tried to push random memories from the weekend out of my head, but occasionally they pierced my resolve. Chris making me a cracker with white cheddar and raw garlic. Chris singing along with my songs. The musing look on Chris's face when he dropped me off, as if he were chewing on some idea, some prospect.

The turquoise sky filled up most of my windshield. I knew I had found Perham when I reached my first traffic light. I opened my windows and inhaled cautiously. No dog food. I inhaled more deeply. Today Perham's air had a hint of spruce.

I passed a store fronted with bags of cow feed piled on pallets and then a building marked Perham Meat Locker. The two buildings summed up the simplicity of life in the country: feed the cows and then let the cows feed you.

I followed Lynn's directions to the town center. The two blocks of Perham's shopping area were flanked with tourist-friendly boutiques and gift stores that sold kitchen wares, handmade jewelry, and Northwoods-styled home decor. Shop owners greeted me with smiles and words of welcome. None of them went for the hard sell. I began to feel guilty for taking up their time. Kindness, at least in a city of millions, was limited. I should only be allowed such kindness from salespeople if I had earned it by making a large purchase.

An hour later, I had visited every shop downtown. I sat in my car, keys poised between purse and ignition. I had planned to take the entire afternoon off as a reward for a productive morning of songwriting, but I couldn't think of anywhere else to go. The only pull was the slight gravity of the artist cottage, and I wasn't ready to return. It was far easier to explore than to write songs, but I had no other destination. I figured I'd return to the artist cottage and read a book.

On my way out of Perham, a brown sign with gold antique script caught my eye: Jerome's Antiques. The sun made the gold letters glow, as if they were flashing to get my attention.

I could always dawdle a bit in an antique store.

The shop's front door was like the ones private detectives have in old movies: top half glass, bottom half wood.

A tall, scarecrow-thin man behind a relic of a cash register pushed too-large eyeglasses up the bridge of his nose. "Well, hello," he said, deep smile carving parentheses into hangdog cheeks. "How are you this afternoon?"

I felt awkward again. There was too much individualized attention from shopkeepers in small towns. "I'm . . . I'm well, thanks. How are you?"

"Just dandy. It's a beautiful day today."

I nodded, running my fingers along the rim of a ceramic bowl.

"You wouldn't be the artist at the Cultural Center this month, would you?"

"Yes. How—"

"Well, first off, you don't look like you're from around here. And second," his ginger mustache twitched. "I'm married to Lina." Lina, the former New Yorker I had met at lunch the other day. "I'm Jerome." His large, calloused hand engulfed mine in a warm handshake. "Welcome to Minnesota! How do you like it?" His Minnesota vowels were as flat as Chris's.

"I'm enjoying it. It's quite the change of pace for me."

"I'll bet. So, I understand you're a musician?"

"Singer-songwriter."

"Are you now? What a wonderful thing to do. Music and lyrics and the chance to put feelings into song. I sure hope to get a chance to hear you perform."

I had never encountered another salesperson who expressed a sincere desire to hear me perform. I thanked Jerome, bought an antique ring that almost fit, and returned to my car.

At the artist cottage, I pulled my favorite guitar into my lap and placed my fingers on the strings. An arpeggio of guitar notes reverberated pure and sweet in the empty living space.

Two hours later, I looked at the clock. Five twenty. Chris would be home from work soon. I forced myself back to my song. The shifting shadows of clouds and sun played on the white walls in front of me. Chris continued to interrupt my thoughts. At 5:30, I set down my guitar and picked up the phone. "Hi, Chris? Yeah, I was just calling to say thanks for taking me canoe camping."

9

Derailed

Can't see what's under my feet
I'd trip over a diamond ring
And not pick it up
– "Lucky for Me"

May

Lynn drove me to the venue for my Tuesday night performance. I chose not to read too deeply into her explanation that it was easier to take me there than tell me how to get there, despite the fact I had already been to Perham. At that point, I had no suspicion she might be trying to fix me up with Chris.

I carried my gear to the makeshift stage in the corner of the cafe. The walls were hand-painted with Italian-style frescoes featuring stone arches, Roman statues, and the bright Mediterranean colors of summer picnics in Tuscany.

I sang a few bars into my microphone to hear how my voice and guitar sounded in the space. I adjusted the tone dial on my amplifier. I waited for the clock to tick down to start time.

When he dropped me off after our fishing lesson, Chris had said he would be here. I reminded myself I didn't care.

I focused on the wall frescoes, and disconnected memories of travels to Italy years before came back to me. There had been a train strike, and I couldn't get back to my hostel in Florence. Every room in Siena was booked, and I knew I would be homeless for the night. When a hotelier recommended I try the local convent, I was skeptical. But the nuns took me in for the night, and in the most unexpected place, I found a temporary home.

People were filing into the venue now, filling up the far tables first. It was almost time for the show. My breathing was shallow. The rubber sole of my shoe caught on a crack between tiles. I stumbled and looked up, surprised to find my eyes directed to the table where Lynn was saving a seat for Chris. Nerves before a show were normal. What wasn't normal was that I kept searching for Chris among the crowd.

I don't care, I reminded myself. I wasn't interested in a man who placed me in a ladybug nest and then laughed when I tried to escape it. I mounted the stage. The cafe's tables had filled. I pulled my guitar strap over my head and felt the comfort of its pressure on my left shoulder. I ran my left hand up the guitar's neck, palm scraping along each fret. I recalled the sound of Chris's voice singing along with me on the chorus of "Marrow." Pushing a lock of hair behind my ear, I stomped hard on my floor-tuner to double-check the guitar's tuning. I shoved Chris out of my mind and muted the metal strings under my callused fingertips. I spread my smile among the cafe tables, casting my eyes across the width of the room.

I strummed my opening chords, stomping my foot to keep time. Well-practiced material allowed me to lose myself in performance, but every time my gaze hit Chris's empty chair, I stumbled over a lyric. Halfway into my first set, Chris slunk in from the front door and slid into the chair next to Lynn.

I spent the rest of the first set trying not to look at him.

At intermission, Lynn said, "Hey, Elisa. I'm feeling a bit tired and need to leave early. Chris is willing to drive you home. Do you mind?"

The frescos around me seemed to blur a little. "No problem." I smiled my confident performer's smile.

The second set flew by.

When the performance was over and I'd spoken to all the audience members who wanted to buy a CD or talk to me, Chris helped me pack my microphone, mic stand, and amplifier into his car. A train passed a few yards away, making a deafening *clickety-clack* that dissipated down the tracks. Chris caught my eye. "Sorry I was late," he said with a roguish grin. "I couldn't get out of work early enough to make it here on time."

Something fluttered in the middle of my chest.

In the car, we fell into the easy flow of conversation we had discovered on the canoe trip. By the time we arrived at the New York Mills train signal, where we had to wait ten minutes for the full length of the Burlington Northern freight train to pass, I was telling Chris about my recent small-town adventures and we were laughing at the differences between city and country life.

At the artist cottage, Chris helped me carry my gear inside. "I have something for you." He ran out to his car and returned holding a dark loaf of bread. "I remember you said you liked baked goods. This is from a great bakery on my way to work. Beer cheddar."

"I've never had beer-and-cheese-flavored bread."

"It's a Midwestern thing," Chris's mouth melted into a half-deprecating smirk. He cleared his throat. "I also wanted to talk with you."

The plastic cellophane under my fingertips moved independently from the bread, so my fingers couldn't grasp the loaf, only maintaining their hold on its sheath with precarious friction.

"Have a seat." I gestured to the folding director's chair and perched on the lounge with the ripped corduroy cover. The white slat ceiling above us felt more oppressive than the previous weekend's ceiling of night sky. Suddenly, the togetherness felt too close, more intimate than sleeping next to each other in the outdoors had been.

"I really enjoyed our canoe trip together," Chris said, voice low. A set of headlights tracked along the blinds and shined for a moment on his face, highlighting a vein that was pounding in his temple. A train hooted in the distance. Goosebumps rose on my arms. I wanted him to leave.

I gripped the seat of my chair, digging my nails into the cushion. I could smell the stale scent of my half-eaten turkey-sandwich lunch reeking from the garbage. The lights and darks in my vision shifted, like someone had adjusted the contrast dial on a TV. The darkness that pooled beyond the lamplight crept toward me; the lamp now blindingly white. As much as I had daydreamed about romance, I wasn't ready for it. I wasn't ready for the risk of falling, really falling for someone, let alone someone who lived fifteen hundred miles away. He might not be an axe murderer, but, somehow, this guy felt more dangerous than the ones I knew in New York City.

Chris's voice lowered. "I'm very attracted to you. I would really like to spend more time with you. Would you be interested in going out on a date?"

Time buckled. It had taken me a year to get over my last serious boyfriend. He had broken up with me before the potted orchid he had given me had had time to die, and he was already sharing an apartment with someone when the last orange orchid petal crackled to dust on my dresser. I had never been very good at caring for house plants. What was the point of starting a long-distance relationship? It was nearly guaranteed not to work. "I . . . I don't know what to do with that." The sound of my voice hung in the motes of dust reflecting in the lamplight between us.

Chris's shoulders dropped, his gaze lowered. A neighbor took out the garbage with a loud clatter. Chris looked up, eyes intense on mine. "That's not a real response."

This man had the depth and substance of a worthy partner, but I couldn't risk a long-distance relationship with someone so far outside my world, particularly with this person who was so clearly, utterly wrong for me. "It doesn't make sense, Chris. We live so far away from each other. What's the point of pursuing it?"

A muscle tensed in his jaw. "If there's a chance something might work between us, it's worth pursuing."

He made it sound so simple. "I just . . ." Color leached from the room. "I just don't think this is going to work."

Chris rose, empty arms seeming to carry more weight than they had when he lifted my amplifier. "I understand." He gave me a sad smile.

The next day, about the time Chris usually returned from work, I found myself pacing the short length of the cottage, bedroom to kitchen and back. As spacious as the artist cottage had felt when I first arrived, today I felt like it couldn't contain me. A train rumbled in the background. I had already completed my writing and practice for the day. The Creamery was closed. There was nothing else I had to do. I thought about starting a song. I found myself out the door walking the block to Chris's house before I realized where I was going. A huge orange van right out of the 1970s seemed to watch me from the backyard. I smelled the unexpected scents of Asian food: soy, fish sauce, garlic. I rapped my knuckles on his screen door, a bright, storm-glass square of green-and-white kitchen.

Chris's face appeared, chiseled by the moving shadows of screen door, then lit up.

"Hi," he said. "I didn't expect to see you tonight."

I cocked my head and grinned shyly. "I felt like coming over to say hi."

He offered me a taste of his homemade Vietnamese food at an antique wood table that had been his grandmother's. He opened the white-painted cabinets stenciled with green leaves to shelves filled with organic grains and products from local farmers' markets. They looked like the contents of my own cabinets in Brooklyn. We sat together in his kitchen talking over train horns that sounded from the tracks down the street.

"Hey," Chris's voice sounded a bit shaky. "I know you don't want to date, but maybe we could, uh, go camping again. As friends." Chris's eyes traced the woodgrain of the table. "I mean, if you like." He raised his gaze to mine. "There's a beautiful state park up north where the Mississippi River starts. I think you'd like it."

I breathed in the sharp bite of lime and fish sauce, remembering how easy it had been to camp with him. How relaxed I'd been. How happy. It was only camping—we'd already been camping as friends. "Okay."

"Really?"

I smoothed my facial features into a relaxed expression. "That would be great."

Chris walked me home, his body solid and strong in the dark next to mine, and said goodbye from the stoop, hands in his pockets.

The next night, at 5:30, all I wanted to do was visit Chris again. *Write a song,* I told myself. I picked up my guitar and tried to compose. An hour later, the chords still didn't make any sense together. I made myself a quick, flavorless dinner and remembered the vibrant Asian flavors Chris had conjured up in his Midwestern kitchen. I found myself on the street, feet pointing toward Chris's place. This evening there was no glow of kitchen light outlining the front door. The dark hulk of a van peered menacingly at me from behind the house.

I returned to the lonely quiet of the artist cottage.

10

Camping Again

I know better than to dive into a tidal wave
I know better than to drive into a hurricane
I don't go wandering in lightning storms
So why
Am I so drawn to you

– "Know Better"

May

Chris picked me up after my second Minnesota gig—this one at the Creamery—to take me to Pam and Gary's house for a barbecue and bonfire. We sat next to each other at the kitchen table in the midst of a havoc of artist supplies, pieces by local artists, and jumbles of shoes and clothing that seemed uncontainable by any room in the house. When I reached for tortilla chips, my calf brushed Chris's underneath the table. A tingle ran up my leg.

He seemed different to me than he had at first sight. Something had changed since I'd met him, and even more since I'd refused him. His cheekbones were more pronounced, his jawline more angled. The way Chris spoke slowly and deliberately, his country accent, his easy smile, his lack of sarcasm: I had never noticed how charming they were.

I wasn't going to fall for some Minnesotan guy and give up my life in New York City, but what would be the harm in dating?

This weekend, I decided, *this weekend when we go on our backpacking trip together, I will tell him I'm willing to try.*

Chris parked the gear-filled Trooper in a thicket of wild plum trees up a dirt road at Itasca State Park. I pulled my backpack out of the hold and tugged at my hip strap, trying to make it comfortable. I wasn't bringing my guitar this time; it was hard enough to walk with a heavy pack. Chris waited at the beginning of the trail. His firm, dependable form was as solid as the tree trunks that surrounded him, but unlike the anonymous trees, he had become familiar to me.

I took a deep breath and walked into the otherworldly quiet of forest. I heard only birdsong, the rustling of wind in the trees, and our footsteps. I looked up to the trees and lost my footing on loose gravel.

"You okay?"

"I'm . . . I'm a bit nervous. My knees aren't very stable, and I've never backpacked before."

"You'll be fine." Chris's smile was as sure as the breeze in the leaves, propping up my spirits. "It's only two miles. And we can take as long as you need. There's no rush."

The constriction behind my ribs eased. *Only two miles,* I told myself. Two miles till the campsite where I would tell Chris I'd reconsidered. I wasn't sure if I wanted the two miles to go quickly or slowly.

Fifteen minutes down the trail, the weight of the backpack had rubbed pain into the soft flesh between my shoulders and collarbone. I tried to shift the straps, but the pack overbalanced and started to pull me down. Chris steadied me before I could fall.

"Okay?" His hand was firm on my arm.

I nodded, not trusting my voice to answer. The shape of his hand lingered on my skin after he had pulled it away. What if Chris had changed his mind?

My feet made hiccups of dust swirl off the trail. I was panting when we reached a hill covered with small white sunbursts of strawberry flowers. Chris carried the heaviest items—a cast iron pot, the apples, the water—and he still bounded up the hill. He called behind him, "You can do it. Not far now."

We walked in companionable silence. The sun was high in the sky when we reached the lakeside campsite. My legs trembled from the weight of my pack, and I groaned as its weight dropped from my shoulders to the hard dirt by the fire ring. Buoyant now, I floated the ten paces to the ledge overlooking the lake.

I smelled loamy earth and the promise of new leaves. The trees' reflections were so pristine that the lake seemed a window into an upside-down Wonderland of aspen, pine, and sky. The image shimmered with silvery light, a magic forest undulating invitingly beneath the water.

"It's beautiful, isn't it?" Chris stood beside me, emanating peace. "There's nothing more satisfying to me than being in the wilderness."

An unexpected twinge of hope pinged inside me. Maybe one day I could love the outdoors as much as he did, be as comfortable in it as he was, and, thereby, be worthy of his affection.

I heard a burble and saw concentric circles spread from the splash of a fish. Chris sprang up and away, upsetting the spell between us like the fish had marred the fantasy reflected in the water. "Looks like a good spot for largemouth bass."

"Are they good eating?"

"Not so much, but they're fun to catch." He walked toward the fire ring. "I'll put up the tent. Why don't you start collecting some firewood?" He pulled poles out of a tent sack and started fitting them into the thin, rugged fabric.

I pushed into the forest to the side of the trail and started gathering the largest sticks and branches I could carry, proud that this time I knew how much wood we needed. When I returned, arms full, I expected to see two bright tents up in the midst of the campsite. There was only one. A shiny thin lasso of anticipation twirled around me.

"Interested in fishing?"

I squinted up at him and raised my eyebrows. "After last time? I'll pass."

Chris smirked. "No waders, no ladybugs."

I pulled a notebook out of my pack. "I'd rather write."

As Chris connected the three sections of his fishing rod and strung his line, I propped my back against an elm and set my songwriting notebook on my lap. I unclipped my pen from the coil binding and lifted it, preparing for inspiration.

With a snap, Chris's line flew out in perfect helixes, depositing his fly in the precise spot where the fish had risen. There was a flash and a flutter in the water, and a hoot from Chris as his line went taut. His features lit with focused glee as he wound his reel, pausing every few spins to let the fish unspool some line. A few more pulls, and the fish was dangling on the end of his rod, flopping and squiggling. Chris's cheeks were pulled wide in an ecstatic smile that showed all his teeth. "Got him!" he yelled with delight, lifting the fish up by its line. He walked the fish over to me. "See the mouth?" The fish's mouth—wider than its body—gaped so much that I could see its ribs from inside its body. "That's why they're called largemouth," he said. Very gently, his strong hands now as delicate and precise as a painter's, he extricated the feather-tipped hook and tossed the wriggling fish into the water. It paused for a moment, then fluttered, and its glistening body melted into the upside-down Wonderland.

While we ate Chris's dinner of fire-roasted "bratillas"—a concoction of grilled bratwurst and shredded cheese rolled in tortillas—the sun painted the lake with colored fire. We sat next to each other on two stumps, talking casually, until the last strip of greenish light disappeared into the horizon.

The fire in the pit popped and crackled, looking as if it were a delayed echo of the ephemeral fire of sun on lake, flaming fingers of orange and red against the black sky. In our small circle of light, with the sound of waters lapping against the nearby shore, it was Chris and me together in a flickering private grotto, darkness surrounding us like ever-shifting walls.

Chris brought out the marshmallows and graham crackers. I had no guitar to shield my body. Cold rippled along my flesh. My forehead tingled at the touch of my hair in the breeze. I steadied myself against the stump.

The end of my marshmallow stick glowed red in the embers. I smelled the stick burn. My mouth wouldn't open. I shook out the small flame at the end of my stick, smoke pouring out and up. *Now. Say something now.* I watched my hand push the stick into the fire, the blackened end bursting red again in a small, perfect flame.

The words I knew I needed to say were dammed up in my throat. "Dinner was tasty. Thanks for cooking." I said instead.

"You helped."

I nodded. Chris watched the fire, his capable hands barely flexed around his stick. My cheek facing the fire was burning, my other cheek was stiff with the chill of night—I didn't know which felt better, the heat of the hearth or the cool of the darkness. I didn't have to say anything. I could let it go, finish my month in Minnesota, and return to New York City with fond memories that would dissolve like ripples on shore.

I cleared my throat. "You know when you came over with the loaf of bread . . ." I paused. "And said you were interested." The fire seared flickers of white and yellow into my vision. "Well, I think I'm . . ." I stole a glance in Chris's direction, and a set of spectral flames came along. "I think I'm interested, too." Chris's face blurred behind the ghost fire in my eyes. "You were right, this is a rare opportunity, and we shouldn't waste it."

I'd said it. Hallelujah, I'd said it.

Chris's brow wrinkled. The air in our private grotto stilled. Lapping waves whispered under small explosions and crackles. My world shrank into the heat between us.

I was too late. I had missed my chance.

Chris's eyes lowered to the leaf-littered floor, then lifted to meet mine. "Are you sure?"

"No. I mean, yes. I mean, I don't know." I looked into the fire, trying to lose myself in the flames. "I'm scared."

"Me too."

Chris's face was surrounded by a nimbus of orange light as he put his arm around my shoulders and leaned in. I closed my eyes. Darkness enclosed us like blankets. Chris's mouth was soft and sweet and warm and full of possibilities.

11

Parting

Road is a river
Reflecting sky
Shining between us
Drive by goodbye
– "Road Trance"

End of May

The day before I left Minnesota, Chris lay on his stomach on the wood floor of the artist cottage living room, knees bent, soles up. We had spent every minute we could together since the backpacking trip. Chris flipped through a magazine an artist had left on the cottage shelves. I folded my ruffled gray vintage dress neatly and placed it into my suitcase. I hadn't worn it—there was nowhere a dress like that would feel right here.

Chris shifted. "I wish you didn't have to go."

"Me too." The swish of fabric against the nylon of the suitcase filled the ever-growing space between us.

"Have you ever thought about living here?" Chris's biceps flexed.

A sound caught in my throat. I *had* thought about it. But wasn't it too early to be talking about such things with a boyfriend of less than two weeks?

"Because, you know," he tapped the toe of a sandal on the floor behind him. His eyes drifted to the drafting table, where the stems of a lilac and a daisy he had given me curled around each other in a jar. "I mean, I know this is premature, and I don't want to say anything to scare you or push you any faster than you want to go . . ." I crushed the dress's delicate black ruffle in my hand. "But, well, if we continue this thing—and I hope we do—at some point, we might want to be in the same place together. And . . ." he ran out of breath and gulped air. The gentle smell of pine wafted through the open window. Chris placed the magazine carefully on the floor. "And if you ever wanted to move here, I wanted you to know we could make it work." A lawn mower buzzed underneath the trilling of birds. "My business is growing, and you could do your music. You wouldn't have to work at a dayjob. You could just, you know, be the artist you want to be."

My insides jumped and wriggled like a loose guitar string, end bouncing violently between fear and gratitude. I liked this guy. A lot. And, yes, I could see—perhaps for the first time in my life—that I might want to stay with him for long enough to consider wanting to be in the same place. But, living in rural Minnesota? What would I do in a place where there was nowhere to wear my vintage dresses to?

Two pine branches rubbed together with a sigh. The answer came to me: I could write songs. A delicious ache spilled down my shoulders and into my arms, the physical sensation of song wanting to emerge. As I had done for the last four weeks, I could dwell in the quiet and space of this faraway place and spend my time doing what I most loved in the world, with a person who seemed more promising than anyone else I had ever met.

But could we make it, this unlikely country man and I? On paper, we didn't work. None of my friends would have ever thought to introduce us—none of my friends *could* have introduced us—no one I knew knew anyone like him. No dating website's algorithm would link me to a country fisherman from central Minnesota. "Urban intellectual artist, too smart by half, seeks country man who loves fly fishing for life-long adventure."

But we didn't live on paper or online.

I imagined myself on the porch of some great big country house, notebook canted on my lap, Chris's Buick driving up the driveway, honking at me to gain my attention, his face wrinkled in a silly expression, me laughing, him tapping a rhythm on the horn, pulling into the garage, then racing out of the car to wrap me in his arms.

But what about the rest of the time? Could I live here, in this slow-paced land with no shops, no theater, with none of my friends, no other songwriters or performing artists? The sunshine highlighted ghostly sponge streaks on the windows. I smelled the sour-cherry scent of the artist cottage. I could wear an apron. I could learn to be a country lady. Would the cost of giving up New York City be worth gaining this man, and the chance to focus on my creativity?

My pause weighed between us. Chris's back tensed. "I'm sorry," he said. "I didn't mean—"

"It's okay. You didn't scare me. And, yes, I have thought about it." Now we were both exposed. Together. Like my two guitars outlined against the window—one bright blue and electric, the other muted wood and acoustic—the silhouettes of their long necks inclining gently toward one another, we were coming together, secure in our own places but part of the same picture.

Chris's shoulders dropped slightly, and his mouth quirked in a self-conscious smile. My mouth mirrored his. Laughter sounded in the breeze. "I really like you, too," I said, voice thick with emotion, mutual risk changing the music between us from gentle swell into fierce and jagged harmony.

Chris's rose to his knees in one graceful motion. He reached for me, pulled me down to the floor, and log-rolled us across the living room, till the kitchen tile was cool on my neck, and his stubble was rough and satisfying on my cheek.

After a gentle Minnesota May, the morning of my departure arrived hot and insistent. The sun baked grass and asphalt into a pungent scent. Chris helped me pack guitars, backpack, and suitcases into my Honda Civic, filling trunk and backseat. When all traces of me, except one of my CDs, had been erased from the cottage, Chris walked me to the car. He opened the driver's side door and leaned in. My breath stopped, and something like a sob clenched my belly. He kissed me goodbye gently. I reached my hands up to feel the roughness of his cheeks and inhaled his grassy, outdoor scent. He pulled away too soon. "I'll miss you," he said, tears threatening to spill out of his eyes.

"I'll miss you, too." A new tightness rose in my throat. My tears stayed inside till I drove across the railroad tracks and saw a tiny Chris in the rearview mirror stop waving and turn toward his house.

My chest was an open pit mine.

It was a long, bitter, three-day drive across Canada to get to New York City. Boreal forests filled my windshield hour after hour, and the newer, better, more artistic shell of me had to split and shatter before I could emerge and reshape myself to my old life. Grief over leaving Chris cocooned and exploded into outrage. *How dare Chris be someone I could care about? How could I have spent so much time mooning over a man when I should have been writing?* In odd moments, distracted by the beauty of a bird soaring high above Lake Superior or the warmth of sun on my face, my fury waned. Small moments of Chris bubbled up from memory: Chris's sure stroke of the paddle, the sound of Chris's laughter as we lay next to each other in our sleeping bags under the night sky, Chris's delicate strength with filament and fish.

My Brooklyn apartment felt unfamiliar when I returned to it; its incense and silk scent had staled in my absence. My cats curved around my ankles and reached their front paws up my legs to be held. It was wonderful to curl them into my arms, but they felt less substantial than the Minnesota man who had held me in his arms less than a week before.

After a couple of days, my old life resumed almost as if I had never left, except now I called Chris every day, picking up the phone and dialing before dropping my bag when I came home in the evening. Chris's velvety voice sent me off to sleep every night.

12

Country Boy in the City

I'm not looking for something so hard and fast
Or looking to stay just to make it last
I'm looking for someone to walk with me
On the concrete waters of the concrete sea
– "Concrete"

June

When the disembodied voice stood, embodied again, at the door to my Brooklyn apartment, it was as jarring as two different songs playing at the same time. The telephone voice against my ear now came from the shape of a person standing in my stairwell. Chris was no longer shaded in the pastels of my daydreams. He was shorter and squatter than I remembered. His nylon pants and polyester polo shirt looked wrinkled, and his skin was jaundiced under the wan hallway lamplight. A passing siren shook my windows in their frames.

I blocked the doorway, staring, trying to make sense of Chris in my New York City. The familiar tree-like solidity of the Chris from my memory had been transformed into a wrinkled, travel-weary stranger. I pushed the door open with my back so he could enter. His backpack caught on the latch, and I stood back as he untangled himself. I darted in for a quick hug. The metal door clanked shut, and I tried to pull away. His arms held me close. I reached for his bag as an excuse to disengage. He held it away from me and set it down by my guitar stand with a thud.

"Are you thirsty? Can I get you something to drink, eat?" I asked.

"No, no, I'm fine. I can't believe I'm in New York City!"

"Neither can I." I jumped into motion, striding to the center of my apartment. "Well, welcome to New York. So, this is my apartment."

One of my black cats *chirruped* a greeting from the couch. "That's Sander. The other cat is Tree. I can give you the whole tour from where you're standing." I turned in a circle, pointing to the thresholds of my city-sized space. "Kitchen. Bathroom. Bedroom." I was speaking way too fast. "This is the living room. The retractable desk with wheels turns it into my office-slash-studio. Have a seat."

Chris put his backpack down on the floor by his duffle and leaned in again to hug me. I tried to keep my body relaxed, but it betrayed my discomfort, stiffening. His arms tried to soften me, pull me in, kiss me. My mouth felt too taut, then too loose. I disengaged and ducked and bobbed under his arm to get away. A new distance had been planted between us, taking root not in absence, but in presence.

Chris cocked his head at me. "Feeling shy?"

A pulse pushed against my neck. I looked down at my feet and then up through my eyelashes. "Yeah."

Chris stood legs-apart, looking too large for my apartment but so much smaller than in my memory. He nodded slowly, took my hand, and pulled me toward the couch. "I can't believe I'm here." He lifted his other arm wide. "I woke up in Minnesota, and I'm in New York City before noon. This morning, I was driving through farmland, and a few hours later I was seeing the Empire State Building in the Manhattan skyline."

That week's copy of *Time Out New York* magazine waited on the coffee table, and I reached for it. "I found all kinds of things we could do. There's a bar in Brooklyn with world music performances. Tonight it's a guitar player from Mali. There are all sorts of restaurants I've been meaning to go to that you might enjoy. What do you want to do now that you're here?"

The pause after my question was worse than the delay on a telephone line. Chris had picked up on my discomfort, and now we were both embarrassed by it.

"Jeez, that all sounds good. Anything would be fine. Whatever you want."

My knees locked. We were still standing, facing each other awkwardly. What did I want? "Have a seat," I said again, gesturing at the couch. It creaked as we sat. I wanted to shrink from the too-intimate warmth of his body. "Are you hungry?" I leafed through the restaurant section of *Time Out*, avoiding eye contact.

"I could eat."

"You name the cuisine and we can find it for you. Japanese, Senegalese, Thai, Afghani . . ."

"Japanese? I love Japanese food."

It was a good enough cue for me. I leapt up, fighting off the cushions that tried to hold me back. I led Chris down my stairwell and across Smith Street to the nearby Japanese restaurant. Chris's head bobbed back and forth, taking in the tumult of pedestrians, buildings, shops. I saw my neighborhood through his eyes—noticing things I had not paid attention to in years. How the green vertical bars of the Brooklyn House of Detention towered above my apartment. How blue the sky looked between rooftop television antennas. The tang of frying onions that drifted down from an open window on the third floor.

"That's the corner where the Dominican guys used to play Dominos." I narrated the scenery as we passed. The Brooklyn summer day was sticky-dirty, city grime adhering to sweat. "That's the storefront where I get ghetto Chinese food to go." The repetition of foot on sidewalk gave me the beat I needed to get back into rhythm. "One block farther down is Saul—it's a Michelin-starred restaurant I eat at whenever I can afford to." We arrived at the Japanese restaurant, and I opened the door for Chris.

Our table was made of polished stone and was topped with a fresh orchid. I pulled the wooden chopsticks apart with a crack. A splinter pierced the skin of my thumb, and I sucked at it. Chris examined the sushi menu. I rubbed my thumb, head in my menu, dawdling over the choice between lunch special or à la carte.

"It all looks so good. I think I'll get sashimi. What about you?" Chris asked.

"Sushi special."

We ordered our food, and I sat back in my chair. "So, how's Lynn? And Pam and Gary?"

"Great, great. You know, it's been beautiful this week. I thought about you a lot."

My ribs pressed into my lungs. I inhaled against the pressure. "Thanks."

"I'm glad to see you."

Something clutched in my chest. "Me too," I said, not sure if I meant it. A nagging voice in my head chided me, *Millions of city men right here, and you have to set up a date with one from Minnesota.* The waiter arrived with the starter course, and I lifted my spoon from the miso soup too quickly, burning my tongue.

That afternoon, I took Chris for a walk around Greenwich Village. We stopped in boutiques and sampled cheeses at the gourmet grocery Dean and Deluca. I pointed out my favorite venues to perform at. Chris requested Asian food again for dinner. When we returned to Bergen Street, it was close to nine o'clock. Chris marveled at the activity around us.

"I can't believe the stores are all still open!" He ducked his head into a woman's boutique and executed a small pirouette at the entrance.

I didn't know how to react, torn between appreciation for his exuberance and disdain for his artlessness. "What are you doing?" I asked. "Do you like shopping for expensive skirts?"

He grabbed my hands and pulled me into another pirouette. "It's so fun!" I let myself get pulled into his momentum.

We neared my apartment building and the inevitable first night together, again. I tried to remember how much I had liked this man weeks, even hours, before his visit. That I had craved his touch during our late-night phone conversations. That *I* had pursued a long-distance relationship. That, two weeks before, I had felt like this man might, just might, be the right man for me.

We arrived at the apartment, and I unlocked the door. Chris followed me inside, then snaked his arms around my waist and kissed my neck, as I stared at the guitars hanging on my wall. I breathed in slowly, noticing how hard it was for me to stay in his arms. "Want some tea or coffee or something?"

"No," he mumbled into my neck. I sighed. I couldn't hold this part of our night off forever. I shut off the light and turned around, letting my mouth meet his. If I could only return to the version of me who felt blissful in his company. Where had that person gone?

Chris kissed my cheeks and hair and I closed my eyes, kissing him back, trying as hard as I could to recall the connection we had had. As we found our way to the bedroom, I forced myself to pretend that my bed was again the bed in the billowing white room of the artist's cottage. In the dark, I managed to forget myself.

When the apartment was bright with morning light, I woke up feeling strangely naked, a set of arms around me. My bed felt like it had shrunk in the night. I turned over and looked at the man next to me, eyes closed, one arm draped under his head. One corner of his mouth turned up, and he reached toward me. I rolled my feet to the floor. His face fell. I put a teasing tone in my voice to make up for the brush-off. "Lots to do today. Let's get dressed and go."

"Come back to bed."

I was grabbing my clothes and on my way to the bathroom. "No way! New York City awaits."

I heard groaning and a thud, and then Chris was behind me in the bathroom.

"Okay, shy one. But tomorrow we get to sleep in."

For two days, I slowed my normal race-walking pace to Chris's leisurely country stroll. Chris was reflected in the passing windows, sometimes stretched tall and thin, other times swelled grotesquely sideways. I wondered how I could have ever imagined myself with him, what spell I had been under in Minnesota.

I tried to recast the spell, rekindle the feelings I had had, but they were Minnesotan feelings that disappeared against the backdrop of my city. Chris looked like he had been Photoshopped into my world, his hiking pants and paunch making him stand out from the elegantly bedraggled hipsters with their long, lean bodies, studiedly casual jeans, and thick plastic glasses. He walked too slowly. He spoke too slowly. When he bantered with the fromagier at the Stinky Cheese Shop, his wide, flat, heartland accent sounded coarse and vulgar. On the street, we were out of step with the rest of the New Yorkers who squeezed around us like obstacles to their city lives.

I couldn't imagine Chris living in my city. Chris belonged in the country. I belonged in the city. It dawned on me that there was no future to this relationship, and that I should try and enjoy these two days as a romantic interlude until I could break up with Chris.

On Sunday, we walked around my Brooklyn neighborhood. Chris pulled a cigar from his chest pocket and ducked into a doorway. He emerged in a blue cloud. We continued down Court Street, the spicy smoke stinging my throat.

Chris led with his stomach and leaned his weight into his heels as he puffed. He was the caricature of the mob bosses who used to run this Carroll Gardens neighborhood. Like them, he greeted everyone we passed, and my anonymous neighbors did double-takes.

"Hi!" Chris nodded at a man in a suit who pretended not to notice.

"How's it going?" Chris addressed an older woman with curlers in her hair under a scarf. She squinted at us.

"Nice dog!" Chris spoke around his cigar. A twenty-something in designer heels walking a toy poodle turned to check if Chris was actually talking to her. "Thanks," slipped from her taut mouth.

Chris was breaking all the unspoken laws of my world. He didn't know how to behave or how to interact. He didn't fit. And the more he stood out, the more I wanted to fit in. Who I was with him and who I was in my city were too hard to maintain at the same time. I needed to get away.

"Hey, uh, do you mind if I go into that boutique for a moment?" Chris's cigar was still smoking.

"Go ahead. I'll wait here." Chris sat down on the stoop next door.

I entered the store and fingered striped silk shirts on neatly spaced racks suspended from the ceiling. I inhaled the scent of perfume, and rejoiced when another customer pushed past me without saying "excuse me." The rudeness felt like a balm. As Chris's departure neared, I wanted less and less to be around him.

I returned outside. From his perch on the stoop, Chris was leading a conversation between three people who didn't know each other and petting a Bichon Frise, a French bulldog, and two matching Papillons.

"Isn't he charming? French bulldogs have such great personalities," Chris said, big country grin widening his face. I watched, shocked, as the bulldog's owner, a woman in a Chanel suit, laughed, her hand touching Chris's on her dog's fur. My urbane neighbors weren't supposed to like his innocent country ways.

Chris was turning everything upside-down.

When the passers-by and their dogs had moved on, I led Chris to a restaurant for Italian water ice. Frozen treat in hand, I sat down at a wrought iron table outside a window with bars on it. Hard chips of sweet vanilla ice scraped my teeth. Chris's rainbow of cherry and lemon and blueberry turned his tongue purple. Melted ice dripped down his hand, vivid colors mixing to a dull gray. A rivulet flowed off his wrist unnoticed and made an amoeba-shaped stain on his T-shirt above a nipple.

"I could live here," he said in his wide Minnesota accent, gesturing to his new fiefdom of Cobble Hill. He settled into the iron filigree of his chair like the Godfather. "I prefer the country but, if I had to, I could enjoy New York. I'd get gourmet cheese every day." He stretched his arms, one landing on my chair back. I slouched to keep his arm from touching me. I prised a chocolate chip loose from my ice with my teeth.

"If I lived here, I'd shop at Pacific Green every day for groceries," he continued. A piece of hard chocolate screwed into my molar, and lemony vanilla ice crystals shot cold daggers through my gums into my temples. The melted paper cup, weakened by the damp, tore and dripped melted stickiness down my hand. I got up and shook off the drips. "Ready to go?" I tossed my soggy cup and started walking without listening for an answer.

"Hey, wait up. Everything okay?"

My eyes were dry stones, hard and unwatered. I blinked to soften them. "We gotta call you a taxi to get you to the airport."

A few blocks later, Chris asked again, "Are you sure you're okay?"

"Yeah, I'm just tired."

I didn't talk the rest of the way back, and Chris seemed to realize that trying to engage me was a bad idea. I deposited Chris in the living room to finish packing his bags and stayed in the bathroom for longer than I needed to. When the car service arrived, I let Chris kiss me for the minimum amount of time that seemed appropriate. "Thanks for coming," I said.

His eyes were clouded with pain and confusion; he knew something had changed. "I'll call you," he said as I held the door for him.

"Right. Safe travels."

I closed the door behind him, fitting the door gently into its frame, feeling the bolts tumble shut in my fingertips. I was waiting for the telltale shuddering of my walls that signified the closing of the apartment building's front door—when that happened, he would really be gone.

The vibration began in my feet, rising up through the floor of my newly empty apartment and into my body. I threw myself on my couch and inhaled the deepest breath I had breathed since Chris had arrived.

I broke up with Chris by phone two days later. Hurt breached the hardness in his voice. "Well, if you change your mind . . ."

"Sure . . ." I said, and hung up.

The day after our break-up, I went to lunch with my friend Jae and reiterated each point on my list of Why Chris Is Wrong for Me. The more I repeated the points, I knew, the more I would believe them. "He said hello to everyone he passed." I ticked a finger. "He tried to make friends on Court Street," I ticked another finger.

Jae interrupted. "How did people respond?"

"What do you mean?"

"When Chris talked to them on Court Street. What did people do?"

I twirled a noodle around my fork and remembered Chris by the stoop, petting the French bulldog with the woman wearing Chanel. "When they had a chance to talk with him, they seemed to like it." The bubble of confidence that had buoyed me since breaking up with my real, live boyfriend burst.

The server came to take our plates. Cutlery clattered against ceramic. Jae's voice was quiet. "Being separated by a long distance is reason enough to end this relationship." She paused. My finger traced a water ring left by a glass on the table. "But there's something about the way you spoke about Chris. You really seemed happy. You had a spark I've never seen in you before. If you choose not to be with him, I support you. But, maybe," Jae's brow furrowed, "maybe you should think about this a little more."

I was tired of thinking about it. I was tired of the tension between my life and Chris's. If I was going to make my life in New York City work, I had to find someone who could be my New York City partner.

Okay, so I hadn't yet found anyone who could do that. And it was true my life in New York had been feeling particularly empty prior to my sojourn in Minnesota. But wouldn't my life be even emptier in the emptiness of the rural heartland? There was nothing there for me. And there was nothing in New York for Chris.

The air conditioning in the restaurant turned on, blowing directly at me, and my skin chilled into goosebumps. I licked my lips. The left-over lime juice from my pad thai stung a cut inside my mouth.

I had thought enough about it. Chris was wrong for me. Absolutely, entirely wrong for me.

13

Stoop Saling

I'm yours for a song
Come back later, I may be gone
You might spend all life long
Trying to find me again
– "Yours for a Song"

June

I woke up alone in my Brooklyn apartment. The bedroom window vibrated along with the vehicles idling at the intersection below. The cheap blind curled in at the edges; two narrow strips of sunlight fell on the wood floor.

I was single again.

Maybe I had made a mistake. Maybe I should never have ended things with Chris.

I stopped the train of thought before it could take over and tried to talk down the peril in my gut. *Single is familiar. I've been single most of my life. Now I can return to my fabulous single New York City lifestyle.*

I pulled myself out of bed. The fridge was empty. I checked the clock again. Eight thirty. I threw on clothing, pulled the strap of my handbag across my shoulders, and vaulted into the brownstoned grid of residential streets.

My favorite weekend activity was to wander through waking Brooklyn streets in search of a stoop sale, the garage sales of the garageless neighborhoods in which I lived. I sailed from one to another, letting signs taped to street lamps guide my way.

Stoop saling was best accomplished alone: no one else had my stamina to keep looking for the next undervalued gem. Why did I want some boyfriend who either didn't want to come or, worse yet, came along and complained about it? I looked up and down Pacific Avenue, seeking treasures to pad my Brooklyn nest: clothing hanging from the finials of iron banisters, carpets draped down stone steps, or gently used knick-knacks stacked on folding tables. Unlike romance, stoop sales were as clear as arithmetic. I either wanted something, or I didn't.

I searched for signs with handwritten arrows and followed them along sidestreets to unknown destinations.

I considered which way to turn on Nevins Avenue. With no one to disagree with me, I let the breeze carry me. I turned right and found my first stoop sale in a quiet section of Wyckoff Street. It was in front of the building that an artist had mosaicked with waves of colored glass and plastic toys embedded in concrete. Every month it expanded, sporting a few more ripples and another doll's head or plastic truck. *I should have brought Chris here,* I thought. *He would have loved seeing this unlikely entryway.* I caught myself. I would not think about Chris anymore. Goodbye and good riddance.

The world narrowed again to the laden tables and rails. Traffic and pedestrian sounds disappeared. I ran my fingers over the bumpy-smooth metal of a jeweled tissue box, stroked the cool fabric of a gold lamé dress that would be wonderful for a gig, and ruffled the scratchy sequins of a pair of high-heels. I balanced on one leg and slipped a hastily un-shod foot into a brick-orange John Fluevog pump. I felt an almost erotic loosening inside; it was exactly my size. I prospected, further ferreting for treasures in dented cardboard boxes. I sorted jewelry and scarves on a card table—yes, no, maybe. I handed over three twenty-dollar bills and the Brooklynite with a nose ring handed me a used shopping bag full of new-to-me designer things purchased for pennies on the dollar.

I was hungry now, a soldier after a conquest.

I turned toward Fifth Avenue, to the Blue Sky Bakery and its freshly baked strawberry-peach muffins. My iced coffee cup overflowed with cloudy sweetness. I remembered how Chris liked to tease me about adulterating my coffee with milk and sugar and started to grin before remembering that part of my life was over.

I returned to my muffin, eating as I walked. I was not willing to miss a minute of searching for the next stoop sale before the goods had been picked over. No matter how many stoop sales I'd already visited, the next one might be *the* one: the sale where I would find the thing I didn't even know I wanted, didn't even know I needed. I couldn't waste any time.

Dating made me doubt myself, but on my way to stoop sales, I felt something akin to belonging. I had a purpose. I had a goal. I knew I'd know what I was looking for when I found it. Another possibility of discovery was just ahead, within grasp, only an arm's length away.

I passed my favorite local brunch place, a flurry of tables laid out on the sidewalk. Everyone sat with someone else, except a lone musician with a scowl who played jazz in a corner on an arch-top guitar. At the closest table, a young couple glowed in disheveled clothing, their easy quiet and hooded eyes suggesting a happy night up too late together. They shared a plate of eggs Florentine, forks tangling. My nostrils flared. I wanted what they had, but that was not on sale today.

A small voice in the back of my mind said, *When you were with Chris, you never felt like this.*

Stop it!

I had made my decision. It was the right decision. Chris and I weren't going to work. It was high time I moved on. Tomorrow, I had a gig to perform. Right now, I was stoop saling. All I had to do was find the perfect thing I didn't know I needed, and everything would be all right.

I drifted alone past the cafe to the relative solitude of the tree-lined cross-streets.

14

Geomancy

Take a man and take a woman
Add some laughter and respect
Some love and conversation
But you know you ain't done yet
Cuz if you want to make it good
The best that you've had
Gotta learn to compromise
Take the good right with the bad
– "A Little Bit of Salt"

July–October

The break-up lasted one week.

I returned from stoop saling to an empty apartment and placed plastic bags of new treasures on my too-small rectangle of kitchen counter. My shoes echoed harshly on the wood floors. My guitars hung static and unmoving on the brick wall. There was no one to talk to. Even my cats were more interested in sleeping than in staying on my lap.

I peered into the brick wall in front of the couch, trying to read my future in the cracked grout. And when I did, I ignored it. All the stoop sale treasures in Brooklyn couldn't add up to a home, but maybe Chris could. I had never felt as peaceful as when we had been together. All I wanted to do was call him. I gritted my teeth and stayed away from the phone.

Sunday was consumed by a gig. For two hours of performance at a coffeehouse, I spent six hours preparing: putting on make-up, warming up my voice, preparing, carrying, and packing my gear into my Honda Civic parked around the corner, and driving to and from New Jersey. It was a slow night. The contents of the tip jar barely covered the gas it took to get to the venue. When I returned to my apartment, I didn't even have the energy to take my guitar out of its case. I let my gear fall to the floor with a thud and collapsed on my couch, arm muscles tired from lugging my gear, cheeks tired from smiling. I tried to read the bricks on the wall again. The straight lines of baked earth mocked my foolishness.

Why had I let my pride get in the way of a rare connection with a wonderful man? I wanted to fall back into the tide that gathered me up in New York Mills, that had led me into Chris's arms. It was an hour earlier in Minnesota. I picked up the phone.

Within two weeks, Chris was in New York again.

We developed a long-distance dating rhythm: daily phone calls and bi-weekly cross-country visits. Once a month, I visited Minnesota. Once a month, Chris came to New York. Each visit was a new adventure. We used our time together to bridge the chasm between our city and country lives. We went on road trips to national parks. We stayed at B&Bs. Chris came with me to a music festival I played in Vermont. When I returned from talking to the stage manager, I was shocked to discover he had set up my gear exactly as I would have, even remembering to curl the guitar cord around the mic stand out of the way of my feet.

On Labor Day weekend, we canoe camped in the Boundary Waters Canoe Area Wilderness. For four days we paddled across lakes and hauled equipment across portages. I carried the paddles and life jackets. Chris hoisted the canoe over his head like it weighed nothing. The one time I tried to carry the canoe, I stumbled five steps before my oblique muscles shuddered, and I dropped it.

We chose remote campsites by which one had the best view. To bathe, we skinny dipped in the cold, clear water, breathing in the scent of pine and spruce. Chris taught me how to build a fire. My early attempts smoldered and failed, but Chris wouldn't let me give up, and when my first fire blazed I whooped and hollered across the lake, scaring a wading moose.

In late October, it was Chris's turn to visit me. I had become used to the abrupt change in my world when his hiking boots clumped into the apartment building and his friendly, sturdy form appeared on the stairs. Now, instead of hiding in my living room till he knocked, I rushed out to the landing, relishing every instant I had with him. I tugged him into my apartment and pushed his backpack onto the ground so I could feel his arms wrap around me and pull me into the safety of his embrace. I dragged him to the couch, where we fitted our bodies around one another and I inhaled his grassy-musky scent. When I was curled in his arms, my Brooklyn apartment felt less like an escape and more like a home.

After we kissed for a little while, I pulled far enough away so I could see his face as I spoke. "So, there's this great new exhibit at MOMA, and I wondered if you would be willing to go with me. Then we'll be right near Fifth Avenue, and I thought you might enjoy seeing the fancy stores there."

His face was soft with reunion. "Anything you want."

MOMA was full of color and light, its roof cantilevered to create a space grand and expansive enough to house masterpieces. When we had had our fill of art and crowds I led Chris past Tiffany's, where he paused to peer at the watches in the luxurious windows. Before we reached Bergdorf Goodman, he said, "I think I need to buy some hipster clothes."

I raised my eyebrows. "Why?"

"Because everyone in Brooklyn looks so well put together. If I am going to keep visiting you in New York, then I need some things to wear to fit in."

I hid a small smile. I had tried to ignore the difference between what he wore and the sleek outfits of my city friends. But I had noticed.

I led Chris to the Mexx store. We wandered the aisles of the men's department and I piled clothes on his arms, pulling hangers from racks of tight collared shirts and hip-hugging jeans. I sat on a padded stool in the vestibule by the fitting rooms while Chris tried everything on.

From behind the three-quarter-door of the changing room, tags snapped against fingers and Chris gasped. "Sixty dollars for one T-shirt?" He emerged from his fitting room and puffed up his chest in front of the three-way mirror. His nylon travel pants and brightly striped polo were crumpled at the bottom of the stall. "I could buy a whole outfit for that at home!"

The dark-green T-shirt showed off the line of his biceps; the dark jeans his shapely legs. "Yeah, but you wouldn't look nearly as good."

Chris turned one way, then another in front of the three-way mirror. "I'm an urban hipster." He grinned at his reflection. "I look like everyone else walking down Smith Street." He flexed his neck backwards and groped his chin with a faux-intellectual air. "Do I look like I'm thinking about philosophy?"

I laughed at his hijinks, then Chris walked out of the store carrying two full shopping bags worth more money than he had spent on all his clothing for the last ten years.

We returned to Brooklyn by subway, and as we exited the F-train at Smith Street, I spotted the signs for stoop sales on the corner bulletin board—people were taking advantage of the fair weather forecast for Saturday, possibly one of the last good stoop sale days of the season.

"Would you come stoop saling with me tomorrow?"

Chris cocked his head at me. "Sure."

I dragged him by the hand out of bed on Saturday. He tried to pull me back in. I resisted. "You promised to go stoop saling with me. Time to get up." I tugged at his arm. He groaned. "Then I'll take you to brunch."

He groaned again. "I don't like brunch."

"What's not to like about brunch?"

"It's boring. There are only so many things you can do with eggs and bacon. I'll take Asian food anytime."

"Okay, if I agree to Asian, will you get up?"

He put a pillow over his face.

I pulled it off of him, kneeled on the bed, and started pushing his body toward the edge.

"Okay, okay!" He rose and tugged at the nylon travel pants he'd left in heap the night before, then paused. "Should I wear my new Mexx clothes?" He walked out of the bedroom in the green T-shirt and jeans that so suited him. He leaned against the doorframe and posed. I wolf-whistled. "Maybe I should wear the other T-shirt." He turned back to the bedroom, but I grabbed his arm and pulled him out the door.

"Come on, you look great."

Our footsteps echoed in the hallway and bounced down one flight of stairs. He held the doors open for me and the scents of the street—cumin, onion, gasoline, dumpster—surrounded us.

The crystals in the sidewalk were sparkling in the sunshine. People were bustling—at a slightly slower weekend speed—down Smith Street. A couple with a stroller laughed as they pushed their charge in front of them, stroller wheels snapping on the cracks in the sidewalk. I bounded to the bulletin board to recheck the addresses of today's stoop sales.

I led us onto Bergen Street and followed the sign with an arrow posted on the streetlight at the next corner. A half block away, a set of folding card tables were propped in front of a small gated garden, fabrics and toys draped up the steps of the stoop.

I grinned widely. "This is a stoop sale," I said.

Chris looked at me skeptically. "It's a garage sale."

"On a stoop. Exactly."

"So what's all the fuss about?"

"Brooklynites have great taste and limited space, which means that you can find amazing things cheap."

He turned toward the stack of CDs on one of the tables. "Hey, it's Sublime. And it's only two dollars."

"See what I mean?"

Once Chris was engrossed in flipping through CDs, I moved to the clothes hanging on the garden gate and banister.

"Elisa!" Chris called gleefully. He was standing by a glass-encrusted box. "A cigar humidor! Pure maplewood. Only ten dollars. It should be at least a hundred."

"Buy it."

"I don't think it would fit in my backpack."

I collected a couple of designer shirts and a silk scarf, and Chris put a cigar lighter on top of my pile. "So I can keep a good cigar lighter at your place." He pointed to the pile in my hands and paid the seller.

"I want to show you something." I led Chris down Holt Street and turned him onto Wyckoff. Halfway to Smith Street I stopped before the apartment building with the sparkling mosaic that a few months ago had made me think of him. The wave design swept up and around the front door, as if to symbolize that from this small Brooklyn entrance, a person could go anywhere, do anything. I took Chris's hand and remembered that day, months before, when I had passed this mural and tried to make myself believe I was happier seeing it alone.

Chris's eyes followed the tidal wave of the cemented collage. "It's beautiful," he said. "I can't believe someone thought to put this on a building." The gingko trees that lined the road were brightening into autumn yellow, and the dappled sunlight through the gently moving branches limned Chris's features with gold. "Thank you for showing this to me."

"I thought you'd like it." I leaned in to kiss him.

A motorcycle passed us with a roar. Chris's lips stiffened, and he pulled away. "Would you ever be able to leave this?"

I remembered our first conversation in the small country cottage in Minnesota about where we would live if we stayed together. It felt so far away, and yet so momentous, so essential to our being together right now, right here, on Wyckoff Street. "Maybe," I said lightly. "But, hey, if I can't leave this, didn't you once say you could live here?"

His eyes clouded over. "I've been thinking about that. I mean, yes, I could. But . . . that would be a lot more difficult than you coming to live with me in Minnesota." He scuffed the sole of his new leather shoes against the curb. "I don't think it will be easy for me to get a job here . . . I have fourteen years of experience, but it's in small-town insurance, in my family's business. Who here would care? I'd have to start from the scratch. You would have to work for money, and I know how much you would rather spend your time on your music. And everything is so expensive here . . ."

I put my hand on his arm. "It's okay." I drew his body closer to mine, my hand to his chest. Under his grassy scent, I could smell sweat, fear. "I understand. If we want us to continue, then we'll figure it out." I let my eyes follow the wave of the mosaic on the apartment wall. "If it makes more sense for me to move there . . . well, if we ever get to a place where it's time for one of us to move, then I am open to coming to Minnesota."

He exhaled. "You would leave this?"

The rhythm of my breathing matched his. "For you, yes."

His stomach muscles relaxed under my hand. He pulled me close to him and looked into my eyes. "I love you," he said.

"I love you, too."

It was the first time we had said it. And it felt like it wouldn't be the last.

15

First Christmas

Gypsy in a taxicab
Don't remember where I'm at
On my way somewhere else
Hope they expect me
– "Gypsy Cab"

November–December

Over Thanksgiving break, Chris and I visited central Mexico. We walked sixteenth-century streets in old silver-mining towns. We stayed overnight in a ghost town. We lingered in graceful Spanish squares and held hands under Mexican moonlight.

Chris was the first travel companion I ever had who made the trip better than it would have been if I had visited alone. He loved to talk to everyone, and charmed every waiter, hotelier, and shopkeeper with his schoolbook Spanish and his gap-toothed smile. He relished stories, and managed to find common ground with everyone our paths crossed. For the first time in my traveling experience, every place felt like it was welcoming me—us—home.

One afternoon, we were eating a lunch of fresh gorditas at a street-food stand. Chris was learning new Spanish phrases, having charmed the kerchiefed woman stirring two bubbling pots into teaching him. As I wrapped my mouth around a fragrant filled tortilla, Chris turned to me and said, "My parents wanted me to invite you to Christmas at their house."

I swallowed. "Christmas?" Sauce dribbled down my wrist.

"Don't worry, it wouldn't be any pressure. Just my parents and my sister and my sister's family. They'd love to have you there."

I swiped at the sauce with my other hand. "I've never been to Christmas before."

Chris's gordita stopped at his mouth. "Seriously?"

"I'm Jewish. Remember? Christmas was family time for all my Christian friends."

Chris stared at me, sauce from his gordita dripping on the counter. "What did you do for Christmas?"

"Chinese food and a movie." I grinned. "The typical Jewish Christmas Eve. Christmas Day is usually my day off from the world. Everything in town shuts down, and I stay home to enjoy the peace and quiet."

Christmas was the one day of the year when the intersection outside my Brooklyn window was still, when I had no responsibilities: no church to go to, no family to visit, no work. It was the day I tuned the TV to Channel 31, watched the continuous loop of crackling Yule log and listened to Nat King Cole's velvety voice singing "Chestnuts roasting on an open fire." On Christmas Day, my Brooklyn apartment became a magical retreat from the world.

"It would mean a lot to me." Chris's hand reached for mine, and our sauce-sticky palms held fast together.

The Manhattan stores all played the same Christmas songs. I had always been careful to avoid shopping this time of year, but now I had presents to buy. The right presents. I bobbed and weaved around tourists mobbing the sidewalks. I forced myself through flocks of Christmas shoppers in department stores. I reached sales-counter islands through moats four people thick. I dialed Chris from the cavernous, perfumed cosmetic hall of the seven-story Macy's. "Do you think your mom would like perfume?"

"You don't have to get her anything," Chris said for the hundredth time.

"Yes, I do."

Chris sighed. "She doesn't wear much perfume, but I'm sure she'll love whatever you get her. She's not expecting anything."

An older woman with a black Gucci purse jostled me. "How about scarves, does she wear scarves? And what should I get your sisters?"

"I don't know."

"Well, I don't know them at all, so I need your help. What do you usually get your mother and sisters?"

"Subscriptions to the local newspaper."

"Seriously?"

"They like it!"

"Uh-huh."

"You don't need to get them anything."

Fat lot he knew. It didn't matter if they were city or country people, they would expect gifts. I was sure of it. "Gotta go. Call you later." I hung up the phone and padded to the escalator on strained feet.

Chris didn't understand. I had a lot to make up for.

When I was five years old and planning what cookies to set out for Santa Claus, my mother told me Santa wasn't coming to our house because I was Jewish and Jews didn't believe in Santa Claus. I cried. My mother tried to console me. "Santa Claus doesn't really exist," she said. "It's a fairytale. Parents put presents under the tree while children are sleeping." She had no idea what a jealous five-year-old might do with that kind of information. The next day I went out to play with my friends, chin high and eyes narrowed. "I know something you don't," I taunted. I dangled my information in front of my friends like a new sticker and destroyed Christmas for an entire neighborhood full of children.

The invitation to the Klein Christmas was my chance for penance. I bought and returned three rounds of gifts before my approaching departure date finalized my gifts for me. JFK airport was in full holiday frenzy, but the sleepy little regional airport in St. Cloud was almost empty. I exited the minimal-security area clutching the yellow ankle-length down coat I had bought on sale especially for my first visit to Minnesota during its legendary winter.

Chris's body felt solid as a totem pole when he hugged me. "It's so good to see you," he said. "So this is the coat?" I modeled it for him, turning around. "You look like Big Bird," he teased.

"Yeah, but at least I'll be a warm Big Bird."

Chris grinned and gestured to his light fleece jacket. I wrinkled my nose at him. He reached for my bags and raised his eyebrows at my second suitcase and the fancy shopping bag marked "Brooklyn Girl Bakery."

"How much did you bring? And what's that?"

"The second suitcase is for gifts. The bag has cookies for your aunt and uncle."

"Are those from the bakery on the corner of Bergen with tiny cookies for three dollars each?"

I nodded. Chris shook his head, appalled. "They won't even appreciate them. They can't imagine anyone would spend that much on a cookie."

"That's okay. They'll see they're fancy and they come from New York and that I thought of them."

Chris lifted my suitcases and walked to the car still shaking his head. "You didn't have to get gifts."

On the afternoon of Christmas Eve, I gripped Chris's arm tightly as we walked down the aisle of the packed Catholic church. He squeezed my hand and whispered in my ear, "Everything's gonna be fine." My lips were sticky with lipgloss. My hair was brushed shiny and I wore a black wool skirt embroidered with an asymmetrical burst of burgundy flowers. "Jingle Bells" rained down from the mezzanine where the choir sang with more enthusiasm than accuracy. Perfume and mothballs mingled in the air. I smoothed my skirt and wondered again whether I had packed the right outfit. I wanted to make a good impression. I needed to make a good impression. It was Christmas. With Chris's parents and family.

Chris caught someone's eye. Close to the front of the church, a small beaming woman with curled brown hair waved to us enthusiastically. The white-haired man next to her also turned, and then a family of four—Chris's sister, her husband, and their two children, Brendan and Cassidy, ages thirteen and ten.

Chris stood aside for me to enter the pew, his hand on my shoulder, and I slid to the space the Kleins had saved for us. "I'm Michelle," Chris's sister whispered to me as I sat down next to her. We shook hands, and I settled my down coat around me, using it to create a couple inches of padding between me and Chris's sister.

The din melted to a hush. A robed priest entered the sanctuary and began the Mass. I could hear myself breathing. My right side tingled, so close to Chris's sister whom I'd barely met. I balanced awkwardly on the bench. Chris took my hand and squeezed it. I sang along to "Do You Hear What I Hear?" Chris squinted at me as if to say, *You know this song? Aren't you Jewish?* I waggled my eyebrows at him. Every American kid learned Christmas carols. I let my voice ring full, and the people in the pew in front of us turned around to see who was singing. I lowered my volume.

When Mass was over, we drove to Chris's parents' lake house for dinner. We emerged from the cars to the frigid silence of a Minnesota winter's night. The crunch of feet on snow bounced across the frozen lake, the quiet deepened by echoes. Christmas quiet in Brooklyn was noisy compared to this.

The door to the house opened in a rush of holiday smells, baked meat and cinnamon. Chris's mother, Betty, motioned me into the warmth, her hand on my back. "It's so good you could come," she said. A ruffled apron was tied behind her with a bow. She pulled plastic wrap off an hors d'oeuvres tray of olives and celery nestled in crystal bowls and offered it to me. Framed photographs of a smiling Chris and his sisters and their families at various ages lined every shelf and wall.

Chris's father, Ken, led us to a long wooden table by a picture window that overlooked a snow-covered frozen lake. I smoothed my skirt under me as I sat, my hazel eyes reflected in the window in front of me, wide and darting, seeking cues about what to do next. Everyone crossed themselves, bowed their heads as one and clasped hands in front of their chests. I clasped my hands, too. Chris's father cleared his throat at the head of the table. The savory scent of turkey mingled with the sweet-tart scent of cranberries.

"We give thanks to the God of Abraham, Isaac, and Jacob for what we are about to receive." Ken looked at me with a glint in his eye. There had been no talk of Jesus in Ken's grace. He unclasped his hands and silverware clattered as napkins were placed in laps. Platters of meat and vegetables began to circulate with clinks, laughter, and murmurs. A warm white casserole dish full of corn touched my fingers. It took me a moment to grasp that Ken had prepared his grace especially for me, to make their Jewish guest feel welcome. My shoulders untightened and a spray of warmth flowed up from my feet.

There were so many platters they couldn't all fit on the table. Ham and turkey and Ken's home-smoked chicken and brightly colored green beans made their way around the table. Cheesy potatoes and roast beef, carrots, and pickles filled my plate.

"What's this?" I asked Betty when a bowl of pink goo was handed to me.

"That's salad," Betty said, watching for my reaction.

"Salad? It looks like Jell-O."

Chris's niece Cassidy giggled.

"It is Jell-O," Betty said, playing along. "Jell-O, cool whip, and raspberries."

"This isn't a salad!" I declared, voice rising comically. "Where I come from salads have lettuce and vegetables in them."

"It's a Minnesota salad," Betty said, eyes twinkling. "I probably should have made you the one with Jell-O and shredded carrots." Cassidy's giggles broke into laughter.

I made a face and gave Cassidy a sidelong look. "You think I'll like it?"

Cassidy looked to her mother before speaking in a quiet voice, "It's really good. You should try the pistachio one, too." Cassidy passed me a glass bowl of mint-green goo. I placed the mint-green gob next to the dollop of pink and tasted. I pursed my lips theatrically and smacked my mouth loudly. "Tasty. But definitely not salad." Cassidy and Betty smiled broadly.

When the dishes were cleared from the table, everyone trooped upstairs to the sitting room. A Christmas tree presided over a mountain of presents, including the gifts I had brought.

Brendan and Cassidy rushed to sort boxes and gift bags into individual piles. Adults claimed seats on couches, and the kids placed small towers of presents at everyone's feet. A heap accumulated in front of me. I touched the curled ribbons and smooth patterned papers. I had never received so many presents at once, even on birthdays.

"How old are you?" Brendan demanded.

"Why?"

"Because we open presents from youngest to oldest."

"Oh, in that case, I'm thirty-one."

"You're third. It goes Cassidy, then me, then you."

Cassidy piped in, "But this is her first Christmas."

Brendan was ordering his presents by size in a line from biggest to smallest. "Her Christmas age is one."

"Does that mean I get to unwrap my presents first?" I asked excitedly.

"No," he proclaimed and sat down in readiness to open gifts. I was almost disappointed.

For two hours, we unwrapped gifts one gift at a time. I stuck a dozen bows on my head in a Raggedy Ann wig of ribbons. My gifts were received with coos and exclamations of thanks. The boxes stacked in front of me opened to sweaters, books, and earrings. The largest box was Chris's present—a wheeled bag for my gigs, handmade by a friend of his who made outdoor gear. By the end of the night, the room was ankle-deep with crumpled wrapping paper.

I returned to New York City with my second suitcase as full as it had been when I left.

16

Naked in New York

Concrete tempest on a rock-hard sea
Concrete cementing you and me
Concrete glistening from too much rain
Concrete leads me home again
– "Concrete"

January 2007
New York City

Eight months into our relationship, the strain of long-distance dating was creating small fissures. It was time for someone to move.

We continued to talk about moving, going back and forth over who would move during lingering phone calls late into the night, sharing our heady dreams of waking up in the same place together every day.

The facts were clear. Chris had a family business and a steady income. I was an itinerant artist supporting myself with freelance consulting. Chris was willing to give up his business and try his hand at getting a job in New York City, but no matter how many ways we shuffled the facts, that scenario had me finding a full-time dayjob to cover New York's high living expenses. If Chris moved to New York City, I would have less time for my music. Living expenses in Minnesota were a fraction of the cost. If I moved to Minnesota, Chris could continue building his family's business, and I could write songs and perform full time.

It was clear it made more sense for me to move. But I still wasn't one-hundred percent sure that Chris was the man for me, that a life with him would be worth giving up New York City, my community, my proximity to my family, and everything that made up my life as I knew it. Doubts corroded the foundation we were building together, flowing water eating away at concrete.

Chris arrived for his January visit on a gray Friday. I wrapped myself around him, welcoming him into my space, into me, now so different from that first stiff embrace in my apartment. We spent the night curled into shapes that fit each others' bodies. In the morning, I draped myself with his limbs, the intimacy of his sour-sweet morning breath warm on my shoulders. It had been almost a month since I had seen him, and I was hungry for his presence.

On Saturday, Chris donned one of the hipster shirts we had purchased at Mexx, and we navigated around curbside slush puddles to visit Ground Zero and Wall Street. At 3:30 p.m., we'd already done everything on our list. I tugged Chris to a stop on the corner of Fulton Street and Broadway, causing a couple of pedestrians behind us to stumble and veer. A fire engine passed in an ear-splitting hullabaloo. Chris jumped away from the curb and covered his ears with his hands. I calmly pulled *Time Out New York* from my messenger bag and flipped through it.

He watched me through squinted eyes, hands over ears, and shook his head. "New Yorkers," he mouthed.

When we could hear each other again, I read a blurb I had marked in the magazine. "'The No Pants! Subway Ride is staged by Improv Everywhere as an international celebration of silliness. Volunteers meet near the Federal Plaza at 4:00 p.m. to remove their pants on the subway.'"

Chris gaped. "We would actually take off our pants on the subway?"

"Yes."

Chris nodded as if to convince himself. "Now that sure isn't something I could do in Minnesota."

I folded the magazine into my bag and took Chris's hand. "Wanna get naked in public?"

"I dunno." Chris looked up the avenue in the direction the fire truck had gone.

"We're really close to where they're meeting. We could find out what's going on and decide later whether we want to do it."

Chris stood up straighter. "Okay."

We walked to the nondescript neighborhood south of Chinatown and east of Tribeca. Chris ran a couple of steps to catch up to me—I was a city walker, trained to cover as much pavement as possible in the shortest time. "Slow down," he grabbed my sleeve. "I'd like to see what we're walking past." To our left, the Federal Building loomed substantial and somber. I smelled cigarette butts and metal, and remembered the feel of concrete on my bare torso. The No Pants! Subway Ride was starting less than a block away from where I had lain in Federal Plaza for Stanley Tunick's naked photograph years before.

If I left New York City, I would be leaving experiences like this behind. I wouldn't be posing in a naked photograph. I wouldn't be able to decide on a whim to go on a No Pants! Subway Ride.

I squeezed Chris's hand for reassurance. He squeezed back. A subway rumbled the pavement underneath us.

It was easy to pick out the crowd waiting for the No Pants! Subway Ride. A mass of young hipsters with goatees and thick-framed plastic glasses gathered on a sidewalk island in the middle of an intersection. Chris's body started to shake, his eagerness bouncing from his hand into mine. The crowd spilled into the three-way intersection. We took a few steps and the crowd consumed us, pulsing with anticipation, a slingshot pulled taut. We pulsed with it.

The chill of the air pushed under my jacket. I drew myself closer to Chris and settled into the familiar adrenaline-infused wait of New York City. Chris fidgeted, bouncy as a tennis ball. He wasn't used to the city holding pattern: waiting for subways to arrive or depart, standing in an interminable line of fifty opinionated and demanding people at the post office. In New York Mills, he also didn't have the excitement of a No Pants! Subway Ride. "Hi," Chris smiled at a man in a red-and-white striped Cat-in-the-Hat cap, who nodded and walked away. "Nice shoes," Chris said to a woman wearing six-inch yellow patent-leather heels. When a man with a top hat climbed onto the railing of a road barrier, Chris lifted his head. Top Hat raised his arms and waved them over the crowd like a conductor, his trench coat billowing in the wind. Chris released my hand and pushed through people to get closer.

"Hey, you," Chris caught the man's attention. "Are you the ramrod of this operation?"

"What?" the man's arms moved in stiff, right-angled arcs.

"Are you in charge?"

The man laughed, top hat tilting. "No, I'm taking advantage of my new height."

Chris peppered Top Hat with more questions, and I turned my attention to the growing crowd that now stretched to the other side of the street. I rubbed my hands together to warm up my fingers.

Forty-five minutes after the event was supposed to begin, a medium-sized white man with a wool cap climbed onto the railing and held his hand in the air to quiet the crowd.

"Hello!" he called. The crowd cheered in response. "It's great to see you here."

Chris's gleaming eyes were glued to the speaker. The crowd murmured enthusiastically. Someone whooped from the back. The leader waited for the crowd to settle.

"You are all going to be divided into groups assigned to Number 6 trains. Individuals in each group will be assigned to take off their pants at each subway stop. By the end of the line, each subway car will be full of people not wearing pants."

Chris elbowed me, his grin as wide as a city block.

"Make sure you do not acknowledge your fellow No Pants! riders before or after disrobing. Everyone act nonchalant. We don't want to telegraph the fact that something's about to happen." There were a few whoops and a gospel-styled "uh-*huh*."

"If someone asks why you took off your pants, come up with a simple answer. For example, 'I was warm' or 'My pants were itchy.' If the person asks about the other No Pants! riders, you don't know them. Now, are we ready?"

The crowd erupted in a spasm of excitement, from hurry-up-and-wait to explosion of motion. The group leaders raised their hands and the crowd thrummed, everyone moving in a different direction. My whole world was moving. I couldn't see the pavement for all the shoes. I reached for Chris, lost in a forest of coats and people. Finally, in the V of someone's bent arm, was the olive of his down jacket. I gulped air and dodged and pushed into the crowd towards his sleeve. I tugged at his arm, pinning us together among the masses of moving people. "Wanna do it?"

He answered by pulling me toward the nearest group leader. We had to move fast now that most of the groups had descended the subway stairs. A red-bearded guy led twenty of us into the bowels of the Brooklyn Bridge station. Unseen subways rumbled the floors. The No Pants! riders walked quickly, no motion wasted, and melted into the crowds of regular 6-train passengers.

Red Beard had assigned Chris and me to the third car and told us to take off our pants before Twenty-third Street. I veered around a guitar-playing busker on the platform. Once, in this very station, I had performed my songs with my guitar case open to receive coins from subway passengers. Today, I would be performing in a very different manner.

I checked the standing map in the middle of the platform. We would have seven stops to prepare to disrobe. We held hands. A departing train pulled a stale breeze across my cheeks. I inhaled the subway's hot, fetid breath. My heart beat in my ears.

The train arrived, doors sliding open with a *ding-ding-shhhh*. My pre-performance nerves jangled. Chris breathed like a runner on a starting block. I linked my arm with Chris's, and we stepped aboard.

My skin was greenish-pale in the darkened window reflection, brown hair tucked behind my ears. Next to me, Chris was radiant, head tilted Puckishly, face angled to watch people streaming through the doors. He kept having to nudge the corners of his mouth downward. I caught his eye in the window. He grinned, then straightened his features to faux seriousness. The PA system crackled: "Stand clear of the closing doors, please."

The train jerked forward, and my body jolted into Chris's shoulder. "Look, there are some of the others—" Chris cut me off with a Popeye scowl—we were supposed to pretend not to know each other—and immersed himself in the subway map poster. I tucked my attention into my magazine and read the same paragraph four times while trying to remember which underpants I had put on that morning. I hoped they weren't see-through or ripped.

We approached the first station. A heavy-set twenty-something with a brown goatee stood up. He unzipped his fly and pulled his waistband to his knees. Balancing on one leg, he lifted pale, hairy legs from crushed denim. Cotton boxers with cartoon bubbles filled with "WHAM" and "POW" fluttered gently before he sat down. He opened a newspaper with a crack, and naked legs jutted out from under a rectangle of newsprint.

No one reacted.

Chris was breathing shallowly, putting visible effort into keeping a nonchalant expression. The rest of the passengers were busy ignoring each other.

"This is Canal Street," the recorded woman purred. "Transfer is available to the N, R, Q, W, J, and M trains."

The doors opened with two pings. Two people exited; ten more piled on. Only one person glanced at the bare-legged man in boxers. I sat down on a seat that had opened in front of me.

"Stand clear of the closing doors, please." The doors whirred shut; the train accelerated. Three No Pants! riders to my right took their hands off the subway poles and reached for their flies, riding the subway's shifting floor like surfers. Hot pink bikini underwear and two pairs of silk boxers appeared over three sets of bare legs. The closest passengers began to turn their heads.

When a dozen riders were bare-legged under winter jackets, people began to notice. Jaded New Yorkers were skilled at hiding their reactions, but I picked up on them: subtle double-takes, an up-and-down jut of a chin, too many sideways glances.

A seat opened next to me, and Chris sat down. He tapped his foot, knee bobbing. It was almost time. I elbowed him. He elbowed back. My limbs moved like wet sand. I slid my butt forward to the edge of the seat, and slipped sock-clad feet out of my Danskos. Chris leaned over to untie his shoes. I pulled my bag strap from around my shoulders and rested the bag on my knees.

"Please stand clear of the closing doors." The door tones sounded: our starting gun.

We were on our feet. I balanced my weight against the shifting of the car as I unbuttoned my corduroys. Chris's arm bumped mine as he fiddled with his fly. The cool air of the subway kissed my thighs as my pants dropped to my ankles. I looked down, relieved to find underwear without holes. Next to me, Chris stood in black boxer shorts.

We had undressed on the subway.

Chris nudged me, then inclined his head towards the khakis bunched up in his hand. I took them and stuffed both pairs of pants into my messenger bag. I tried to make my eyes say: *Isn't this crazy?* Chris stifled a grin and returned to cell phone Solitaire.

The skin of my thighs curved into the shape of the molded plastic seat. I smelled the sour-sharp scent of yesterday's alcohol from the man in the blazer three seats away. A large woman's elbow jabbed me in the side as she squished herself into the space next to me on the bench.

Throughout it all, an invisible thread joined me to Chris. Today, I was not going through the subway motions alone.

I recalled the subway ride a year before when I had watched my old friend Jodi and her husband, Ron, reading next to each other, Ron's body shielding Jodi, Jodi's foot touching Ron's. Separate but tied inexorably together. I had craved that sensation, knowing on some level it was part of what had been missing for me in New York City.

Today, for the first time in my life, I had it.

Chris nudged my shoulder, and his thrill traveled through me where his body touched mine. I had an urge to pull him into both my arms and hold him close, but here, together, already attached at a level more fundamental than physical, I didn't even need to. Instead, I nudged him back and let my leg linger against his as I pretended not to be paying him any attention.

Chris and I filed out of the car at 125th Street, the end of the line, in a parade of pantsless people, an elongated kickline of mismatched Rockettes that stretched down the platform, bare legs in all shades and sizes. Chris was beaming like a golden retriever.

A downtown-bound train dinged open, and we followed the rest of the pantsless people on.

"What now?" I asked over the rumble of the accelerating subway.

Chris smiled into my eyes. "What do you want to do?"

"Dinner?"

He nodded, and I pulled the wad of our intertwined pants from my messenger bag and, standing in a moving train, balancing on our half-removed shoes, we put them on. By the time we got off the subway in SoHo, no one could have guessed we had just been pantsless.

We held hands as we walked up the stairs and clattered through the turnstiles. The wind was fresh and bracing as it welcomed us aboveground, renewed, reborn. The concrete was sturdy under my feet and Chris was walking beside me, and all of a sudden I knew. This was the man for me.

This was a man willing to take off his pants in public for fun. This was a man who brought me unadulterated, child-like joy. This was a man worth staying with.

Chris was a man worth moving for.

Part II

The Topography of Sky

March 2007–July 2008

17

The Move

I need to keep on going
It's only moving that I feel at home
– "100 Miles to Nowhere"

March 2007
New York City

My apartment was a warehouse of cardboard boxes. My father had traveled north from my parents' home in the D.C. suburbs to help me pack the weekend before. My international urban parents were still unsure about my move to the rural heartland, but they were happy their thirty-something daughter had finally found a man she thought was worth introducing to them. They had almost given up hope that I might get married someday. Another bonus of my move: my mother had stopped trying to set me up with distant acquaintances of her synagogue friends.

Cats sprawled on the highest cardboard towers. For a week, I navigated my apartment by narrow, box-lined paths.

Because of work obligations, Chris hadn't been able to make my goodbye party at a local bar the night before, but he was coming this morning by plane to drive the moving truck cross-country with me.

Cubes packed with books filled the space where I used to lay my yoga mat out on the floor. The gaping mouth of the wardrobe box dribbled mismatched autumn-hued fabrics. The intercom buzzed. This was it. There was no turning back. I squeezed myself between a box and my disassembled desk chair to open the door. Chris pulled me into a hug in the doorway. My heart fluttered like a dying moth against the trunk of his chest.

I pulled out of his arms, blinking my eyes hard. "Gotta finish packing up the cabinets." I lifted my leg high to step over the box marked "Dishes." My heel caught on a cardboard flap, and I stumbled gracelessly into the kitchen. I righted myself sheepishly. "How was your trip?"

"Fine. You know, a part of me is sorry I won't be coming to visit you in New York anymore. I'm going to miss it."

The cords in my neck tightened. I blinked tears away, so close to the surface now. Chris reached over a box to touch my shoulder.

"Will it be okay?" I asked, voice breaking.

His voice was gentle. "It's already okay."

"Right." Blinking no longer worked. Tears were acid. I pulled a plate out of the cabinet, placing the circle of smooth ceramic on a blank square of packing paper. The plate, cool to my touch, felt sturdy and solid, but I knew one blow would break it into hopeless shards. Without padding, it wouldn't survive this move.

Chris wrapped his arms around me from behind. "Hey, let's sit down. I'm here for you." He led me through the boxes to the couch and I curled my trembling body into the circle of his barrel chest and bough-like arms. Chris would be my protection, a gentle embrace around the brittle edges of my fear.

Once the spilling innards of my cabinets and closets had been wrangled, folded, and stowed, Chris took me out for a goodbye New York dinner. "Wherever you want to go." For my last meal before I moved to a place where the only restaurant in town—a diner—closed at 3:00 p.m., I chose Saul, the Michelin-starred French restaurant two blocks away.

Chris looked too sturdy for the fine wood chair and filmy white tablecloth. The base of his stemmed water glass caught on his plate and clinked as he lifted it. He wore the beige checked shirt we had bought for him on our Fifth Avenue shopping spree months before. The candlelight lingered in the folds of fabric that were starting to pucker around the buttons.

The room suddenly felt too warm and close. I shifted in my seat. *What am I about to do? Is this guy really the one for me? Is moving the right decision?*

I reached for the butter when Chris did. Our hands bumped, and Chris's fingers hooked mine over the bread basket.

"I love the butter at Saul," I said, voice tight.

"I love you," Chris said back, squeezing my fingers.

"I love you, too." The familiar words tasted different today, like cream a little off.

Chris must have sensed how fragile I felt, that anytime now I would explode into a puff of dandelion seeds and flutter away in the wind. He held my hand firmly, anchoring me to him as we walked to my apartment. Opening the door, the space smelled like someone else's—its normal spice-and-candle scent overcome by packing tape and cardboard. There was nothing more to pack. My whole life had been compressed into twenty-four cardboard boxes and a bed. The alarm was set. The only thing left to do was to prepare my apartment cats for a three-day drive. The veterinarian had suggested giving the cats a trial run with the sedatives in a familiar environment before getting on the road.

I held the cats' mouths open, and Chris placed a small tablet of sedative on their rough tongues. I gently closed mouth over pill until their furry necks bulged and swallowed. When I let go, the cats leaped from my lap, tails twitching with dissatisfaction.

"Think it's working?" Chris asked.

I stared at the thin strip of sky at the top of my windows, dark now. The corner traffic light reflected faintly on my wall, morphing from green to yellow to red. Engine noises shifted from drive to idle to drive again.

The cats began to run into walls. Sander's legs moved in the wrong order. He tripped and collapsed, scrabbling his legs to get himself upright, falling again. *Meow,* he whined. *Meow meow.* Tree's head wobbled on his neck like a bobble-headed doll on a dashboard. Their yellow eyes were half-closed, pupils dilated. Chris teased the cats with a strip of packing tape, and they pawed the air a foot away from the tape. Tree's eyes crossed as his paws reached nothing. Chris melted into laughter.

"Stop teasing them!" I picked Tree up and cuddled him in the protective circle of my arms. I felt as discombobulated as they looked.

Chris stopped twitching the tape, a once flat strip now crumpled into a tangle of plastic and adhesive. His face bunched with concern. "They're fine. Just drunk."

"Please don't tease them. They're scared."

Chris righted Sander gently and put his hand on my arm. "Are you scared?"

I couldn't answer. I pulled away from Chris and lay down on the bed facing the window. The cats curled next to each other in warm circles on the flowered coverlet I would pack in the morning. My mind circled through all the questions I couldn't answer yet. How would I survive in a town of 1,100 people? Would I be able to make myself a home there?

"Are the cats scared about the move?" Chris asked.

I snorted a chuckle through my tears and nodded.

"It's okay, honey." The bed bowed as Chris sat down beside me. He folded his body around mine. "Everything will be fine."

I slept fitfully in neon-tinged darkness, strips of light flickering behind my eyes, downy duvet trapping me as I tossed, dreaming of a version of me dressed in a gingham apron.

When I woke, fear pinned my eyes wide open. The morning light on cardboard made my apartment look sterile, uninhabited. My Brooklyn sanctum was no longer mine. I rustled toward Chris, pulling his arm across me and snuggling into the crook of his elbow.

"Goodbye, apartment," I said.

"You can still stay, if you want to." Chris said, playfully.

I elbowed Chris in the stomach and shoved myself out of bed. "Let's get this over with."

We took the F-train two stops to the Penske Truck Rental I had not known about till I needed to move. I handed a man behind a desk my credit card and driver's license and wrote down the address of the dealership in Fargo where we would return the vehicle in three days. Fargo. My nearest delivery point was the subject of a movie titled to represent emptiness and isolation. A movie about a place so remote that a character gets shoveled into a woodchipper in a backyard. I slid the yellow moving truck into the metered space under my apartment window and waited the few minutes till parking was permitted. Chris placed my songbooks and guitars in the cab of the truck. Hired movers arrived and hefted boxes on their shoulders two at a time down the stairs. Sander and Tree yowled in counterpoint from two cat carriers in the corner of the apartment where my stereo used to be.

Jae and Maggie came over to say goodbye and keep me company as I watched everything I owned parade into the back of the truck. Empty of furniture and all my belongings, the apartment that had once been my sanctuary now felt bigger, anonymous and alien.

It was time to go. Jae handed me a paper sack of natural-food snacks for the road. Maggie gave me a boisterous hug that lasted till the strength in her arms gave out. With a lump in my throat, I turned to open the passenger door. Chris's voice stopped me.

"You should drive," he said.

"Can't you? I want to curl up with the cats."

He blanched. "I don't think I can manage the truck on city streets."

I walked around the cab of the truck, waiting for the traffic to stop for the red light before opening the driver's door. I dwelled in the mundane tasks of fastening seatbelts and adjusting mirrors. Small silvery versions of Jae and Maggie waved at me from the side mirror. The terror of crashing the truck distracted me from the terror of my destination—a new, unfamiliar life—as I pulled into the traffic on Atlantic Avenue.

The center of the windshield where the rearview mirror was supposed to be was bare, the view ahead bigger and more daunting in the uninterrupted rectangle of shatterproof glass. There was no longer anything separating me from my new life. At the entrance ramp to the Brooklyn-Queens Expressway, I made a kamikaze run into a tiny space in the stream of traffic that never stopped. The cats yowled at the acceleration.

"We're on our way!" Chris's voice bounced exuberantly. Hairline cracks formed on my shiny ceramic surface. I tried to let Chris's enthusiasm cushion me so I wouldn't shatter from the truck's vibrations. The scent of gasoline and the Gowanus Canal snuck through the windows. Conversation fizzled into silence. The cats cried in long, deep moans.

By New Jersey, the sedatives started to do their job, and the cats quieted down. That night, Chris aimed the truck sideways across three parking spots at a commuter motel in eastern Ohio. After a final glance at the yellow truck that contained everything I owned, I put my guitar on my back and one cat carrier on each shoulder and walked down a musty motel hallway. Blood coursed through the veins in my temples, and I couldn't calm down no matter how tightly Chris held me on the lumpy bed.

We left the northeast behind on the second day. Miles of strip malls and refineries melted into forests lined with trees just beginning to bud. The cats meowed less, and Chris and I played I Spy and Spot the License Plate. We chose lunch and dinner restaurants by whether or not there was a parking area large enough for the truck. On the third day, we crossed the invisible Minnesota border. Everything looked the same as it had in Wisconsin and Illinois, except the Minnesota trees were still bare of leaves, branches twisted and threatening. The "Welcome to Minnesota" sign felt like an afterthought.

18

How Not to Be a Midwesterner

Below the rise of my instep
In the scrape on my knee
In the dip of my waistline
Or the hole in my jeans
In the sight of my neck raised high
In your hand released
You will find my strength
—"Find My Strength"

April
Minnesota

The summer after I met Chris, we had heard a professional mountain climber speak about his ascent of Mt. Everest. His presentation covered the expected ground: base camp, inclement weather, extreme conditions, death-defying climbing maneuvers, and the thrill of summiting. The most vivid part of his story, however, was when he described the death zone.

At 8,000 meters of altitude, the thin blue air left in the atmosphere has only one-third the pressure it has at sea level. Only one-third as much oxygen to breathe. From twenty-five breaths per minute, human respiration increases to eighty-five breaths per minute. A person is exhausted just by breathing.

I had thought that crossing the border from New York City to New York Mills would be as simple as taking a step over an invisible line. Instead I discovered it was a death-defying climb up a record-breaking mountain, and before I could reach the other side I had to pass through the death zone. Stranded between my life before and my life to come, I couldn't breathe. No, it was more like I was hyperventilating and still not getting enough oxygen. I could not go forward. I could not go back. I was neither here nor there. I had left New York City behind, and I had not yet found a new home. I was in the middle of nowhere. I was in the death zone. I was exhausted by breathing.

"Took you long enough to get here," Jack said gruffly from behind the counter of the Creamery coffee shop. "What'd you do? Walk?" He glanced pointedly at the counter. Cheryl, co-owner, watched me from behind Jack. Tented in front of the cash register was a folded piece of paper with my name scrawled across it. I unfolded it to find a photograph of the road sign that said "New York Mills. Population: 1152." Jack had crossed out the two and handwritten a three above it.

I dropped my head, letting my long side-swept bangs veil my eyes. My thumb pressed the cheap copy paper into my index finger. It was smooth and thin as gauze, and I knew I was about to crease it with the pressure, but I needed to hold onto something.

"Thank you. This was exactly what I needed." Jack wrapped a dishtowel around the mug in his hands, grunted and turned away.

Cheryl rolled her eyes at Jack's back and beamed at me. "It's so good to have you here! An official resident of New York Mills."

A rush of cooler air came from the front door, and Cheryl shuttled her head from the newcomers to me. I waved and shuffled toward my favorite table, the one next to a sackcloth-covered column where Jack had pinned a poster for my concert the year before. I tried writing, and managed a couple pages of useless words. I left the Creamery and returned to what had once been Chris's house and was now where I lived.

The gray cottage with white trim was a little bit larger than the artist cottage, but far less spacious. On the ground floor were a kitchen with stenciled cabinets, a dim bedroom too long in one direction and too short in another, and a living room with a previous owner's lace curtains. A precarious stairwell led upstairs to two tiny connected rooms under the eaves. The interior of the house had been painted so many times by so many different hands the walls had the texture of a raised relief map.

While the house had felt welcoming when I visited Chris from New York, now that I was living here it was like a pair of jeans that didn't fit right. The rooms were tight and cramped. Air seemed to get caught in doorways, trapped by furniture too large for the space. Chris's polyester sheets squeaked and pulled at my skin. The living room was filled by Chris's beloved overstuffed black leather couch and loveseat, which clashed with the lace curtains.

The upstairs rooms were empty save a few of Chris's cast-offs, so I chose to make the far one into my studio. I placed my guitars on their stands and piled notebooks and pens onto a small desk I appropriated from the garage. I banged my head on the angled ceilings every time I tried to turn from my writing desk to a guitar.

Chris was back at work, and I was desperate to establish the minor daily routines that add up to a life. "What are you doing today?" he asked each morning.

"I don't know," I said. "Writing, I guess."

One morning after I had cried myself to sleep in Chris's arms, Chris looked at me with concern. "Are you going to be okay?"

"Sure," I grinned with more confidence than I felt. "I'll go to the Creamery later."

When Chris left for work, I went upstairs to my makeshift studio and tried to write. I didn't have a regular job to give a rhythm to my days. I had no office to go to, no colleagues to pretend were friends, no office politics to chew on when my loneliness got the better of me. Instead I had the strange new creaks of Chris's cottage-like house and the regular thrum of the train barreling down the tracks five blocks away. I had the hollow spaces of lonely rooms while Chris was at work. I had an awkward corner with my computer, guitars, notebook, and pens. And I had a lingering uncertainty about whether moving had been the right decision. Life in New York Mills began to feel as lonely as the moments before I went onstage for a show. Disconnected from my audience, I had to prove myself before I could be accepted and embraced.

I sought out activities to help me forget how terrified I was to fill the blank pages of my new life.

Two weeks into Minnesota, the trees were still bare, but the fields had become verdant with the green promise of upcoming blooms. Chris invited me for lunch near his office, which was in the basement of the house Chris grew up in, a former corner church two blocks off a sleepy main street. I drove forty-five minutes to Eagle Bend, population 512, on long, empty, sixty-mile-an-hour roads through bright-green farmland. Chris's daily commute had scenery I would have once paid to vacation to.

The town's only restaurant was also its gas station and grocery store. Chris opened the glass door for me, and the smell of gasoline transitioned to the scents of fried food and mildewed fridge. The restaurant's windows overlooked the cars filling up with gas. Chris greeted the waitress and cook by name as we walked in.

We slid into a molded plastic booth by the window. The laminated menu advertised a "taco salad" special. My other options were fried chicken, steak, or hamburger. The only non-potato vegetables on the menu were in the taco salad, so that's what I ordered. The lettuce was shredded iceberg. The dressing came out of a plastic pouch.

A man and a woman with gray hair and rough hands finished their lunch and came over to our table. Chris introduced them as two of his insurance clients and introduced me proudly as his girlfriend who had moved here from New York City.

"How do you like it here?" the woman asked.

"It's great, but quite a change."

"Ooh, ya. I can imagine." Her nasal "ya" made a glissando down and up and down the scale. "What kinds of things are different?"

"Everything. The food. The people. And, what is that color everywhere? That strange shade in the fields?"

The woman looked at me blankly. Her brow furrowed. She turned to her husband. He looked confused.

"It's so green," I said, lamely.

There was a pause. Our conversational rhythm was off, like a motor that wouldn't catch. The woman's mouth twisted. She shrank into her husband and the two of them, without taking any steps, seemed to move further away from me.

"In New York City there's not much greenery," I tried to explain. I didn't have the strength to pull the rope of the motor hard enough to get it going again. I stopped trying. "The farmland here is beautiful."

The woman's mouth moved in the direction of a smile. Her eyes didn't. "Good to meet you," she said unconvincingly. The two walked out of the restaurant, through the gas pumps, and to their car.

Chris's forehead creased. "You can't say things like that around here. People here don't understand sarcasm."

"But that wasn't . . ." I trailed off and pushed iceberg lettuce across my plate. It wasn't sarcasm, but that didn't matter. He was right. I lived here now, and I would have to learn how to talk like everyone else.

"Hey," Chris stretched his hand across the table to take mine. "I didn't mean to make you feel badly. I only want to help."

I nodded and pushed the remains of my salad away. Chris went up to the counter to pay the bill, and I stared out the window at the pick-up trucks and farm vehicles and the men in work shirts and wondered how I would ever fit in here.

On my way back, I stopped at the Creamery. I sat at my favorite table by my poster. There I was again, the two-dimensional me staring confidently out on the world from the sackcloth column.

I spread my notebooks and pens over the smooth wood table. Everyone arrived and greeted other people in the room. No one greeted me. Everyone knew each other here. Only a few people knew me.

"What are you wearing?" Jack grunted from behind me.

I swiveled my head and followed Jack's gaze down to my jeans, bell-bottoms artfully patched with tapestry. I ran my hands against the nubbly fabric. "Pants."

"Those aren't pants. Those are tablecloths."

Cheryl bustled over with the scone I had ordered. "Oh, hush, you," she said. "Those pants are beautiful. This man doesn't have enough fashion sense to fill his pinky."

"Woman, what do you know about my fashion sense? Those pants are ridiculous." Jack swaggered away in Wrangler jeans, turning his head to wink at me as he left. Cheryl placed my mocha in front of me, rolled her eyes and followed him to the kitchen.

I put the brimming mug to my lips and closed my eyes in anticipation of the first sip. My eyes flew open. Too-hot coffee seared the tender flesh of my mouth. I forced it down and felt the liquid burn from throat into chest. I sucked at my tongue, rubbing burnt tastebuds against wounded gums. The waistband of my fancy jeans dug into my side. I set the mug down with a thud.

"Nice blazer," Lynn gestured to the flower-embroidered corduroy jacket as the front door of the Cultural Center clicked shut behind me the following week. Her body overflowed the rolling chair at the front desk behind the cash register. The buzz of voices filled the gallery space. "Where's your man?"

"Chris is out of town on a fishing trip." I held a plastic grocery bag, handles stretched taut with the weight of tortilla chips and salsa. Bringing a contribution for the spring auction buffet was my first official duty as a newly elected board member for the Cultural Center.

Lynn placed a price sticker on a basket donated to the silent auction. Her eyes sparkled mischievously. "Have you two lovebirds been following my advice?"

I sucked at my teeth. "Not exactly." The plastic shopping bag twirled, and the handle garroted my fingers. "Our shower isn't very big."

"Ooh," Lynn trilled, waggling her eyebrows. Her voice dropped into the growly seduction of Mae West. "A small shower makes it even better! My sister swears the secret to keeping her marriage vibrant is to shower together every morning. She's been married twenty-nine years. She should know."

I shifted my eyes to the metal shelves behind her where Scandinavian glass bird sculptures glowed like round jewels. In New York City, I would have parried with a retort like, "Why don't you tell me about your recent shower companions?" But Chris had made it clear my "sarcasm" didn't fly here.

Lynn's tone was coy. "I even told my daughter that's what she should do with her boyfriend."

I raised my hands in laughing surrender. The plastic bag twirled in the other direction, and the handle loosened its hold on my fingers. "Gotta find a bowl for these chips."

The light-filled gallery space had once been a furniture store and had the hardy feel of a well-built antique building. Sculptures had been pushed aside to make room for tables covered with garden-themed auction donations: potted plants, metal buckets, and the fancy new flowered cushion covers I had brought from New York that didn't match Chris's leather couches.

I walked across the section of wood floor that would be my stage when I performed here next month. I smelled the rich oniony scent of home cooking coming from the buffet table at the back of the room. I had thought about cooking or baking something, but it hadn't seemed important enough. On my way to the Cultural Center, I whisked by the three-aisle supermarket in town and grabbed tortilla chips and salsa.

In the center of the buffet table, homemade fudge and cookies were laid out in neat squares on a fancy serving platter. Two slow-cookers sat like mismatched sisters. The orange one was squat and filled with Swedish meatballs. The tall green one held a slurry of miniature hot dogs in barbecue sauce and trailed a well-worn electrical cord.

I found a bowl on the utility shelves and shifted a warming dish of spinach dip to make room for it on the buffet table. The tortilla bag deflated in a puff of salty air. I should have spent less time choosing my outfit and more time baking. I upended chips into the plastic bowl. I had no bowl for the salsa—*How hard would it have been to bring serving containers?*—so I twisted off the tops to the jars and placed them in front of the chips. They looked like what they were: fake food, entertainment for the purpose of staving off hunger, a bait and switch, a delay. I tilted my head and squinted. Through blurred vision, I tried to see the chips and salsa as part of the homemade whole. It didn't work. I stood there, tortilla chip bag crumpled in my right hand.

I didn't have to make anything for New York City parties. Brooklyn roof soirées offered catered canapés and views of the downtown Manhattan skyline lit up against an orange-gray sky. Small hipster gatherings took place in studio apartments in the East Village, with radiators banging and guests claiming angles of space between the coat-piled bed and candle- and alcohol-covered kitchen counter. I might pick up a bottle of Belgian lambic from the Korean deli on the corner or, if the host was a close friend, stop at City Girl cookies down the block for a dozen teardrop-shaped delicacies. Mostly I never brought anything at all. I met artists and authors in leather booths at mirror-lined bars that served white chocolate martinis.

The tortilla bags crackled as I stuffed them into the plastic waste bin by the office. A voice from behind me said, "I love chips and salsa. I'm so glad you brought them." I turned to see one of the board members smile at me. I cleared my throat and dipped a tortilla chip into the salsa and crunched it between my teeth. The tangy salsa and the salty corn mixed in my mouth, the combination better than either of its parts.

As I walked across the gallery, I took a moment to appreciate the way the ceiling of the first floor was cut away to reveal skylights on the roof. I could almost imagine a Jewish marriage canopy suspended from the balcony. The thought came unbidden, *If Chris and I ever get married, this room would be a lovely place for it.*

19

Fish Fry at Lina and Jerome's

Treasures can hide in plain sight
A trifle's a prize if you look at it right
Once you place me where I belong
Everyone will see what you saw
– "Yours for a Song"

May

My rear ached from the press of porch step; my back throbbed from the ridges of the cottage's gray siding. Chris was supposed to have been home fifteen minutes ago to take me to Lina and Jerome's house for dinner. The sun glared off the foil-covered paper plate of homemade cookies on the landing next to me. Lilies of the valley exhaled perfume into thick summer air. I reached to pick a stem from the patch by the front door and twirled the miniature white bells under my nose.

He loves me, he loves me not. The petals were too small to pluck. I stood up and paced across the narrow width of driveway. I swatted at a mosquito and felt the resistance of air. A sting pricked my calf. *Damn mosquito.* I slapped and missed, skin smarting red around the raised bite.

Where is he? I inhaled more lily of the valley, its bouquet now thick and cloying. I threw the rigid stem into the weeds.

A car honked. I raised my head. Chris was roaring down Main Street in the Buick LeSabre, grinning wildly behind the windshield as rock music blasted out of open windows. I picked up the cookies. Chris leaned across the passenger seat to unlock the door for me. "You're late," I said.

"Grrrrr . . ." Chris answered with a maniacal look, whites of his eyes showing.

I kept my face stern. "Is that supposed to scare me?"

"You're the scary one," Chris whispered theatrically, widening his eyes even more and shrinking back in a parody of fear.

I tried to stifle my giggle under a frown, but he caught it.

"Don't smile," he said.

The hard angles of my face softened.

"Got you!"

I scratched at the mosquito bite. "I hate being late."

"We're going to be there in ten minutes. No big deal."

"But . . ." But what? But there was too much riding on this evening. But there was too much riding on everything in Minnesota. But there were some things about this man that made me love him more and some things that made me want to go running back to New York City. "But I want to make a good impression."

"Elisa, they already like you."

I curved my body to get into the car and stopped half in and half out. Chris followed my eyes to the passenger seat's nest of magazines, CDs, and insurance forms. His car was always a chaos of clutter, like his dresser, his closet, the kitchen table, and the bedroom floor. I straightened and raised my eyebrows at him, my hard-won cheer hardening into frustration again. We had had words about this the night before. He was visual, he claimed. He needed to see things to remember where they were. I was ambulatory, I responded, I needed uncovered floor where I could place my feet so I could walk.

"Oops," he said sheepishly. He scooped everything up and threw the pile into the backseat next to another pile, a striped towel and a pair of swim goggles. With splayed fingers I tossed a piece of plastic wrap with sticky brown crumbs from the passenger seat onto the floor and entered the car.

He tried to lighten my mood with an upbeat tone. "It's my mobile office. It has everything I need to work anywhere, even on a boat."

I bit the inside of my cheek, knowing anything I had to say would only lead to a resumption of last night's argument. Chris pulled onto Highway 10, and a stray can of Diet Coke knocked against my left foot with a hollow clang. I wanted to kick it. Hard. I had imagined being a couple would be easier, somehow. That any conflict would be over important issues, like whether to have kids, or how to spend money, not about where to put one's dirty laundry (i.e. not on the floor).

I opened the window a crack and shut my eyes, letting the breeze blow the hair away from my face, hoping it would also blow away my irritation. When we parked outside Lina and Jerome's Victorian, I had almost composed myself. I opened the door and the acrid scent of old meat stung my throat. Perham was having another dog-food day. I inhaled shallowly as I followed Chris onto the wrap-around porch. The front door swung open to a pair of twinkling tea-colored eyes. "Come on in," Lina said. The scent of frying oil wafted out behind her.

Chris and I entered one after the other, each of us pausing in the awkward space between doorframe and door to hug Lina. I could hear the clatter of meal preparation from deeper in the house. I handed her the foil-wrapped plate of homemade cookies—at least I'd managed to make something to bring this time.

The small front hallway opened to a parlor filled with musical instruments. Sheet music was piled on top of a carved piano. A phalanx of brass horns paraded across a dark wood table. I stepped into the hush of this altar to music and stopped. I ran my hand against the top of a red-velvet chaise lounge carved in the shape of a sleeping swan.

"Are these yours?" I almost whispered. Lina nodded. "I didn't know you were a musician, too."

Her eyes twinkled as she touched the piano keys with affection. "I studied music in New York City." Lina led us out of her music room and into the living room, where a worn velveteen chair faced the TV and an end table was hidden under a jumble that included a man's reading glasses, a couple of empty mugs, and fishing and antique magazines.

Jerome peeked his long, Ichabod Crane body from the kitchen. One hand was gloved in a flowered oven mitt; the other wielded a metal spatula. His too-large glasses were tipped sideways and fogged. "Hi! Sunnies'll be ready in a few minutes." Lina placed my cookies on the sideboard and bustled up to Jerome with a gilded china platter. Jerome's rail-thin frame towered over Lina's shorter roundness.

"Where'd you catch 'em?" Chris asked.

"Otter Tail Lake. We went out yesterday. Fish were really biting!"

I stared at the mismatched pair, and the similarities between us hit me: Lina was a musician from New York City, and Jerome was a local Minnesota boy who fished. Chris and I were Jerome and Lina, thirty years later. I rubbed my thumbnail across my index finger.

"Do you fish, too?" I asked Lina.

"Of course. I love fishing. I find it very relaxing." My thumb jumped and my nail dug into the flesh of my finger. My brief bubble of hope popped. Lina and Jerome might have managed to bridge the gap between them, but I wasn't Lina. I didn't like fishing, and I didn't think I ever would.

Lina directed us to chairs facing an English garden where green herbs surrounded a stone fountain. The dining table was covered with a white tablecloth; antique silver salvers held carrot and celery sticks. Jerome came from the kitchen with a platter full of golden-brown fish fillets. "So, you're still in Minnesota. We haven't scared you away yet, eh?"

I swallowed, grateful that years of experience amplifying my thousand-watt performer's smile made it easy to hide my discomfort. "Not yet."

Lina placed herself between Chris and me put her arms around both of us. "We are so happy you're here. You are wonderful together."

I bit my lip and turned the antique plate in front of me a couple of inches clockwise.

"Now we gotta make a Minnesotan out of you," Jerome added and turned to Chris. "Have you taken her out fishing yet?"

"Yes," Chris patted me on the back. "I've been trying to make a fly fisherwoman out of her." He paused for a beat and looked mournfully at Jerome. "I don't think it's working."

Chris told the story of our first fishing trip and the great ladybug massacre. I paid special attention to taking and passing the serving platters. Jerome chuckled. Then both of them laughed. I looked up, clinking fork against ceramic. Lina and Jerome were leaning back in their chairs, enjoying the story so much they had stopped eating. I crunched a carrot. Chris, a natural storyteller, built up the tension as he led Jerome and Lina to the funniest part—me jumping around the parking lot trying to get the waders off so I could get away from the ladybugs. I speared my fish cutlet with my fork. My cheeks felt hot, but everyone was laughing joyfully, not at me, with me. I hesitated, then joined in."I thought that was it right there." Chris's eyes were soft with affection as he looked at me. "It's a good thing she gave me another chance." I smiled back at him.

When the plates were cleared and my cookies were passed around, we started talking about how Jerome stocked his antique store.

"Sometimes I go to antique shows, but the best stuff is here, in the Midwest."

"Here?" I asked, cookie crumbs dropping into my lap.

"Yep. The East and West coasts have been picked over. Out here you can still find gems."

I swept the crumbs off my thighs and felt Chris adjust in his seat, his body strong and solid beside me. "Are antiques how you met?" I asked.

"Not exactly." Lina leaned back in her chair. "I was a few years divorced, and Jerome worked at the local supermarket. I kept going to the supermarket more than I needed to. I would forget an ingredient on purpose and return later to pick it up, to make sure I had a second chance to say hello."

Jerome chuckled and pushed a crumb around his plate with his fork. Chris slipped his hand into mine. His eyes were fixed on Lina. He had the gift of making people feel heard, as if there was nothing more important in the world than what they were saying. I had originally thought this was a trick, but I was beginning to learn that the secret to his gift was that he truly believed, in those moments, that there was nothing more important than hearing what a person had to say. And at this moment, I was certain all he wanted was to be right here, next to me, listening to Lina and Jerome's story together.

"I waited for Jerome to figure out I was interested. He didn't. Or if he did," Lina said as she cast a hooded look toward Jerome, "he was too shy to do anything about it. When I got tired of waiting, I asked him over for dinner." She took a sip of water. "One afternoon Jerome stopped by when I was in the middle of painting the barn. I asked Jerome to hold the ladder, but the moment he took hold, my elbow smacked into the paint bucket. The bucket overturned, spilling red all over Jerome's head. I was mortified, convinced Jerome would leave and never come back, after, of course, shaking the ladder so hard I fell off and broke my legs." They exchanged a look. Jerome was grinning. "Instead, Jerome opened his mouth, face dripping paint, and laughed. He laughed like buildings shake. And then I laughed. We laughed and laughed, and I thought, if we can laugh over this, then I have to marry this man."

Lina reached over to take Jerome's hand. For a moment, the matched pair looked into each others' eyes: a New Yorker and a rural Minnesotan who had found happiness together. I wanted what they had. I wanted to be able to laugh at domestic difficulties, at an overturned paint bucket, at a bedroom floor covered with dirty clothes. Maybe, just maybe, Chris and I could find a way through our differences and create the bond I saw between Lina and Jerome.

Chris was watching me. I squeezed his hand.

When the dishes were done, Chris traded final fishing tips with Jerome, and Lina walked me to the door. "You know, Chris reminds me a lot of Jerome." She hugged me and whispered into my ear, "I'm so happy he found you."

As Chris said his goodbyes behind me, I crossed the threshold into country darkness. A wind chime pealed from the backyard; the porch swing creaked in a gentle rhythm. The scent of lilac floated toward me from Lina's garden. Chris's laughter carried through the doorway. Maybe I could get used to the way Chris kept his things. Maybe I could learn it was okay to take a little bit of time to get places. And maybe one day, years in the future, we too would sit next to each other on a porch swing, holding wrinkled hands, a New Yorker and a rural Minnesotan showing another mismatched couple that differences can be overcome.

20

Once Upon a Time in the Vanagon

I know the northern lights
Dance pink and green
Though I've never seen
Them shine

I thought that night
You first spoke to me
I knew what was to be
By and by

But the space between
What I thought I'd seen
And what now I know
Could fill with all the stars in the sky
– "Northern Lights"

May

I knew spring came late to Minnesota, but I hadn't anticipated how much I would crave warm porch breezes and lilacs before they arrived. Leaves unfurling from budded branches quelled in me a longing I didn't even know I had, and, in the way that lemonade both quenches and triggers thirst, Minnesota spring delighted me and made me itch to travel.

The old orange camper van that loomed indifferently from behind Chris's kitchen began to draw my attention. Crouched over a rectangle of crunchy brown in the midst of the otherwise verdant backyard, the 1981 pop-top, air-cooled Volkswagen Vanagon Westfalia was capped by a white beanie of roof. The year before, I had seen Chris lovingly sweep branches and leaves off of it, but I had never known him to drive it.

The week before Memorial Day weekend, Chris materialized by the couch where I was reading, took my hand and pulled me half up to sitting. "It's time to see the sunset."

I groaned and curled my book closer to me.

Chris wrapped his arms under my shoulders and lifted me up to standing. "It's beautiful out, and you are always glad you went outside."

I grumbled, but let Chris pull me into the yard. Sunset had striped the sky in watercolor hues. The air was gentle, full of the scent of pine and freshly mowed grass. The last rays of sun gilded the Vanagon in glowing red-gold, and I was drawn to it as if to a beacon.

"It's got everything you need," Chris said admiringly from behind me. He ran his hands over the door in a caress. Behind hand-sewn curtains, I could see a miniature stove, sink, and gas-powered refrigerator tucked behind the driver's seat.

"How about a toilet?"

"Who needs a toilet when you have the woods?"

"So why don't you ever drive it?"

"I do so drive it."

"I've never seen you."

"Okay, maybe not since you've known me."

"Why don't we take the Vanagon somewhere for Memorial Day?"

Chris twined his arms around my middle from behind and kissed my ear. "Where do you want to go?"

"How about the Black Hills in South Dakota?"

A bat zig-zagged overhead. "No, that's way too far."

"We've driven further."

"The Vanagon can only drive fifty-five miles an hour. It would take so long to drive there we'd have to turn around as soon as we arrived."

The glow was fading off the van as the sun dipped below the horizon. "Okay, how about the North Shore of Lake Superior?"

"No, forecast says it's likely to be cold this weekend. The heat doesn't work so well."

I sighed. "What if we took more time off and went to Glacier National Park?"

"Way too many mountains. The Vanagon is air-cooled. It overheats on mountains."

I elbowed him in the gut. "You've got to be kidding me." I extricated myself from his arms and faced him squarely, enumerating points on my fingers. "So, you're saying we can only take it" (one) "slowly" (two) "in perfect weather" (three) "a short distance" (four) "on flat roads?"

Chris crossed his arms and leaned protectively against the vehicle. "Hey, don't put down the Vanagon! You just have to find the right kind of trips to take it on."

"I'm sorry." I leaned next to him and pulled his arm through the triangle of mine. Finding a destination that accommodated the Vanagon's special needs was like matching the glass slipper to Cinderella's foot. The whoosh of the breeze was the same pitch as the distant sound of a lawn mower, and the answer came to me at once. "The North Dakota Badlands aren't too far, and it's flat all the way there. The weather there should be pleasant all weekend."

Chris's body softened. A sound came out of Chris's mouth, then stopped. "I guess we could," he said slowly, as if trying each word on for size. "But, you know, North Dakota's boring. I don't think we'll find enough to do for four whole days."

"How do you know?"

"I've been there."

"To Theodore Roosevelt National Park?" I knew the answer was no, and I could see Chris was about to relent by the way the skin above his left cheekbone quivered. Foot into slipper, a perfect fit.

"No. Okay, fine. I've always wanted to go there. But if it's boring, I get to say 'I told you so.'"

Chris's enthusiasm built as we prepared for our trip. While we piled clothes we would pack on our respective sides of the bed, Chris told me stories of trips he'd taken in the Vanagon. Each was memorable mostly because the Vanagon broke down and left Chris stranded in the middle of South Dakota or Montana. Chris tended to gloss over what happened then, but I gathered that each breakdown led to many-day adventures of trying to find someone to fix the Vanagon and someone else to give him a ride to the someone who could fix it. Once, Chris got stuck seventy miles west of Bismarck, and Chris's father had to drive six hours to pick him up.

The songwriting notebook I was about to pack hesitated above my duffel bag. "Are you sure the Vanagon is going to make it to the Badlands?"

"Yeah, don't worry. I had it repaired last year."

West of Fargo, the Vanagon shivered and shook as we drove fifty-five miles an hour in the seventy-five-mile-an-hour zone. Cars whizzed past. The air blowing through the front windows made the back curtains *thwap*. The plastic door lining had cracked away from the bolts and clattered noisily against its metal frame. A repetitive metallic creak came from the hinge of the folding back bench.

Chris's fingers beat a tattoo on the hollow plastic console that was no longer bolted to the floor between the front seats. The console tended to vibrate backwards into the body of the van and required regular repositioning.

"How fast are you going?" Chris peered at the speedometer. I eased my foot off the gas, and the indicator dial floated down from fifty-seven to fifty. Ten minutes later, indicator nudging sixty, Chris leaned across the lopsided console. He cleared his throat and flashed the whites of his eyes at me. I eased off the gas again.

"Does the Vanagon have a name?" I asked, only partly trying to distract Chris from his critique of my driving.

"No, *I* don't tend to name my inanimate objects." Chris liked to poke fun at me for my penchant for naming things, like my Honda Civic (Serendipity) and my Goodall guitar (Kahea).

"But it has so much character. It ought to have a name. It's also a lot easier to say a name than 'Volkswagen Vanagon Westfalia.' I can't believe you haven't named it. It's your baby."

"It's not an *it*, it's a *her*."

"That's a start." I noticed the speedometer dial moving up again and slowed. "If you were going to name *her*, what would you choose?"

Chris considered.

Jumping in before he was done thinking—as usual—I added, "It should be a timely name, something from the '70s or '80s."

Chris glared at me. His eyes said, *Duh*, and returned to the road in front of us. I waited. A few more miles of flat prairie grass passed by. I pressed my lips together and bobbed up and down to keep myself from talking.

Chris said, "How about 'Esmeralda'?"

The wind trilled through the crack in the door. "That's perfect!"

Seven hours later, a billboard announcing our destination swelled into huge block letters in front of us: "Medora: North Dakota's #1 Vacation!"

We curved off the highway and stopped at a cowboy barbecue buffet for dinner before the Vanagon grumbled over gravel roads into the park's campground.

Once parked, Chris stuck his hands in a depression in Esmeralda's ceiling. The roof clicked and bounced free. From a hinge over the rear door, the ceiling tilted upward forty-five degrees, creating enough space for two adults at full height.

I stood. "Nice!"

Chris tugged at the bottom of the back seat, and in moments the seat was lying flat, the shape and size of a double bed. He clicked open a cabinet at the back and pulled out a set of sheets, two pillows, and a blanket. The scent of lavender wafted from the sheets as Chris, pretending to be all matter-of-fact, arranged the bed. The Vanagon was a magic box, full of hidden tricks.

"This is so great!" I did a little tap dance to the accompaniment of my own humming.

"Isn't it?" Chris's cheeks were flushed. "This is the greatness of the Vanagon." He spread his arms across the space, eyes sparkling in the fading light. "I think you're starting to get it."

I was. We'd driven for hours through another state, and now all I had to do to complete the living room was turn the driver's seat backwards to face the tiny house behind the dashboard. I was so tickled by the transformed Vanagon, it took me a little while to get to sleep.

"Time to wake up, Sleeping Beauty." I flickered my eyes open to see Chris's stubbled face. "Time to see North Dakota."

I blinked away the remnants of a song that had risen in my head overnight and lumbered to the door. My bladder was full. Thankfully, I would be spared peeing in the woods as the campground had an actual toilet. I got as far as the door handle when a bison the size of a Volkswagen Bug nearsightedly peered through the sliding window at me, snorting.

"Chris," my voice squeaked. Chris jumped into a kneeling position on the mattress.

He started to giggle.

"I have to pee!"

Chris's laughter shook the bed. "I don't think you're going to be peeing until he decides he's good and ready to leave."

I started to giggle, too. The buffalo took a few more sniffs of the van and then lumbered through the fire pit toward the river. I ran for the group toilet, legs tight together.

We spent the day driving and hiking past the colorful rocks and grazing buffalo of North Dakota's badlands. By late afternoon, we'd seen everything we wanted to. We had two full days left before we were supposed to return to New York Mills. Esmeralda had warmed up under the afternoon sun. The heat amplified the damp stink of two pairs of muddy hiking boots, old sweat, and dirty carpet.

"What now?" I asked. Chris and I looked at each other across the wide front of the Vanagon.

"I don't know. What do you think?"

There was a whole state between the badlands and home. "How about we go on a road trip around North Dakota?" I imagined a two-day adventure full of scenic vistas, craggy buttes, and small towns with cute restaurants. I pulled the map of North Dakota from the center console and started to unfold it.

Chris groaned. "There's nothing to see in North Dakota." The granary smell of wheat wafted through the window along with a musky fug of dried buffalo scat.

I straightened the map with a slap against the dashboard. "You can't be sure of that." I looked at the relatively few pink dots representing towns scattered irregularly around the vast state. "You haven't been to every single part of the state. Anyway, we're here. Unless you want to drive to Montana?"

Chris groaned again. "We don't have enough time to drive to the good parts of Montana. And, anyway, I told you, it's too hilly and far for the Vanagon."

"Fine. North Dakota, then. There's got to be something to see." Brown and green splotches of townless land took up most of the map.

"You're wrong. But, okay." He sighed. "We've got nothing else to do." He opened the driver's door and walked around the front to open the passenger door. He took the map from my hand and gestured for me to get out. "You're driving."

*F*our hours of empty, flat farmland later, interrupted by a tiny town where we ate pancakes in a diner last decorated in the 1950s, I pulled down the window, turned my head toward the endless waves of amber grain and screamed, long and loud. When I was done, I tucked my head into the car. The plastic door lining clattered. The back seat creaked.

"I told you so," Chris said.

I collapsed into my seat. Chris was right.

I was hungry again. We hadn't seen a restaurant since lunch. The sun had dipped precariously close to the horizon. The map showed we were approaching Four Bears Village, and the size of the pink dot on the Missouri River suggested it might be large enough to have a restaurant.

The only structure at the intersection that made up the town was a huge building that poked up in acute angles over the fields. When we were close enough to read "Four Bears Casino" on the sign, Chris cheered. "I love casinos!"

I turned the car toward the gaping entrance maw. A generically Native American mural was painted above the front doors. In the large parking lot along the side of the building, was a mismatched collection of RVs, each taking up four or five parking spaces.

Chris's voice was gleeful. "We could park for the night at the casino. Then I could play a few hands of blackjack."

I was too tired to protest. There wasn't another town on the map for miles, and my eyes were blurry from driving. "You ask at the front desk." I clicked off the ignition, and my head slumped into the headrest.

"Come on." He pulled me past the large carved wooden poles to a set of glass doors that opened to a head-thumping clanging.

Chris went to the front desk. I found a bathroom behind a blinking, buzzing, dinging row of slot machines.

"We're on!" He was waiting for me outside the ladies' room, perky as a newly watered plant. "I'm going to play me some blackjack."

"I'm going to the Vanagon to read."

"Here." Chris peeled three twenty-dollar bills from the bill clip on his wallet and handed the rest of the wallet to me. "So I can't bet away the house."

I turned to escape the Febreeze-masked smell of tobacco smoke and the glazed faces of people losing money. I aimed myself through the parking lot toward Esmeralda. In my pocket, I fingered the smooth leather billfold I had bought Chris as a birthday gift from the overpriced Brooklyn boutique where he had twirled me around when I still lived on Smith Street.

A few minutes past North Dakota's late summer sunset was the Magritte time of day, when the sky is still bright but the ground has grown dark. My flip-flops clumped over the wide expanse of parking lot. Children shrieked happily from the park behind the casino. As I got closer to the Vanagon, the generators of three RVs overpowered all other sounds. The air smelled wide and open, the hint of diesel suggesting the roads went on forever.

I hummed a promising blues melody. The orange Vanagon was David to the Goliaths of stainless steel RVs trailing Subaru Foresters and motorcycles, but its torpedo shape felt inviting, comforting, homey. Esmeralda had been loved and cared for. She was right for me. Not too big, not too small. Just right.

I scooted the curtains shut and enclosed myself in Esmeralda's cocoon, protected from prying eyes. I grabbed a cookie from the bag of assorted road food we had collected, too tired to find anything more nutritious, changed into pajamas and curled up with Chris's headlamp and a paperback mystery.

The bed embraced me with its twin scents of dust and detergent. I floated on the buzz of the generators and was lulled into the space between sleep and waking, the space of romance and fairytales. I was Cinderella, Sleeping Beauty, Goldilocks.

Once upon a time there was a singer-songwriter who lived in a big city. One day she traveled far away to a land without cities. A land full of grass and trees and lakes and animals. There she met a man who belonged to the land and the lakes. They fell in love. And the woman left the big city and moved to the place of the land, to be with the man who belonged to the lakes. Then the man from the lakes took the singer-songwriter to the parking lot of a Native American casino in North Dakota.

The parking lot of a casino!

I lifted my head from the flat pillow. I was about to sleep in an old Volkswagen van in a parking lot in North Dakota behind a casino, waiting for the man I loved to join me in the fold-out bed in the back of his beloved jalopy.

The generators buzzed. I was miles and lifetimes away from where I had planned to be, a world away from where I could have envisioned myself. But I was okay. I was okay because Chris was a few yards away. It didn't matter where I lived, where I was. Because I was home. Chris was my home. He was my home, and he was there, inside that casino. He would return with lights in his eyes and stories about the gamblers he'd met and drawn into conversation. He'd come back eager to talk, smelling of other people's cigarette smoke and his own sweet musk.

Somehow, miles away from where I started, and worlds away from where I ever thought I would be, Chris made me feel like I had come home.

21

Guitar String Blister

I like to leave a trail of broken hearts behind me
That way I know I left them wanting more
I like to see them lining up to find me
As I sneak out by the other door
– "Trail of Broken Hearts Behind Me"

June

Holding on to the feeling of home was like trying to catch a minnow in a bucket. One moment I had grasped it, and the next moment it slipped right out of my hand.

"You're leaving again!" Chris let his half-packed canvas briefcase fall against the chair. We had been back from North Dakota for two days, and the red-gold glow of our time together was fading under the fluorescent glare of everyday life.

I nested the milk-rimed cereal bowls together. "I know, but I told you I had to go to New York. I have gigs." My voice sounded strained. I put the cover on his insulated coffee mug and held it out to him. He wouldn't take it.

"I thought you'd be home this month." His voice had an edge to it. "*I* thought we could go camping up by the North Shore, maybe even take the Vanagon, but clearly *you* have better things to do."

The mug made a paltry shield. I slammed it down. Liquid sloshed and coffee arced out of the small drinking hole onto the table. "I *told* you about my tour when I was booking the flights to New York."

"I guess I forgot." His voice was acid. I had only seen hints of this version of Chris before. "I'm sorry for not being able to keep track of the details of both of our lives." He shoved his leather document case into his briefcase. It wouldn't fit. He shoved harder. A seam ripped.

I tried to keep my voice calm. "My tour schedule is on my website. You can always check it when you want to know where I'll be."

Chris swung around to face me. "I guess I have to look at your website just to know when I'm going to see you."

The guitar-string blister that had formed on the tip of my middle finger the day before began to throb. I had started daydreaming about marrying Chris. Now I wanted to scream at him, to throw everything in his face. To say, *I came all the way to Minnesota for you, and you have the nerve to get upset because I'm doing my job?* I pressed my thumb into the blister and focused on the sting. "I know it's hard. I don't like being away from you, either, but I already booked these gigs."

"Clearly you don't really love me."

My mouth opened and closed. A big bucket of bitterness in my center toppled, no safety cover to keep the contents from sloshing out over my insides, and too many words poured out in a loud rush. "You knew I was a touring songwriter when you met me. Why in the world would you think doing my job meant I didn't love you?"

"Because you were just gone!" Chris yelled back.

"It was an artist residency, not touring!" I had spent four weeks at an artist residency in Washington State in late April and early May. "And you said you were fine with it!" My voice echoed on the hard ceramic behind the stove.

Chris turned his back to me. If he dared to come up with another reason I was wrong for going on tour, I was going to tell him what I really thought about his behavior, about him, about his damn hometown.

He said nothing.

Argument I could participate in; argument I could win. His silence cut the thread that connected us. A thick emptiness pooled between us.

His document case had come to a stop at a steep angle, refusing to fit inside the briefcase. I dabbed my finger at the constellation of coffee splash marks on the table. I painted a trickle of coffee between two drops and watched them fuse together.

Chris gave the document case a final shove, and the briefcase bent underneath the strain though the case still didn't fit. "You know, one day you are going to have to figure out what you really want in life."

I wiped my coffee-moistened finger on my jeans and tried to will the angry tears stinging the corners of my eyes not to come out. Chris dug his hand in his briefcase pocket and removed a small plastic container of yellow trout-fishing flies. The document case slid smoothly into the briefcase.

"It's only for a week."

Chris's feet thumped across the linoleum. The door slammed shut with a hard gust of air.

"Have a good day!" I sing-songed to the splash marks on the table. I was alone with two dirty cereal bowls, a box of shiny yellow trout flies, and the bitter taste of our argument.

As I balanced the bowls on the dish mountain in the sink, the edge of one pushed into the blister on my left middle finger. The sting was all-consuming. As it receded, the dull, melancholic ache from my fight with Chris returned. I pressed my finger down on the counter and leaned into the searing, smarting clarity of sting.

I climbed the stairs heavily and pulled the guitar over my shoulders. I pressed pitch into steel wire. The blister on my middle finger screamed. The tingle of upcoming blisters bloomed in other fingers—index, ring, pinky.

Every new guitarist passes through this initiation of pain. When I stopped playing for too long, I had to endure the hazing again, my fingers smarting anew at every chord change, lines of metal drawing furrows into flesh.

I kept playing.

Even if I had had the time to stop and wait for the blisters to heal, it was better not to. If I kept playing on the blister, then the skin above it would thicken and harden, giving me a strong, leathery patch of skin the size of a sunflower seed, a rugged pad that held strings down painlessly. For now, as for every beginner, each chord change felt like a stab. On the other side of that pain was strength. The more pain I felt, the harder my callouses would grow.

I alternated between minor and major chords. The major chords filled me with the focus of righteous anger. The minor chords sent me into a glum thrall. Trying to balance my new community, my music career, and the desires of this man whom I was coming to depend on felt worse than the point after a gig when I lost the bliss of audience connection to the dismal solitude of a hotel room. Maybe I needed to curtail my music travel, to give up some of the career goals I had had when I was single and music was the only thing I had to make me feel like I had a purpose. Maybe a relationship with Chris was worth some more sacrifices.

Then I remembered the new, scathing tone in Chris's voice.

Anger took over like prairie fire, burning away everything but righteous indignation. Why would I sacrifice music when I wasn't even sure Chris and I could make this city-mouse, country-mouse experiment work?

22

Wendy and the Gnomes

Can I recognize my hunger
With my Geiger counter gut
Or is the apparatus rusty
Cuz I'm thinking too much
– "Thinking Too Much"

June–July

Chris returned from work the day after our fight carrying a bouquet of daisies. "I'm sorry," he said. "I didn't mean to make you feel like you had to choose me over your music. I just . . ." he fumbled with the vase under the tap. "I just enjoy my time with you so much."

We resumed our country-city experiment, sometimes penitent, sometimes tepid, always having to work to find ways to accommodate one another. I traveled to New York City to perform. Chris went on a fishing trip to the Canadian wilderness with his father. He was out of phone and email contact by the time I returned from New York.

The house was empty, my guitar moaned in echo-y dissonance when I dropped its case by the kitchen door. I fell into Chris's black couch and leather stuck to my bare legs, releasing with a stinging rip when I tried to get up. I was alone, in the middle of nowhere. I hadn't expected to feel so isolated without the substance of Chris's physical presence, the sound of his voice making up silly songs from the other room, even the disagreements we scuffled through on a weekly basis.

Once the tears started, they didn't stop until my abdomen hurt with the effort of sobbing. I couldn't even call Chris to hear his voice for comfort.

"Why don't you meet the visiting artist while I'm gone?" Chris had suggested during my last crying jag before we both left. A new artist was arriving the next day to stay in the small cottage I had lived in for one life-changing month the year before. Maybe meeting her would make me feel better.

The gentle morning breeze smelled of peonies as I walked up the road the next day. I arrived at the Cultural Center to see the visiting artist opening up the doors of a beat-up Jeep.

"Hi, I'm Elisa. I was an artist-in-residence here last year. Then I fell in love and moved here. I'd be happy to show you around, if you like." The words all tumbled out of my mouth before I could edit out the enthusiasm that must have telegraphed my loneliness like a billboard.

"Hi, I'm Wendy." Jet-black eyes flashed over a sly smile. She stifled a yawn. "Sorry, I've been driving since Alabama, and I slept in my car last night. I'm a bit behind on sleep." I had learned from the Cultural Center that Wendy Deschene was a conceptual artist and art professor. In person, I could see she was about my age and that, even tired, she gave off the energy of a just-lit firecracker.

I put my hands in my pockets and tried to pitch my tone between nonchalant and welcoming. "I meant to say, if you ever need a break from creating I'd be happy to take you for a wander."

She suggested I call her the following day, when she had caught up on sleep. Over the phone, I proposed a lake visit, and Wendy suggested a picnic, which was how, that afternoon, I was driving Wendy to my favorite swimming lake an hour away, playing songs to her off my most recent CD.

Eagle Lake was spring fed, cold, and clear, with a gently sloping swimming beach in a tiny county park. Wendy brought a picnic of turkey sandwiches and home-brewed iced tea in recycled glass juice bottles. I brought beach towels and two oversized styrofoam noodles we could float on. We sat at a picnic table at the edge of the beach in the shade of a large white pine tree and talked about art and music. Whoops came from children on float-toys in the swim area. The iced tea tasted bitter-sharp, and the glass bottles clinked against our teeth.

"What are you working on while you're here in New York Mills?" I asked.

"I'm drawing—working on this project with my three-year-old niece. I give her markers and she draws with them, then I take what she's created, enlarge them, and use them as the basis for my own work."

I nodded as small waves made hypnotic lapping sounds against pebbles. We finished our food, swept the crumbs off the table, and twisted the lids onto the bottles. We pulled off the shorts we wore over our swimsuits and left them on the picnic bench.

Wendy and I waded into glowing blue water, cold nipping toes then settling around feet, ankles, knees, thighs. Wendy plunged in headfirst. When she surfaced, she tilted her head backwards so her hair fell away from her face in a solid black curve. We moved through waves made by a gaggle of shrieking kids playing tag, toward the far end of the swimming area. The water's chill turned to comfort. My feet lost the sand below and pedaled. We treaded water in the deep end, our movements carving mountains and valleys into the surface of the lake. We emerged onto the beach dripping waterfalls and sat on towels on the lawn to dry off in the sunshine.

"This was just what I needed," Wendy said.

"Me too. It's been too long since I've been able to talk with another artist like this." I rolled up my towel and set it in the picnic bag.

Dry and dressed again, we wound up the access road, windows open, gravel crunching beneath the wheels. A mile down asphalt, we passed a sweeping property that was covered with a small city of papier maché garden ornaments. Gnomes and butterflies, frogs and fountains posed on the lawn, a dozen rows deep.

"I have to take a picture of that," Wendy exclaimed.

I pulled the car to the shoulder underneath an oak. Wendy burst out of the car and skipped across the field with her camera. She was lining up the best angle for a photograph of a plump plaster pig when a large man in Carhartt overalls emerged from the farmhouse. He pushed a large paunch ahead of him down the lane-like driveway.

"Hi!" called Wendy. "Do you mind if I take some pictures of your beautiful collection?"

"Nope." A breeze made the grass rustle in a soothing wave.

"Do you make them?"

"Yep. My wife helps me."

"Are they for sale?" I asked.

"Sure." He paused for a beat, then added, "If you like these, you should see what I have in the barn." The gray-haired man pointed at the aluminum pole barn on the other side of the driveway.

"Hello!" a small high-pitched and strangely accented voice called out from the direction of the house. "Howie, you show them statues?"

"Yes, dear." Howie turned to us. "This is my wife, Mai." A small, wrinkled Asian woman in her sixties pranced over. She was half Howie's height and one-third of his weight. She wore a form-fitting silk skirt and looked completely out of place in front of a rural Minnesota farmhouse.

"Hello! You come see statues? They beautiful, yes?"

"They're lovely. So you help make them?" I asked.

"I have ideas, then Howie make."

Wendy was photographing a boulder-sized frog with a pink tongue sticking out in the air. I couldn't keep myself from asking. "Mai, where are you from?"

"Thailand."

"That's a beautiful country."

"You go to Thailand?"

"Yes, I've been there a couple of times. Bangkok, Phuket, Chiang Mai, and a few other places."

"You know my country," Mai's smile smoothed her face into a moon of pleasure. "Come. The barn has more pretty to see."

What was Mai doing here, on a farm deep in the middle of nowhere? A Thai woman in the outposts of rural America where there were few people of any color other than white. Mai led us into a barn filled with statues, garden benches, and wishing wells.

"How did you end up in central Minnesota?" I asked Mai.

Howie answered. "I served in Vietnam, and I met Mai when I was in Thailand for R&R. We fell in love, and I brought her here." He smiled at Mai. "This was my parents' farm, and we've farmed it for forty years, now."

I looked at Mai with wonder. She was probably the only Asian woman for miles. How had she made a home for herself in this desolate, foreign place for four decades? Her effervescent grin grew even larger as she wrapped Howie's huge hand around her tiny one.

23

The Proposal

I know better than to dock before the end of the cruise
I know better than to stop before seeing the view
I don't stay inside 'cause the water's too cold
So why
Don't I just say yes to you

– "Know Better"

July

I took Chris's hand across the cracked formica table at the Eagles Cafe. He was back from his trip, and I was relishing a shared morning together in the coffee- and hash-brown-scented restaurant. After we ordered breakfast, Chris rose from our booth without explanation and walked to the door. The table bounced with his sudden motion. He returned with two newsprint real estate brochures. He thrust one at me across the table and cracked its duplicate open in front of him. It took me a moment to understand, and then I did. My harangues about how little I liked living in the gray cottage had finally swayed Chris. He didn't like change, but, for me, he would make himself ready to look for a new house.

The newsprint made satisfying *shirring* sounds as I flipped pages of potential homes. "How about this one?" Chris turned his magazine upside-down to show the miniature house right-side-up underneath a coiffed still of a posing realtor.

"I like it." I pointed to the facing page. "How about this one?"

"Definitely doable," Chris said. He put an index finger on the realtor photo and proffered his cell phone with his other hand. "Will you call her?"

"Why don't you?"

"Because you can use your New York City superpowers."

"What?"

"You can be pushy and aggressive and make things happen. I can't do that. I'm Minnesotan." He fluttered his eyelashes at me.

"I thought you didn't like it when I was pushy."

The vinyl seat squeaked as he shifted. "It has its uses."

I glared at Chris as I took his cell phone.

The next afternoon the live and less-coiffed version of the realtor took us on a tour of houses, describing their features in a flat-voweled Minnesota accent. The houses ran into each other like the blur of rectangles in the real estate brochures. None of them felt right. It was almost sunset when she dropped us off at the parking lot by Otter Tail Lake where we had left our car.

The lake sparkled. The air was thick with a hint of evening chill and had the earthy scent of oolong tea. My hand drummed impatiently on the handle of the passenger door, waiting for Chris to unlock it. He placed a hand on my arm. "Wait, it's a beautiful night, let's go walking."

I was tired from the parade of houses. I craved my bed and a book, and was about to say so when I looked at Chris. His face glowed with an unusual combination of eagerness and trepidation. He had his hand out to me, inviting me to take it.

I took his hand. Grass tickled my ankles; the sky was wide and clear and shell pink at its edges. Chris pulled me close and led me to steps carved into the lake's steep bank. "Look how lovely the sun looks on the water." Chris leapt down a few steps toward the dock. He usually moved languidly, taking time to ground himself before his next step. Now, Chris's gestures were quick and sharp. I dropped his hand. At the top of the stairs, a gentle breeze from the lake cooled my face. "I don't want to go down the stairs. I'm tired, let's go back." I turned to the car.

"No!" he begged. "Please stay. We don't have to go all the way down to the shore. Just—please. Will you watch the sunset with me?"

There was an unfamiliar pleading tone in Chris's voice.

I sighed and returned to the top of the stairs. The sun was a white coin behind the trees across the lake. A line of sparkles trailed across the water to where we stood. Chris took both my hands and pulled me toward him. "I'm tired," I said. My voice sounded feeble against the firmament.

"You are very important to me, and I love you very much." A multicolored sky mirrored his multicolored eyes, and his voice held a certainty I had not heard before.

"Oh," I said. My eyes widened, and my ribs pull together. A breeze lifted tendrils of my hair so they floated about my face. "Is this it?"

"Yes."

Water tinkled against rock where lake and shore came together. It was time to commit. Not only to this man who had planted roots inside me, but to my new life, my new career, to Minnesota.

"I'm scared."

"Me too." Our shared fear steadied me. Chris held my hands tightly; I held his hands back. Chris's chest rose and fell. The wind whispered secrets to the trees, and the scent of fresh new growth surrounded us, oak, pine, and maple.

"Will you marry me?"

My lips parted, and I sipped fragrant air. I pictured Mai's small hand enveloped in the large, rough hand of her Minnesota husband's. I imagined Lina and Jerome laughing by a ladder while red paint dripped down Jerome's face. I remembered the moment in the Vanagon when fairytale and reality had fused.

The answer came to my lips like a truth I had always known. "Yes," I said, face half smiling, half crumpled. Chris made a sound and pressed me to him, wrapping himself around me.

"Oh, my God, did we just do this?" I asked into his shoulder.

"Yes," Chris answered into my hair.

I pulled back to look at him, setting my hand against the stubble of his cheek. I wanted this to be the face I would smile up at for years to come.

"I almost forgot," he said. "I don't have a ring yet, but . . ." He reached into his pocket and pulled out the red paper seal from one of his cigars. "This is for you." He pulled my left hand off his cheek and gently splayed my fingers. He fitted the red cigar wrapper around my ring finger. "It's temporary. Till we have a chance for you to choose your own."

I spread my hand and modeled my cigar-wrapper ring for both of us. "We're getting married," I said, dazed by the sight of a ring, paper or not, around my finger.

"Yes, we are." Chris beamed.

24

Bingo!

It's not about the bumper cars
That crash but never meet
It's not about the flashing arcade
Or the kids who keep getting beat
It's not about the hollow music
Piped in from the carousel
But the wish that I could go
Somewhere else, which is really
Not about them, it's about me
– "Ferris Wheel"

August

The morning after my sleek New York City actress friend Maggie arrived for a summer visit, Chris slapped his hand on the table with a thud. "I completely forgot," he said. "It's East Otter Tail County Fair weekend. We should go to the fair tonight."

The home-painted stencil of green leaves on the kitchen cabinets seemed to blur into the white background. The Vanagon peeked in at me through the kitchen window as if to remind me Maggie was not a country kind of girl. I rubbed at the faded kernel shapes of the burn I had made on Chris's grandmother's table when I had thoughtlessly placed steaming cobs directly onto wood. How would my city friend handle a country fair?

I imagined Maggie, dark wavy hair over Italian features, Mediterranean-tinted décolletage in a low-cut designer dress, aiming a miniature bean bag at a goldfish bowl next to a bearded man in a straw hat. "I don't think she'll like that . . ."

"Like what?" Maggie called hoarsely, her feet thumping down the stairs. She wore black pajamas, and her pixie 'do was pillow-flattened. Without looking at us, she beelined to the self-grinding coffeemaker.

Maggie and I had met in seventh grade when I braved the crossing of the middle school cafeteria to say hello, and we soon found ourselves taking acting classes together and sharing book recommendations. Maggie moved to New York City for college, and we visited one another via the easy MetroNorth commute between New Haven and Manhattan. By the time I followed her to New York City after graduate school in London, Maggie was thriving in the underground theater scene at night and eking out a living doing odd jobs during the day. It took me another few years to cast off the corporate sheen of my dayjob and pursue songwriting. By that time, she was a veteran of the New York City art scene, and it was clear she was bound to New York City for life.

"Going to the county fair." I lifted my voice and tried to raise one eyebrow in a show of cynical solidarity with what I imagined her reaction would be. I ended up with two raised eyebrows and a twisted up forehead.

Maggie hummed thoughtfully, clattering a spoonful of coffee beans into the grinder basket. "I don't think I've ever been to a county fair. Sounds good." She hit the power button, and the coffee maker buzzed into a deafening grind.

Chris gave me a triumphant look over the corncob burn.

The early evening was bright with northern sun. Wire cages in the fair's entry area held a selection of local wildlife under a sign announcing that the exhibit was sponsored by the local 4-H club. The anteroom had the neglected feel of a lost-and-found cubby, animals misplaced, relocated mistakenly from their forest and field homes. A porcupine dragged its quills in sawdust. A red fox hung its head by its paws. The fisher hunched in an indignant lump, lips curled above sharp teeth, fur matted and dull.

I backed away from the cages, as if from a version of myself I did not want to contemplate. Chris, Maggie, and I walked into the endless green lawn of fairground, exchanging the anteroom's scent of sickness and dung for funnel cakes and cotton candy. The toy-piano music of an ice cream truck beckoned.

Chris tugged at my arm from behind. "Food later. First, we have to go to the animal barns before they close for the night." He led Maggie and me over candy-wrapper-strewn grass to a series of pole buildings on the other side of the fairgrounds.

I was seeing everything through Maggie's eyes. People migrated in bands like tribal groups: mothers and children, elders, and teenagers. Girls with too much liquid eyeliner held their faces in stiff expressions of studied boredom. Adolescent boys in athletic T-shirts jostled each other to be close to the girls.

I didn't just want Maggie to like it here, I needed her to. If my best friend didn't approve of my new life, then it would mean I had made the wrong decision to stay.

"This reminds me of Coney Island." Maggie smirked. "At least, sort of."

I bit my lip, tried to laugh. "It's like the equipment from Coney Island arrived, but the people didn't." My tone remained too thick, too wary. The last time we'd been to Coney Island together was for the annual Mermaid parade, in which all kinds of New Yorkers dress up like mermaids and creatures from the sea. I could not imagine my New York Mills neighbors dressed up like mermaids, naked breasts painted blue and green, parading at the county fair.

Here, dull-eyed moms pushed strollers from which two or three small children hung, mouths sticky, helium balloons dragging listlessly from their wrists. Fathers walked in pairs some distance away, eyes glassy, beers in hand, bellies pushing ahead like sentinels.

My hip joint caught and stiffened as I tried to sidestep an overturned paper cup of brightly colored sugary slush. I limped for a few steps to get the hitch out.

"Come on," Chris yelled, panting. "We've only got twenty minutes before they close." I quickened my pace to catch up. The first red tin building was marked "Rabbit and Poultry Barn" in neatly painted white letters. Quiet clucks and the sloughing sounds of small animals made a gentle song of greeting. Towers of cages, two and three high, covered long tables down the center of the room. The cages on one side of the room were filled with rabbits, on the other chickens, ducks, and geese.

Chris moved on to the horse barn, and I stopped by a cage holding three Angora rabbits, fluffy as coats. "Awwww . . ." Maggie pointed to another cage, with two fuzzy white chickens with poofs on the tops of their heads. "It looks like they're wearing fur hats."

A blue first-place ribbon was affixed to a cage in which two polka-dotted birds flaunted black-and-white feathers. A sign on the cage door identified the birds as the guinea fowl Matilda and Fred.

"Why did Matilda and Fred win over the furry white chickens?" I asked, tone serious.

Her voice matched mine in gravity as she agreed. "The white ones with the powder-puff hats are much more attractive."

A giggle wound its way up my torso. We were evaluating the appearance of farm animals. Maggie caught my laughter like contagion. In an instant we were curled over by the bird cages, clutching our bellies, laughing so hard we stopped making sounds. I held the nearest cage to steady myself. The two white geese inside started honking. Maggie pointed at the geese and erupted into guffaws at a higher pitch. An older couple moved pointedly away from us. We caught our breaths, wiped our eyes, and put our arms around each other to catch up to Chris.

After the three of us had visited horses, goats, sheep, cows, and a few pigs, we moved out of the animal barns into a colonnade of game-booths. Armies of stuffed animals hung from awnings. A stone-eyed carnie waved a scratched-up laser gun in our faces. "Hit three ducks, win a purple lion!" he intoned as if he'd forgotten the meaning of the words.

A shriek of metal on metal pulled my attention to a mud-filled arena past the game booths. Dozens of people surrounded an oval of fencing around dirt mounds and heaps of metal. Chris stopped at the edge of the crowd. I leaned in to be heard, my arm touching his. "What's this?"

"Demo derby," Chris yelled back. A sickly hum, a roar, and a clatter came from one pile of metal. I smelled something chemical, like burning plastic, and one of the metal heaps in the middle of the arena started to spew orange flames and black smoke.

"What?" I yelled to Chris over the whoops and cheers of the crowd. Beer sloshed from bucket-sized plastic cups in applauding hands. Maggie was squinting, her head tipped toward the smoldering metal heaps. I looked closer. The heaps had once been cars.

"Demolition derby," Chris said, focusing on the action in the ring.

Two of the crumpled cars were still moving, galumphing forward on misshapen wheel beds, rubber tires flattened or peeled away. I jerked my head to Maggie. Her mouth was ajar, her eyes glued to the inevitable crash. Dizziness overcame me like motion sickness.

Clank-shriek-bang. I whirled my head around. A sympathetic hiss escaped from Chris as a driver's body jolted forward at impact. My mind told my body to run, to drag Maggie by the arm away from whatever we were watching, but a voyeurism as strong as animal instinct kept my feet planted.

"This is crazy." Maggie's voice was breathy, jubilant. The metal fence bounced hard against my elbows as Maggie leaned in.

The car that had once been green revved, rear wheels spraying mud in a perfect half circle. The engine, visible under a torn-off hood, bounced loose. The rear wheel caught, and the car spiraled up a mound of metal and mud, engine tilting dangerously. With a wrenching crack, the engine toppled out of the vehicle. The car jerked to a stop.

There was a moment of silence.

An official raised an orange flag, and the crowd started screaming. I closed my ears against the noise with my fingers. Someone moved to my right. Maggie. I jerked to the side, words ready to quell her reaction, whatever it might be.

She was staring at the arena, watching the driver limp out of the car, held up by another man. "Wow," she said, face beatific, voice like prayer.

Chris grinned. "It's like trying to take your eyes off a car crash."

I cleared my throat and pushed a weak voice out to say something—anything—neutral. "That was something."

"That *was* something." Maggie's eyes were large, her mouth pulled toward a grin.

The humor returned to my voice. "Yeah, country life has its own excitements."

"I can see that," Maggie said.

I linked my arm into Chris's, sending him a silent thank you with my touch. He leaned his head against mine and made a "*bop*" sound when our heads touched. "Mini-doughnuts!" He sprang forward and yelled over his shoulder, "You have to try mini-doughnuts." He race-walked past vans selling cotton candy and hot dogs, French fries, and fish to a stall marked with a cartoon doughnut.

The first time I had introduced Chris and Maggie in Manhattan, Maggie breezed into the chocolate cafe as if she owned the restaurant while Chris sat close to me, back stiff in the midst of the city buzz. In rural Minnesota, Chris led the way, while Maggie's eyes darted from one side to another.

The heady scent of fried dough filled my lungs. Chris waved a five-dollar bill at the yellow-aproned attendant who extruded pale rings of batter from a metal cone into a fry-oil bath. She herded the rings with paddles, a game of edible pinball, to arrive at the far end of the assembly line cooked to a golden brown. The paper bag filled with thirteen papery thumps and a spray of sugar.

"Maggie, have some." He opened the bag toward her. I tried to reach in, and he jerked it away. "Guests first."

I wrinkled my nose at him. He widened his eyes in manic glee. Maggie grinned wickedly at me, then gingerly took a bite of donut. Her eyes rolled with pleasure.

"Good, right?" Chris reached into the bag, head dipping possessively over it.

"Hey! My turn." He playfully batted my hand back, pulled out a doughnut and dangled it in front of his mouth with one hand while whipping the bag in front of me with the other. I grabbed for the doughnut. He laughed, stuffed the doughnut in his mouth, and handed the bag to me.

My teeth eased into hot dough, sweetness bathed my mouth. The three of us *mmmmed* together. Our hands scrabbled into the bag for more.

"Bingo!" Chris exclaimed. He threw the now-empty bag into a garbage drum and took off toward a picnic shelter with open sides and tall, narrow tables.

Maggie and I exchanged a look, shrugged *what the hell?* at each other and followed.

The editor of the local paper wore a black visor and apron with pockets filled with wads of cash. The collection of tables and chairs looked like someone had upended a church basement and resettled it into the picnic shelter. We sat down, and Chris ponied up three one-dollar bills. "Hit us," he said.

The editor handed each of us a long paper sheet with three photocopied Bingo grids and gestured to a basket of tubes. I didn't want to admit I didn't know what I was supposed to do.

"So what do I do?" Maggie asked. I rocked on my stool, pretending I didn't need to listen to Chris's answer.

"Haven't you ever played Bingo?"

"At kindergarten birthday parties."

Chris laughed and put his wallet in his pocket. "It's the same thing. You listen for the numbers and letters, and mark the ones you have on your card. You use these." Chris pointed to tubes that looked like the love children of felt-tip markers and jumbo stamp pads. Maggie laid her Bingo grid sheet on the table and reached for one. Chris thrust another into my hand.

I pulled the cap off my marker and pressed it to the blank part of my Bingo sheet. It made a satisfying round green splotch. I hummed a clownish tune at Maggie and splotched a few more times to make a happy face. Maggie giggled.

"Will you stop that?" Chris's hand stilled my marker and I stopped mid-note. "It's not for making happy faces, it's for marking the Bingo card."

Maggie made a show of putting a frown on her face and sitting up straight. I widened my eyes in overdone innocence and lifted my hands slowly.

The Bingo caller's voice crackled over the portable loudspeaker. "Okay, last call for Bingo cards. This round is now closed. Players ready. Pot for this round is seventy-five dollars."

"That's nice," Maggie hissed at me.

"Sure better than a birthday party Tootsie Pop," I whispered back. We started to giggle again.

Chris elbowed me. "Shhhh."

A large man was sitting in front of a glass aquarium full of balls marked with numbers and letters. He pressed a button. A ball whooshed up and plopped down. "G-58," the man said into his microphone.

Maggie happily splotched at two grids. I turned to my own sheet. No G-58 on the first grid. No G-58 for the second grid. "I-32. I-32." The caller was onto the next number, and I hadn't even gotten to my third grid.

"What was that first number again?" I whispered to Chris.

Chris flicked his eyes over my sheet. "You don't have it," he murmured.

I stole a glance at Maggie's sheet. It was filling up with hot pink splotches. My best grid only had three green splotches in a row.

"Bingo," someone called. Air whooshed out of my lungs. A woman with white hair and brown glasses waved her sheet in the air. The attendant ran over and took the sheet.

"Bingo has been called," the announcer purred.

"This is really exciting," Maggie whispered into my ear. My feet began to tingle

"Please stand by as we check the winner's grid." A pause. "The Bingo is good. Seventy-five dollars to this round's winner." The woman whooped, and her friends yelled and clapped. Chris looked over at Maggie's sheet. "Maggie, you had Bingo!"

"I did?" Maggie looked down at her sheet and, sure enough, there was an almost complete diagonal. She had left the "free" square unsplotched.

"Yes," Chris said. "That middle spot is a freebie."

"Oh." Maggie splotched her free slot, finishing her winning diagonal. "I won!"

The Bingo caller's voice introduced the next round. "This is our Blackout game. Winner must fill in the entire Bingo grid."

Maggie's face broke into a huge grin. "I got Bingo!" she called out loudly. A few people at the next table turned their heads toward us.

Chris looked pained. "It's too late. You missed the window. Once they start the next round, you can't claim the winnings."

Maggie's shoulders drooped, and I held my breath. "Oh, well." She settled into her stool. "I'll just have to win again."

The editor came around with new sheets. "How many for the Blackout round?"

I put my hand on her grid. "You know, we can always do something else."

Maggie gathered her Bingo cards and arranged them in front of herself with care. "I think I'll try six grids this time."

There she was, my New York City friend, joyfully playing Bingo at the East Otter Tail County Fair.

25

Oak Hollow

We're made to bend
So we don't break
We're made to learn
From our mistakes
Don't give up now
You're halfway there
It's just another way
To get there
– "Lean into the Curve"

September–November

Maggie left me with the faint memory of my former life of urban sophistication. But soon enough I was back to my country rhythm, writing by day, visiting warm tree-lined lakes in the late afternoons, occasionally driving across the state to perform gigs in faraway rural towns very much like New York Mills.

Chris and I continued our search for a new house. Though I had the nest-egg of a down payment I had saved during my Brooklyn rental years and Chris had a dependable monthly income, the lake homes we liked were too expensive for our budget.

Then one sparkling fall day, when crimson sumac lit up the green of the roadsides, Terry the realtor called with a house she was sure we would love.

The first thing I noticed were the columns. After a long, curved gravel driveway, the white Grecian columns stretched up like graceful arms coupling the six-acre stretch of spacious lawn to the wide blue sky. The red, two-story Southern plantation-like home had five sets of French doors that opened onto white verandas. Centered in front of the house and taller than the upstairs veranda, a hundred-year-old oak tree held its branches out to us in welcome.

The breeze hushed like a lullaby and brought the scent of autumn leaves from the surrounding woods. "I don't know," Chris whispered in my ear when Terry left to fetch the key from the lockbox.

A few crumpled leaves fell from the oak. "What do you mean, you don't know?" My hands were on my hips.

"This house is in the country. It feels so isolated. What if something happened?" The wind picked up. "I don't want to live in the country. I'd rather live in town. The country scares me." I squinted at Chris. He had grown up in the country. He fished, hunted, and backpacked in the wilderness.

I shook my head fast, sharp edges of my hair windmilling into the corners of eyes and mouth. "Chris . . . New York Mills *is* the country."

"No, I live in town." Chris's head pulled backwards with emphasis. "The country is totally different." He sensed my indignation and fell back on his trick of using humor as deflection. He lowered his voice to a dramatic whisper. "There's no one nearby to hear you scream."

A piece of gravel skittered across the driveway. "Are you serious?" I had left the buzz and energy of eight million people for the middle of nowhere, and already this property, with its privacy, its trees, and the gentle sounds of the country that would inspire my songwriting seemed like it had the potential to make up for my loss.

Chris's voice rose to normal volume. "Yes. I'd be scared to be home alone. I mean, did you see the neighbor's house?"

Across the road was a wood skeleton of a house jacketed in flapping plastic. Three cars were parked in front in litter-strewn mud. Two horses with their ribs showing were caged in a paddock at its side.

"I'm sure they're in the midst of renovations."

"Did you see any building materials? I think it's been an eyesore for a while. And did you see the graves at the foot of this driveway?"

In the triangle between the driveway and the gravel road, two gray headstones sat stoically under a wooden trellis in a rectangle of lawn.

"Is it okay to have human graves so close to a residence?"

Chris laughed harshly. "This isn't New York. There aren't any zoning laws in the country."

I made a clicking sound with my tongue. Terry returned with the key. She led us through a heavy oak front door inset with cut glass, and we found ourselves in a foyer with hardwood floors. The house felt airy and spacious. It held the scent of candles and freshly baked cookies.

Terry opened a closet off the foyer, "And here's the elevator."

"Elevator?"

"Yes, I believe there was a handicapped child who once lived here, so they put in an elevator." Terry closed the door with a click, and we moved past a library with built-in bookshelves to enter a family room paneled, wall and ceiling, in glossy wood.

"That's quarter-sawn oak." Chris exhaled a whistle. He ran his hand over the paneling and glanced sideways at me. The house was beginning to wield its magic on him.

It was one of the upstairs bedrooms that made up my mind. The square room had two closets large enough to fit my guitars and hand drums, my boxes of yet-to-be-sold CDs, my stacks of reference books, thesauri, and rhyming dictionaries. A ceiling fan moved lazily between where I would put a writing desk and where I would place a couch. A set of French doors opened onto the upstairs veranda, where I could envision sitting and writing on warm days, watching deer from between its railings.

For a price that wouldn't cover half of the cost of a studio apartment in Brooklyn, I could have three bedrooms, three bathrooms, two verandas, two fireplaces, and quarter-sawn oak walls.

Chris's fear of country isolation was no match for the house's grace, its verandas, and the oak-paneled family room. By the time we had finished the tour, neither the eyesore across the street nor the two graves at the foot of the driveway could dissuade him.

Our offer on the house was accepted. After closing, we visited what was now our new house. I ran up the stairs, whooping with glee. Chris whooped back. We jumped and sang nonsense songs and danced in the master bedroom. Chris stopped singing and looked thoughtful. "A house this fine needs a name."

Outside the bedroom window, the oak tree waved branch-shaped silhouettes across a bright, wide swathe of Milky Way.

"Let's name it Oak Hollow."

In the weeks between closing on the house and moving pick-up loads of boxes from Chris's cottage to Oak Hollow, I painted the upstairs bedroom that was to become my studio. The quiet of my soon-to-be home had a pulse like a heartbeat, soothing me into calm.

Until a vehicle roared dissonance into the groove. The motor quieted, and small muscles I hadn't known I'd tensed released. I cocked my head, trying to place the sound. The doorbell rang and my hand jumped, spraying a mist of paint droplets. Someone was here.

Who would be visiting my isolated house on a weekday afternoon? I was used to neighbors who shared my apartment walls and pedestrians only feet away from my window. But they were never a threat: our proximity was tempered by the separate trajectories of our lives. In the country, no one was supposed to be anywhere near me, unless they had business with me. I put down my brush and wiped ghoulish streaks of green on my gray sweatshirt. I tip-toed down the stairs, hoping my socks weren't tracking paint.

Through the paned windows, I could see the broken vision of a well-built man of fifty, with cool blue eyes and weathered skin. A young boy, about four years old, clutched his hand.

In Brooklyn, I would have only unbolted the door with the chain fastened. I was in the country now, and there was no chain. I opened the door.

"I'm Robin Wells," the man on my doorstep said. "I'm sorry to bother you, but I used to live here."

November cold whipped against my cheeks as I recalled the name. When I told people in town about my new house, they recognized it, "You live in the old Wells house," they would say. The house that was built by Robin Wells, the man standing in front of me.

The hairs on the back of my neck twitched, and I wasn't sure if it was from the cold or because there was no one else around for almost a mile. I folded my arms in front of my chest in a useless attempt at self-protection. I was beginning to share Chris's concern about isolation.

"You're the one who built this house. Thank you. I mean, it's a great house."

The story of the house began fifteen years before, when Robin's eight-year-old son, Buck, sustained brain damage in an accident. Robin installed an elevator to transport his son between floors. A year after the accident, Buck died, and the family moved out. Robin sold off the farm property, then the house. He kept a green rectangle of grass at the bottom of the driveway where his son and his mother were buried, the graves I saw every time I drove up or down the driveway.

Robin lifted his head up, standing up even taller. "We were visiting my son's grave and, while we were here, I wanted to show my youngest son, Kyle, the house I built." Robin patted the shoulder of the small form hiding behind his legs.

By my city barometer, the conversation was getting too intimate and my arm muscles twitched, eager for a swift city door slam. My new sense of country etiquette fought against my city instincts. Robin was a neighbor, or at least sort of; I was probably supposed to invite him in. The boy poked his head around his father's leg, a sparkle of sunshine reflecting off his irises.

How dangerous could a man be with his young son? "Would you . . ." My voice wavered. "Like to come in?"

Two branches in the oak tree creaked against each other. I pulled the door closer to my body and wedged myself in the space between door and doorframe.

"No," he said. "Thank you. I don't mean to interrupt. I only wanted to bring Kyle out here." Robin turned his head toward the loop of driveway in front of the house. "I built the driveway in the shape of a teardrop. For Buck." Robin walked his new son to the far end of the veranda. He pointed to the floor where, finger-grooved by a child's hand in once-wet concrete, was Buck's name.

Something in my center buckled. "Are you sure you don't want to come in?"

Robin said, "No, we're just leaving. You know you need to fill the fuel tank every three weeks, right?"

I nodded.

Robin gathered Kyle and led him off the veranda to the four-wheeled all-terrain vehicle parked out front. "Just wanted to let you know that I'm around regularly to keep up the gravesites, and I live in the RV by the graves over the summer."

The roar of the four-wheeler going down the driveway vibrated up my spine in a shiver. As soon as I thought I was getting the hang of this country thing, something new arrived on my doorstep.

26

Paper Ballots

Those officials said: you're not like us
We don't want to hear your preachin'
Don't try to fight us
We've got the might of right behind us
– "Hold On—the Dr. Bronner Song"

November

In the rearview mirror, I caught a last glimpse of white columns over red siding. I had figured out how to handle the driveway, braking slightly into the deep curve after the teardrop loop. My new house disappeared behind a privacy screen of trees and brush so thick it blocked the view of our house from the road even after the leaves had fallen and faded.

Beyond the curve, the Wells cemetery came up quickly on my right. The two small graves were magnified by the field around them, like a tragic miniature augmented by a heavy frame. I sped up and gazed ahead, trying to ignore the reminder of Buck's death.

It took a few minutes of driving before the car warmed up. I bopped along to a new album I had traded a CD for at a performance with another songwriter the week before. The car hadn't heated up enough to remove my wool cap when I arrived at my new Minnesota polling place. I rolled my vehicle off the empty two-lane road and bumped onto the flattened grass parking lot of Bluffton Township Hall. The upbeat song was silenced with the turn of my key, and the wind made a low whistle across the plains.

The light gray paint of the former one-room schoolhouse blended into the overcast sky of early winter purgatory. Two Buick Regals already in the lot were unobtrusive shades of silver and slate, and two pick-up trucks were so covered with dust they looked gray, too. In the monochrome landscape of faded farmland, my burnt orange corduroy pants were the only sign that color hadn't drained from the world. I huddled my shoulders against the November wind and speed-walked to a single-width door cut into clapboard.

For a moment, I wondered if I had come to the right place. Unlike the line of people I had waited in when I had voted the year before in Brooklyn, there was no one waiting outside. In New York City, queues ran for blocks out of the entrance to the local elementary school. On the clipboard for last names beginning with "K" and "L," I helped the volunteer flip through dozens of pages until they found "Ko." From there I moved into another queue where a chorus line of people waited for one of the voting machines that ran in pairs from one end of the gymnasium to the other. In Bluffton, I parked on dried grass and walked into a one-room schoolhouse that smelled of woodsmoke and pencil shavings.

Five older white people sat at a folding card table by a 1930s-era furnace. I could tell by the words "buck" and "stand" that the conversation was about the upcoming deer season. I stood, waiting for acknowledgment. The conversation was animated for Minnesota. Deer season seemed to get people excited. A man with a red face noticed me first and peered at me suspiciously. Two other men turned, eyes flinty under feed caps. Conversation ceased. Everyone stared at me for a long moment. I felt like a student who had been sent to the corner for misbehaving.

"Do you need to register?" the white-haired man asked, with a tone that meant, *Are you sure you're in the right place?*

"No, I'm already registered." I pointed at my name on the clipboard. The first feed-capped man scanned the sheet.

"That's you?" he said doubtfully.

"Yes."

He hesitated for a moment, then proffered the sheet for me to sign.

"Where do you live?" The lady with the eyeglass lanyard cocked her head at me.

I scrawled my name on the signature line. "On 475th, near the curve."

"I don't know these new-fangled street names," the other feed-capped man said. The township had renamed the roads thirty years ago. "Which house are you?"

"The old Wells house. The big red one you can see through the trees."

"Are you Chris Klein's girlfriend?" asked the red-faced man with stubble.

I nodded. The room seemed to exhale, now that I had been placed in relational context.

The red-faced man stopped scowling. "I live just up the road from you. I went to high school with Kenny." My father-in-law, who had grown up in New York Mills. "I'm Vernon. You're from somewhere else, aren't you?"

"Yes. New York City."

"Wow." He laughed, rubbing one heavy-lidded eye. "From New York City to New York Mills." The two ladies resumed their conversation, now talking about a fish fry at church planned for the following week.

"So, what do you do?" asked one of the farmers from under his feedcap.

"I'm a songwriter."

"A what?" The ladies stopped talking.

"A songwriter. I write songs."

A chair leg squeaked against the floor. "So, you're a housewife."

"Uh, no. I'm a songwriter. I compose music and write lyrics. I create songs, like the ones you hear on the radio."

"Have I heard any?"

"Probably not."

The guy in the feedcap grunted, dismissing me. The woman with the lanyard turned away. No one said anything. I could almost smell the acrid scent of schoolroom glue, almost feel the pointy dunce cap on my head. I wanted to get out of there. "So, where do I vote?" I couldn't see any voting machines in the tiny room.

The lady with bright white hair handed me a sheet of paper and pointed to the chest-high shelf that had been sectioned by planks into four niches. From what I could tell, a person faced the walls and used the shelf as a standing desk. I looked at the paper in my hand and read the word BALLOT at the top. I had never actually seen a paper ballot before. In Brooklyn, I pressed metal buttons and pulled a lever and I was done. "How do I fill this out?" My voice cracked.

"Color in the bubbles and, when you're done, feed your ballot in there." Vernon pointed to a machine that looked like a copier.

I filled in my ballot with a black ballpoint offered by the lady with the lanyard. The election volunteers returned to their conversation. I heard Vernon say, "Last year, I got an eleven-point buck at the end of my driveway. Just walked right up to me. Good thing I always keep my gun by my side and loaded." He laughed. I stifled a shiver. I finished marking my ballot and held it carefully behind my body, trying to make myself really big to hide it from view. Vernon reached for it. I jerked it away, then blushed. I put the ballot into the slot of the machine. The machine sucked it in slowly enough for Vernon to get a good look at my votes. I could have sworn he drew away from me after seeing them.

The LCD counter on the front of the machine clicked up from sixty-two to sixty-three. It was 4:00 p.m., and I was the sixty-third person to vote in Bluffton Township. Vernon handed me a red "I Voted" sticker and waved goodbye. I walked out into the monochrome world and inhaled the winter scent of frozen dirt. I wondered if I'd dreamed the last few minutes of color, and absent-mindedly drove toward town for some coffee.

The Creamery clattered with the sound of espresso makers and conversation. At the counter, Jack gestured with his chin toward my sticker. "How'd it go?" he asked.

"Fine, but I think they saw my votes. I didn't want anyone in Bluffton to know how liberal I am." I pulled my knit hat off and let the warm air of the cafe soothe my cold ears.

Jack looked me up and down. "Elisa," he said. "With those pants? They already know."

27

The Importance of Being Furnaced

Snow's coming down
Too cold to go out
I could almost drown
In the sound

Of whitewashed horizon
Wind whipping outside
Blanket around me
And you by my side
– "Winter Song"

December

The Minnesota winter weather of legend arrived with temperatures that hovered at twenty-six degrees below zero and winds that shrieked by the outer walls at forty miles per hour. With windchill, it felt like fifty degrees below zero. I slipped out from under the covers, leaving Chris snoring lightly on his side of the bed. Despite the indoor heat, I felt unusually chilly in my flannel pajamas. I stepped barefoot into the bathroom, and my feet ached against cold tile. The digital thermometer in the bathroom read forty-three degrees. My sleep-fuddled mind only registered the thought I should probably change clothes downstairs, where it was usually ten degrees warmer than the upstairs due to faulty ducts.

The doorway to my studio was dark and quiet. Traipsing downstairs, I vaguely noticed the absence of the usual wind tunnel caused by the temperature difference between the two floors.

Cold had dampened the scent of the house. Wind whistled through the cracks between the French doors. I cringed, anticipating the shivering moments between the warmth of the shower and the cover of the towel. I wondered whether I really needed to shower at all that day.

The main floor didn't feel any warmer than upstairs. I considered staying in my pajamas all day and wondered how many layers I could physically put on at the same time. I walked past the library to the thermostat. Next to the target temperature, sixty-eight degrees, there was a larger number for the current temperature. It read forty-two degrees. For one instant, before the meaning of the measurement sank in, I was slyly impressed with my ability to live in forty-two-degree air in light pajamas.

Then the weight of my discovery landed like a icicle to the chest.

The furnace had stopped running.

Broken furnace.

Negative twenty-six degrees.

Bad.

"Honey!" I called shrilly up to Chris. He mumbled something from the bed.

"The furnace broke!"

There was a second of quiet, then the thump of Chris's feet hitting the floor of the bedroom. Footsteps pounded down the stairs, and Chris stood next to me at the thermostat, his body tense and uncertain.

It still read forty-two degrees.

Chris stared at the thermostat for a full minute. He jiggled the power button from on to off, his head cocked to listen for the sound of the furnace starting. We heard nothing. Chris raced through the kitchen and banked the turn down the stairs to the basement. I followed. In the unfinished utility room, behind a nest of wires in the furnace's bowels, a tiny red indicator light was the furnace's only sign of life.

It was 7:00 a.m. Our furnace was broken. The temperature outside was hovering at twenty-six degrees below zero. There were at least four months left to Minnesota's winter.

"What do we do now?" I moaned, following Chris up the basement stairs.

"We call Mike's Plumbing and Heating." Chris ran back and forth between the fireplaces in family room and living room, gathering odds and ends of wood that had collected during our few experimental fires.

I stood motionless between rooms.

"Call Mike's." Chris pitched his voice as he would to a frightened child, crinkling paper between logs. "I'll work on starting some fires in the fireplaces."

The phone was cold, its plastic brittle and unyielding.

"Mike's Plumbing and Heating."

"I'm so glad you answered," I babbled. "Our furnace stopped. Can you help?"

"Who am I speaking to?" Flame whooshed as it caught paper in the fireplace.

"Elisa. I live at the old Wells house, on 475th Avenue."

Jeremy the heating man agreed to come over first thing.

I replaced the phone in its cradle at the wrong angle, and it clattered to the floor. I bent down to get it and bumped my head on the counter. I dropped the phone again. I picked it up and placed it on the table. My hands were shaking. It was Minnesota. It was winter. Our furnace was broken. These thoughts cycled on repeat.

Chris dashed into the living room, hands cradling more logs.

"What are you doing?" I called as I scurried to the laundry room to get my fuzzy robe.

"What does it look like I'm doing?" Chris squatted over the pile of logs he'd arranged in the second fireplace, his wool coat puckering out behind him.

I stood above him. "Can't we find a hotel and stay in it until it warms up a bit, and then we can deal with the furnace?"

Chris adjusted a log. "No. We need to keep the house heated. If we don't, the pipes will freeze and burst. You think this is bad? If the pipes burst, we'll have a real mess on our hands. Talk about expensive. We're really lucky this happened while we were here."

Cold air blew in from the chimney. My ears and fingers were starting to numb. I stumbled by Chris to get my mittens and hat as he rose. We bumped into each other.

"Oops, sorry," I said, head hanging, hands clutching and opening, holding nothing.

"Why don't you make us some tea?" Chris said gently.

I took the kettle to the sink, knocking over a plate and a mug on my way. Once both fireplaces were ablaze, Chris ran around the house to close bedroom doors. "Conserving heat," he explained. I finally filled up the kettle and put it on the stove. I barely noticed that the wrong burner was glowing red. I moved the kettle. I poured orange juice into dried oatmeal. Chris blew on the fires to get them as hot as possible, and I walked in circles around the kitchen trying to remember which cabinet I'd put tea bags in.

"Can you get some more wood?" called Chris.

I found my ankle-length down coat in the coat closet and went outside to the woodpile.

The wind seared my cheeks, facial nerves traveling through pain to numbness. Logs scraped my deadened fingers. The heat was gone. There was no way to make enough heat. The house would freeze. I would freeze. Even if I managed to find shelter, the pipes in my new house would freeze and burst. My dream house—the first house I ever owned, the home I had lovingly imagined as my Minnesota refuge, my haven—had failed me.

Only a small gradient of warmth met me at the threshold of transition from outdoors to indoors. I dumped the wood by the fireplace. I left my coat on. In the kitchen, I took the steaming tea kettle off the stove, forgetting to turn off the burner.

Chris entered the kitchen wearing his business clothes. "You might want to turn that off," he said toward the stove.

"Wha-what are you doing?"

"I'm going to work," he said. "It's eight o'clock."

"But, what do I do?"

"You wait for Mike's to come, see what they say, and then try to keep warm."

"But, you can't leave me here to do that alone!" I was ashamed by the screech in my voice.

"Elisa, you're perfectly capable of handling this. It'll be fine." He bussed my cheek and went out the door. I sat down at the kitchen table in my coat and nursed my tea, trying to breathe down my heartrate. The two cats burrowed together on the couch in a furry heap.

Twenty minutes later, the doorbell rang. "I hear your furnace stopped, there." The man in the coveralls stamped the snow from his boots onto the rug in the foyer. "How do I get to the basement?"

I led Jeremy to the furnace and hovered at the top of the stairs with my forgotten tea. Metal tools clinked echoes against the furnace body. I moved to the family room and pretended to read a magazine while quarter-sawn oak walls leaned in around me, trapping me in a wooden icebox.

For an hour, I shuttled between kitchen and family room, winding a trail around the main floor trying to keep myself occupied, before remembering I ought to check whether the cold had affected my acoustic guitar. I was putting the guitar into its case when air wheezed through the ducts. The furnace had come back to life. I put my hands above the vent and a small, cool sigh tickled my fingers.

"Yah, I got her going again. She needed a new fuel nozzle." Jeremy's voice came from the top of the basement stairs, where he was wiping grimy hands on his coveralls. "Should be fine now. It'll probably take all day to warm up."

"*All* day?" I asked.

"Yah. Should work fine after that." Jeremy gathered his tools and walked out the front door with a wave.

The house smelled stale as a meat freezer. I had intended to use my day to write a song about winter, but I couldn't face staying in the house, nor the cold-induced slowness of my fingers on the guitar. I couldn't even face the moments of bare skin against the air when changing out of my pajamas. I thought about how quickly my Honda Civic heated up. No one would see my pajamas under my coat, and my winter hat would cover my bed-tousled hair. I grabbed my keys and my purse and piled into my car. With the heat cranked to high, I headed to the nearest Target store, one hour away.

I spent the day in well-heated stores purchasing blankets, oil heaters, rope caulk, and draft dodgers. By the time I returned that evening, the thermostat of my house read sixty-five. I flung my coat off, switched on my new space heater, and curled up in the warmth of my new blanket to write lyrics about the fierceness of Minnesota cold.

28

Cursing

So, who was I?
Who was I?
Who was I?
Tell me something about my life
– "Who Was I"

January 2008

Winter was surprisingly productive for my creativity. The long, languid cold days were defined more by waking and sleeping than by a sun that, like a fashionable guest to a party, entered late and left early. I could spend all day in my cozy studio, writing and playing, seeing to the business of maintaining my music career, and making a game of not leaving the house from when I woke to when I went to sleep. The outside sounds were muted by snowfall, and the hum of my repaired furnace was a soothing drone behind my melodies.

In the evenings, Chris returned from work and cooked me dinner. We had figured out that the domestic arrangement that worked best was to have him cook and me do the dishes. He loved to cook and hated to clean. I was tepid about both, but when I cooked, he always found better things to do than dishes, and I ended up doing both. Chris prepared Vietnamese and Japanese dishes out of recipes he'd collected from Asian friends, and winter was no obstacle to his love of grilling.

In my world, grilling was only a summer activity, but Chris threw a down coat over his apron, stomped a trail through the snow from the back door to the grill, and returned to the kitchen with red cheeks and a steaming plate of steaks we had sourced from our farmer neighbor.

Every week, I let errands collect untended to. When I had enough of them for an efficient outing, I left my creative cocoon and ventured into the white landscape to buy groceries, visit the post office, stop at the Creamery and the Cultural Center.

"Hey, Buzzer, can I move our mailbox?" I called across the post office counter, letting the glass door shut behind me. "The fu—" I stopped myself in the middle of a curse and restarted the sentence. "The dogs across the street keep trying to bite me whenever I approach my mailbox."

Our mailbox was across the street from our driveway, at the foot of the sidingless house. Chris and I had taken to collecting our mail from the car in order to protect us from the growling dogs. When Chris was away, I let mail collect for days before I mustered the courage to get it. When I worried the mailbox was packed so full I wouldn't be able to open it, I veered my car to the wrong side of the road, grabbed the mail, and squealed into my driveway before the pack made it, barking and howling, to the side of the car.

"The dogs at the house across the street from you?" Buzzer raised his eyebrow and gave a knowing little grin. "Sure, you can move it."

"I'm going to do it right now!" I pulled the glass door open in an arc, cold winter air whipping my hair.

"You might want to wait a few months." Buzzer's voice followed me out. "It's mighty hard to hammer a mailbox into the ground while the ground is still frozen."

My step stuttered. The door caught on my foot, leaving a throbbing ache in the bone that jutted out of my ankle. "Damn!" My voice caught in my throat. I looked around to make sure no one had heard me. Buzzer was sorting through the mail. I let the air out of my lungs and limped to the car.

Unlike my former New York City neighbors, inhabitants of rural Minnesota did not curse. Last time I said "Oh, my God!"—a staple of a New Yorker's lexicon—Chris had glared at me and proceeded to explain, in the tone of a lecturing schoolmaster, that one did not take the Lord's name in vain in central Minnesota. It was hard to believe but, then again, the worst thing I had ever heard come out of Chris's mother's mouth was "Sheesh." Sticking to a clean lexicon was difficult in my worst moments; "gosh" and "golly" didn't offer the same satisfaction as "shit" and "fuck."

I missed cursing.

After stopping to talk to Jamie at the Cultural Center and pick up a mocha from the Creamery, I drove the seven miles to my red-and-white sanctuary in the country. I realized it had been a few days since I collected my mail, so before turning into the driveway that now represented peace and creativity, I sighed deeply and directed my car toward the mailbox. No work had been done on the sidingless house since we had seen it the previous fall, and every day took more of a toll on its structure. The roof had lost shingles. The exposed frame was rotting. Without its siding, the house loomed monstrously, a body without skin, all its sinew exposed.

Three members of the dog army lolled by the front step. When they saw me they leaped up, barking. Soon a collection of dogs crowded around my mailbox. I threw the mail in the passenger seat and reversed in an explosion of engine noise. The pack chased my car up my driveway, only slowing and scattering at the end of Robin's small cemetery.

"Fuck you!" I yelled. A little of my tension released. "Fuck you!" I yelled louder.

I needed to calm down. I needed some exercise. And I needed to prove to myself that the neighbor's dogs would not prevent me from enjoying my new house in the country. I decided I would take a walk. It was a relatively warm fifteen degrees and hadn't snowed in a week.

Most of the ice and snow had withdrawn to the edges of roads and driveway. Chris had dragged me outside to wander our yard under the Milky Way–covered sky the night before, and shown me how to throw stones at the dogs to keep them away.

Getting ready to go outside in Minnesota took longer than it ever had in New York City. I changed into long underwear and multiple fleece layers and laced up snow boots over wool socks. I clad myself in a down jacket, scarf, neck gaiter, insulated mittens, and double-layered wool-and-fleece hat. At the bend in my driveway, I picked up a couple of flat stones and held them, awkwardly, in my mittens.

The two headstones in Robin's cemetery watched me like sphinxes. The skinless house came into view behind them, white plastic flapping in the wind where siding should have been. Twenty yards from the end of my driveway, a fist-sized stone ready in my hand, the first dog caught my scent and howled. The rest of the dogs joined in a chorus of barks. One large black-and-brown dog ran to me, jaws snapping. Three half-grown puppies followed a few feet behind.

I threw a stone. It landed short of the dogs in a small spray of snow. The puppies stopped. The mother kept coming. I threw another stone, my heart starting to pound.

A man's voice screamed through a boarded up window. "Molly! You get back here."

My heart was beating in my head. The dog paused. I didn't hesitate. I ran toward the road, trying to get past their territory. A smattering of disappointed barks petered out behind me. The dog named Molly glared at me from the edge of the property. The rest of the dogs lay down.

I slowed, breathing clear, cold air into my lungs. I sang a hard, angry rock song to the fast beat of my footsteps. I was okay. I had made it past the dogs. I was walking down my country road. At least the confrontation had served to get my heart moving. I pulled off my hat to cool myself.

A vehicle rumbled into the turn onto 475th Avenue. A gray Buick crested the hill, a small cloud of dust rising from the bare gravel between two parallel strips of ice that tires had welded into the road. I moved to the side. Like a good New Yorker, I put my head down to avoid catching the eye of the driver. I listened for the car to pass. Instead, the ticking of the engine slowed, and the car eased to a stop beside me. I lifted my head and found myself looking directly into the hooded eyes of the man from the polling place: Vernon, the man who always kept his gun nearby and loaded.

A cold wind picked up, and ice cracked as the branches of the trees bent and snapped. Vernon rolled his window down with a whine. He jutted his chin at me. "I heard you're Jewish."

The dove-gray clouds seemed to sink closer to me. Jewish people were rare in rural Minnesota. I knew of only one other Jew in Otter Tail County. Most people here had never met a Jewish person, leaving me unsure how they would react.

I looked up and down the road. There was no one else around. Did he keep a gun in his car? My teeth clenched together so hard my jaw snapped when I opened my mouth to speak. "Yes."

Vernon tilted his head to the right, his eyes not blinking. I was so close I could see the blue veins crawling across his nose. I stayed very still. The wind stopped. The world was silent, waiting.

"You and I believe in the same God," he said. A dim circle of sun appeared like a portal from behind a scrim of white-gray. "So you're okay by me."

I let the air out of my lungs and tried to smile. A crow cawed and flapped out of a tree nearby.

"The Messiah is coming again." Vernon lifted a red-stubbled face to the overcast sky. "And it's important that we believers stick together so we can work together against Satan." He lowered his eyes, and they bored into mine.

"Oh," I said. Now was not the time to explain that Jews believed that the Messiah hadn't even come once. I moved my weight to my other leg. "What church do you go to?"

Vernon shifted his car into park. "I don't go to church. People run churches, and they get things wrong. I prefer to stick directly to the Word of God, take my teachings from what He said in the Bible."

"I see." The wind picked up and its sound filled in my silence.

"You know, the Great Battle is coming." I could hear the capital letters. "You can see the signs everywhere." Vernon lounged in his seat. "The world is coming to a head. The time of the Messiah is nigh."

"Mmmm," I said, noncommittally, and placed my cap on my head.

"I'm glad we were able to talk about this." His eyelids lowered to half-mast. He shifted the car into drive. "It was good to see you." He drove off, shutting his window against the cold.

I stared after him. Motes of ice hung in the clear, cold air behind Vernon's car, suspended and twisting in the light.

I walked fast to get home, keeping my attention on where to place my feet between strips of ice and humps of frozen mud tractor tracks. An excited bark came from the direction of the across-the-street neighbors. I slowed. My house was at the far end of the field to my right. Though bumpy and snow covered, a route through it would circumvent the dogs.

My boots crunched a trail through the sharply scented old snow. My breathing became uneven; walking through snow was more exhausting than I had expected. My foot caught in an unseen hole, and I wrenched the same ankle I had knocked at the post office. "Goddamnit," I said as I bent my knee and twisted backward to rub the ankle. When the throbs subsided, I limped to the barbed-wire fence and contorted my body to fit through the top and middle wires. A twist of sharp metal scraped my wrist, and another snagged my favorite fleece pants, ripping a hole. "Fuck!" I yelled.

I opened my front door; defeat plucked at strings in the back of my throat. I needed to talk to someone. I needed to talk to another New Yorker, someone who understood the disorientation of country life. I lifted the phone and fought to keep the wistfulness from my tone as I greeted Lina.

"I'm almost done at the museum," she said. "How about you come over to my house for tea?"

At Lina and Jerome's painted Victorian, I stood under the roof of the back porch on a faded Astroturf doormat that said WELCOME in white cursive. Lina's muffled voice answered my knock. "Come in!" The vestibule door opened with a comfortable creak into a yellow kitchen with an iron stove and pottery jars marked FLOUR and SUGAR.

"I just put on the water." Lina swept into the room wearing a long kaftan. Her soft, dark hair brushed my chin as she enveloped me and held me close. I breathed in Lina's clean scent of roses and sandalwood. "It is so good to see you," she said into my ear. "It sounded like you needed to talk." She clattered in a cabinet and brought out a box of Lipton tea.

"It's been a weird day."

Lina led me into the dining room and gestured to a chair at the carved table where a half circle of papers circumscribed a comfortable workspace. The top page of a notebook was filled with Lina's neat handwriting, and the leather seat of the chair looked like it had been molded to Lina's shape.

She stacked the papers together and moved them to a pile on the sideboard. "Looks like you have a lot to do," I said.

A muscle in Lina's jaw tightened. Her face looked weary. "There's always more to do for the museum than I can get done. And then there are all the projects I want to do for me—writing, photography, grant applications. I'm always playing catch-up."

I searched for a cue to a new, more cheerful topic. The dining room walls caught my eye. They were an antique beige with vertical vines of maroon, cobalt, and goldenrod flowers. Though it looked like wallpaper, on closer inspection I saw warp and weft. "Why are your walls covered with fabric?"

Lina moved her eyes from the sideboard to the walls. "When Jerome and I bought the house, we found crumbling plaster under the original wallpaper. There was no way to hang new wallpaper without further damaging the wall."

I rose from the chair to touch the walls, running my fingers over the fabric's threaded crosshatch.

"At the antique store, I came across wallpaper reproduction fabrics that were exact copies of period wallpaper. So we pinned it on over the plaster."

My finger pushed on the fabric until I touched the roughness of broken wall. For the slightest moment after I pulled my hand back, the indentation left by my finger remained.

The tea kettle began to whistle. Lina pushed her hands down on the table and levied herself up. I slouched in my chair and stared at the dining room walls. The fabric hung the slightest bit askew, so the vertical stripes of flowers angled infinitesimally sideways. I tilted my head to align my vertical with the wall-fabric. Everything else in my field of vision angled. The sideboard swayed. The floor tilted.

I sighed, righted my head, and looked away from the vexing walls.

Lina returned to the table with a china teapot illustrated with a sprig of lemon-yellow flowers. The teapot had no top, and its inside surface was covered with webs of slender tea-stained cracks.

"Have you noticed that everyone in Minnesota is super careful not to swear? No one says a bad word around here."

Lina swished three teabags in the pot. "I've noticed."

"I have to catch myself before any New York language comes out of my mouth. How did you do it? How did you stop cursing?"

"It took a while. I turned a few heads with some blue language when I first arrived."

"Do you ever miss it?"

Lina poured the tea into two china cups. "Who the fuck said I ever stopped cursing?"

A laugh burst out of me. Lina's f-word was a medicinal splash from a secret stash of whiskey.

"Sometimes, I'll watch my language all day and then I'll get home and scream like a sailor." She puckered her mouth mischievously. "It took Jerome a little while to get used to it." She pushed the sugar bowl toward me. The spoon was sticky and rough with half-melted sugar granules. "Feel free to curse."

I took a deep breath and spoke to my teacup. "God, I hate my fucking neighbors and their fucking dogs!"

"Fuckers," Lina said.

My head jerked up. "They are fuckers. *Fuckers.*"

"Fucking assholes!"

"Yes. Fucking assholes!"

Lina grinned at me. "Sometimes, cursing is exactly what you need to make yourself feel better."

I grinned back. I tipped the cup to test the temperature of the tea on my lips. Perfect. The tea's sweet warmth flowed down my throat and radiated from the center of my belly.

"So, what did the fucking dogs do?"

I closed my eyes, readying myself to return to the experience. I opened them again and planted my feet on the ground. "You know the house without siding down the driveway from me?" Lina nodded. "Right, so they have a pack of insane fucking dogs. I went for a walk today and picked up stones to throw them at the dogs."

"Good idea." Lina chuckled into her teacup.

"I went down the driveway, and the evil demon bastards came after me. I threw stones at them, but that didn't stop them. They chased me till the owner came out and yelled at them."

"Damn dogs!"

"Right? And I thought that was bad enough till another neighbor drove up to me in the middle of the fucking street, with no one else around, and he stops his car, and I'm like, what the fuck? And he tells me that he knows I'm Jewish. And for that moment right then, I think

I'm about to be mauled or molested or lynched and, shit-fuck-damn, if he didn't then tell me we believe in the same God and that I was okay by him."

"Shit-fuck-damn is right. That's a crazy fucking story." Lina banged her cup on the table for emphasis.

"Damn straight. My neighbors are fucking crazy, right?"

"Fuck yeah." Lina pulled the teapot off the quilted tea cosy and held it over my cup. "More tea?"

"Sure." I reached for the sugar bowl.

29

Satellite Dish Snow Bowl

Bring me winter
Freeze the ice on the lake
Give me quiet
And a place to hibernate
– "Winter Song"

February

Among endless fields sprinkled sugar-white, the house at Oak Hollow was a candy-cane confection of white columns and red walls.

The dove-colored sky had shattered into bits and floated down to cover the earth in blankets of tiny, cruel diamonds. Sky fragments glittered on the roof between the twin pearls of tundra and sky. The oaks were many-armed gods, black calligraphy on a white page. In the black-and-white beauty, cold was the slicing jab of a broken bottle, its sharp edges keen for one who had not known cold before. It met me, and stole my breath.

"Have you been here through a winter?" was the second thing all Minnesotans asked upon meeting me, after "Ooh, yah, New York City to New York Mills, eh? Didn't want to change the address too much then, didja?" When I answered I hadn't yet lived through a Minnesota winter, the locals shook their heads and turned away.

"Don't worry about it." Chris pulled me close. "Winter's not that bad here."

Despite the focus that a quiet January had given to my songwriting, it was now February, and the sheer willful doggedness of winter was "that bad." There were at least a couple of months more left of ceaseless, white cold, and I couldn't be a real Minnesotan until I had lived through winter in its entirety and chosen to stay anyway.

The cold of negative twenty degrees Fahrenheit burned like molten glass. Exposed skin seared as if blistered. Eyes pricked and ached. Nostrils tightened and stretched. Lungs stung. Hardened mucous pulled nose hairs and blocked airflow. I struggled to inhale frigid air. I breathed glass.

My new life in Minnesota was outlined in cold, circumscribed by cold, defined by cold, and determined by cold. Cold was my rubicon, my crossroads, my final test. If I could make it through the Minnesota winter, I'd be able to live here. Permanently.

*T*he Internet went down during a snowstorm before a brilliantly sunny stretch of weather with skies clear as glass and turquoise as tropical seas, blue-bright as only cold could make it. The outside temperatures were ten to twenty degrees below zero. The wind blew in gusts. The two feet of snow on the ground had hardened into rockscape. My boots left jeweled caves in the sparkling sediment, foot-sized sinkholes with igloo-solid walls.

The Internet satellite dish was a bowl of snow.

On the first day of my life without Internet, I drove twenty miles and back through a snowstorm to a meeting that had been canceled over email. On the second day, I called friends to remind myself they still existed. Despite Chris's absence on Friendster, and later Facebook, I learned that some in the rural Minnesota community were online. The Internet was now the arbiter of my social life, allowing me to contact the world I had left behind in New York City and keeping me current with my new friends in rural Minnesota, many of whom had disappeared behind snow-covered driveways. I was getting antsy.

A week into our Internet fast, we were invited to dinner at Chris's parents' house. We arrived early. Chris's mother Betty was still cooking, and Chris joined his father in the garage to tinker with a boat engine.

"Do you mind if I use your computer?" I asked Betty.

"Not at all," she cooed, waving her left hand so the modest diamond she wore glittered in the lamplight. I left the kitchen for the computer desk in the front hall. "Dinner will be ready in an hour," Betty said from the other room.

When dinner was called, I was only halfway through my inbox. "One more minute!" I yelled, trying to speed up my typing and making a hash of spelling. I closed out of the Internet and walked to the dining room.

Everyone was already sitting at the table. Even Chris's eleven-year-old niece and fourteen-year-old nephew had been peeled from their video games and were sitting politely, napkins on laps. Chris glared at me from across the table.

"Oh, um, sorry. I haven't had Internet in a week."

Chris's father Ken asked, "Has the world ended while you were offline?"

I blushed. I wanted to explain about driving through the snowstorm because of the missing email, but the family shuffled in their chairs, impatient to eat.

We bowed our heads for grace and passed bowls of food around. I took small portions and scarfed down too-large bites while the others talked about Minnesota sports. I was finished first, but when I pushed my chair back, Chris glared at me. I scooted my chair back under the table. When everyone rose, I put my dishes in the sink and darted to the computer desk through the kitchen, but Chris beat me through the living room. I wheedled like a kid. "I wasn't finished!"

"Too bad."

"Honey!"

"You were already on it for an hour. I want a turn."

In that moment it was clear as diamonds that I needed to get online, and that someone needed to remove the snow from the satellite dish. In my mind, that someone was Chris.

After breakfast the next morning, Chris built a fire in the family room and lay on the black leather couch he had purchased off the back of a truck. It suited the oak-paneled den much better than it had the lace-curtained living room of his gray cottage. I put my hands on my hips and stood over him. The heat of the fire made a warm pool on my back. "Will you please fix the Internet?"

"Nope." He sipped green tea out of a pottery mug. "I'm not going out there." He pulled the faux-fur blanket farther up his chest. "It's way too cold out."

The fire snickered behind me. I swallowed a small scream of frustration and tempered my voice. "Come on, please?"

Chris nestled into the couch cushions. "I don't need the Internet that much. I'd rather wait for the snow to melt than go out in that cold."

Snow wouldn't melt till spring, which I understood might not arrive till May. I set my jaw and dug my toes into carpet. A log snapped and settled. I could look at this as an opportunity, my chance to redeem my poor performance with the broken furnace.

Chris put down his mug and fiddled with his cell phone. I assessed the situation. The satellite dish was attached to the roof above the garage twenty feet up from the ground. There was snow. The wind was blowing.

I needed a ladder and a lot of warm clothes.

I brushed snow off the ladder and lifted my heavy boot to the first rung. I transferred my weight slowly, testing the hold.

Boot met ladder. Sole met step. My foot held. I inhaled. Cold outlined my lungs in pain. My face set with determination. As the pain of guitar strings had dug calluses into my fingers, the pain of the cold would callous me to Minnesota's winter. I lifted my other foot to the second rung and climbed. The third rung. The fourth. I looked out on the white world of Oak Hollow from a new vantage point. Emptiness. Clean white under turquoise. Glorious.

I reached the top of the ladder and stretched my body up. My mittens made jazz hands well short of the snow-filled satellite dish.

I needed more height.

I was resourceful. I was desperate. I could figure this out. I went back inside, wriggled my feet out of my boots and shed my outermost layers. In the laundry room I collected more supplies: a telescoping cobweb duster, a broom, a broom handle, and duct tape. Chris was singing one of my songs to himself in the kitchen.

After duct-taping duster, broom, and broom handle together, a twenty-foot pole reached through the doors of three rooms, flexing and dancing in my hand. I wriggled my new tool in victory.

"How's it going?" Chris asked through the wall cut-out from the kitchen to the family room.

"Check out my homemade snow-removal tool."

"Nice!" he said.

"Wanna come see?"

"No thanks." A spoon clattered in the sink.

I suppressed the name I wanted to call him and threaded the extended pole through the door to the garage, muscles tightening against the cold. I pulled against the tool's weight to balance it upward, and watched the far end draw bouncing circles in the air over the tops of our cars. I teased the whole contraption out of the house and closed myself out with the cold.

The javelin quivered into stillness. I climbed. Then I was up the ladder in my puffy yellow coat, perched in slippery boots on a windy subzero day.

I was a long way from my Brooklyn apartment.

I took a steadying breath. From the top, the end of the duster barely reached the satellite dish. I stood on tiptoe, my right arm extended as far as it could go. One clump of snow fell into the space between coat collar and bare skin. Blood pumped cold through my neck.

I stretched farther. My boot slipped. I clutched the rails of the ladder and stabilized. I could do this. I twirled my spear upward in an arc. Broom met bowl. Grenades of snow dropped in explosions of sky dust. I inhaled diamonds.

My arms ached. My abdomen shook. My fingers were numb. The satellite dish was half empty. I hoped it was enough.

I carefully aimed the end of the pole to the ground in a curve that arced from white driveway to white roof. The oak tree regarded me, naked, brown, and grizzled, and I felt a new connection to it. I could be out here in the cold, too.

I pranced into the house, pride lifting my step despite the heavy snow boots. I smelled the warm, honeyed scent of Chris's homemade caramel sauce.

"How'd it go?" Chris's voice rose over the sound of clattering pots in the kitchen.

"It worked, I think. Hey, could you come outside and check that I've removed enough snow?"

I reached to unlace a boot. Chris's footsteps scrambled up the stairs. "What are you doing?" I yelled.

"Checking the Internet to see if it works." Chris's voice came through the section of ceiling under my office.

I pulled at my boot, laces constricting sock at my ankle, pulling it off. I hopped on my half-socked foot, melted snow sliding off me to the floor, until my other boot released with a pop, and I ran, dripping and half barefoot, up the stairs.

In my warm, candle-scented studio, Chris sat at my French writing desk, my computer loading Gopher basketball scores.

"All right!" I yelled and tried to shove Chris out of my chair. He pushed me right back.

"I'm not done yet," he said, grinning wickedly at me.

30

Roadkill for Dinner

A little bit of salt will make it sweeter
A little bit of rain will make it bloom
A little bit of sand will make it smoother
A little bit of harm can do us good
– "A Little Bit of Salt"

March

Call me the Grim Reaper." Chris's voice crackled with excitement into the phone. "I killed two birds on my way to work."

"What kind of birds?" I tucked the handset into the crook between shoulder and neck. The sunny March day held a false promise of spring against the whiteness that extended in every direction. I was in my favorite writing position, lying on my lime-green couch under the Thai marionettes on my wall, my head and back propped by down-filled cushions, laptop in my lap.

"A sparrow and a grouse."

"Can you eat grouse?" I knew from Chris that you couldn't eat sparrow. I settled my fingers into typing position on my laptop. My citron-scented candle glowed.

"Yep. And I already have it in the back seat."

My hands went slack. The phone slipped from its perch on my shoulder. I grabbed at it wildly, catching the phone somewhere around my lap. I placed it against my ear. "You picked it up off the road?" My volume rained static into the mouthpiece.

"Yep."

"Seriously?"

"Sure." Chris paused. "Hey, don't worry. It's safe. I mean, it was a fresh kill. It was still warm."

My jaw hung open like a hatch.

"Still there?"

"What were you planning to do with it?"

He chuckled. "Eat it, silly."

Chris's family lore included a story of how Chris's dad used to stop the car on family trips to check if roadkill by the side of the road was still warm. If it was, he used to put it in the back of the car and take it home for dinner. The story had been told to me by Chris's sister with the cadence of a fairytale. I hadn't thought it was true. Now I knew that it was. And I was living the son's version of it. The cereal I'd had for breakfast sank in my stomach.

The city had not prepared me with a way to respond to a hunter bringing back dinner for his woman. I swallowed. A good country woman would probably try to sound appreciative. I pitched my voice upward. "You are certainly bringing home the bacon tonight, honey!"

"It's grouse, and that's Mr. Honey, sir, to you," Chris said with faux dignity and clicked off. My head stayed crooked against the phone as I stared out the window at decomposing snow. My neck cramped, and I returned the phone to its cradle. I tried to put dinner out of my mind and work on the flyer for my upcoming concert, but flashes of a flapping grouse, wings splayed in panic, kept blocking my view of the screen.

Chris brought the scent of wood into the house with him. His button-down shirt was wrinkled and beginning to come out of his pants. I was slicing carrots. The roasting pan was ready on the countertop, and the oven pre-heated.

"Hi, honey!" I forced myself to smile. "Where is it?"

Chris dropped his briefcase on a wood-slatted chair. He pushed aside spools of fishing line cluttering the kitchen table and pulled a plastic-wrapped package out of a brown grocery sack with a cartoon flourish. One hand glided with a magician's flourish to reveal the other holding a naked pink carcass of a bird in a plastic bag. A few tufts of down puffed from bare and bumpy skin.

I reached over the sink to take hold of the package and hefted its lightness in my hand. "It's so small."

"That's how big a grouse is." He looked up at me. "Nice apron." I grinned and snuck a glance at my aproned reflection in the bay windows.

"What's that?" Chris was looking at the counter, where a pile of carrot coins trailed away from a stub of carrot like fallen dominoes.

"I figured we could cook the grouse with my mom's chicken recipe." I put knife to carrot and a new slice ricocheted off the backsplash and onto the tile floor with a snap. "Rub the grouse with vegetable oil, set it on a pile of sliced onions and carrots, and roast it at 350 degrees."

"That won't work." My knife paused mid-slice. A glimmer of light was still visible over the white field dotted with corn-stubble. In the window glass in front of it, I could see the reflection of my disappointed face.

Chris pulled a can with a red-and-white label out of the grocery bag. "We pour a can of Campbell's cream of mushroom soup over the top and bake it."

I set the knife down so hard it vibrated in an extended clang. A second piece of carrot jumped off the counter. "You're kidding."

"Nope, that's the traditional way to cook grouse."

My hands were damp and itchy. I wiped them on my apron and retrieved carrot pieces from the far corner of the floor, smooth orange surfaces now marred with dust and crumbs and cat fur. I dropped my weight into a chair. The wood rails dug into my shoulders. "I wanted to surprise you by being prepared," I said plaintively.

Chris leaned toward me, the motion making his body smaller, softer. His eyebrows moved together sympathetically. "Nice job, honey."

"Can't we use my mother's chicken recipe anyway?"

"It would dry out." He patted my shoulder. "You need to add a lot of fat to grouse." He looked behind us at my pile of vegetables. "Thank you for getting everything ready. We can use the carrots for a side dish."

The oven beeped, and Chris put down the *Sierra Trading Post* catalog. A gust of heat hit me like a khamsin desert wind. A pool of thick mushroom-soup gravy sloshed over the steaming bird. Chris rested the pot on a trivet alongside the bowl of sautéed carrots and onions already on the table. I watched the pool of goo come to rest around the island of poultry.

The dish gave off an aroma of salt and mushrooms and gamey meat. My head started to spin. My hand pressed the flat of my chair.

He looked at me over the platter, waiting for a reaction. I stretched my mouth up with effort. "Smells great!"

He raised his right eyebrow. "Want some?" The knife in his hand hovered over the pot like a guillotine.

"Of course." My voice was pitched a little too high. I pushed my plate toward Chris, trying to maintain an expression of pleasant anticipation.

He pulled a small ribcage covered with white meat out of the pan and sawed at it with his knife. Flesh ripped from bone. He placed a chunk dripping lumpy goo on the smooth ceramic circle of my plate.

When I lived in New York City, a five-star restaurant could render unfamiliar meat into an exotic dish with French calligraphy on the menu and an artful drizzle of balsamic reduction on the plate. We didn't have a menu, and Campbell's mushroom soup was not a good enough sauce to make me forget that the meat on my plate had been roadkill that morning.

My throat swelled shut.

I slowly served myself a heaping portion of carrots in multiple careful spoonfuls. I handed the bowl to Chris. I placed my hands on my lap.

The left corner of Chris's mouth twitched. "Dig in," he said.

I leaned over my plate, smelling the strong scent of unfamiliar meat. My stomach felt as small and wrinkled as a walnut. "You first."

He slitted his eyes. "Are you chickening out on me?"

"Me? No!" I picked up my fork and pushed the hunk of bird an inch across my plate. "Chickening out! Ha! That's funny. You're funny, Chris."

"Your weak attempts at distraction are not going to work." He tilted his head and softened his voice. "You are going to try it, right?"

"Right," I answered too quickly. I tried to swallow away the constriction in my throat. I stabbed the grouse with my fork, gray liquid drooling off the white gob of meat. From two feet away, the smell was woody and tangy. I brought the fork closer to my face and inhaled a hint of rancid. My mouth went dry.

Chris chewed heartily.

"Is it good?" I asked, fork hovering halfway between plate and mouth.

He considered. "A little dry, but not bad for not having cooked grouse in a while." He set his fork down and turned toward me, waiting.

I looked down at the forkful of grouse. My hand was moving it toward my mouth. My lips stayed pressed together.

Chris waited, each passing moment putting more emphasis on the question of whether or not I would eat it.

My elbow pressed into the table, the table his mother had given us, the table on which Chris had eaten his meals since childhood. Behind him, on the refrigerator, I caught sight of the photograph, edges curling, of Chris and me clowning around at the lake. His dirty socks dangled from the back of the far chair. On the thin strip of wall between the windows, a set of bird-watching binoculars hung from a hook on the wall. He had brought them from the basement for me so I could watch the birds that gathered to collect birdseed near the patio every morning.

I had moved across the country to share a life with this man. I had journeyed across worlds. Moved from concrete to cornfields. Daily, I was filled with doubt that I belonged, that I had what it took to stay. I wanted—no, I needed—to prove that I could share Chris's world with him.

I took a deep breath and blew it out slowly. I relaxed my lips and opened my mouth. The lamp over the table bathed me in yellow light. The fork placed the piece of grouse on my tongue, and I started to chew. Gamey, strong and sharp, the flavor filled my mouth. My teeth ripped the meat into fibers, dense, chewy, and tough.

I swallowed.

The hunk of grouse slid down my throat.

I reached for my glass, feeling its smooth cool surface in my hand, the rim slipping against my greasy bottom lip. I gulped. The grouse stayed down. My face broke open with triumph and I grinned at Chris. I turned to the window expecting to see the reflection of a couple smiling blurry smiles at each other.

Instead Chris pulled a bottle of hot sauce toward him and examined the label. "You are going to eat more, aren't you?"

31

Prairie Chicken Theater

See them look at you
And then make them look again
Make them not want to turn away
If you've got them by the second glance
You've gotten them to stay
– "Trail of Broken Hearts Behind Me"

April

I was dreaming of small brown birds when the beeping of the alarm clock jarred me upright. Chris groaned next to me. Yellow numbers blurred into the scrunched-up slits of my eyes—2:30 a.m. I slammed my hand against the clock and fumbled the sound off. My mind stumbled to remember why I had set the alarm for such an hour. Oh, right: I had signed up to sit in subfreezing temperatures on the Bluestem Prairie at dawn to watch prairie chickens mate.

After one year of living in Minnesota, when people asked me what I missed most about New York, I still answered, "Gourmet baked goods and performing arts." I couldn't do much about the baked goods, but Jamie at the Cultural Center had promised me that the mating dance of the prairie chickens was "can't-miss theater" that Nature displayed for only two weeks every April. I was so starved for the performing arts I was willing to wake in the middle of the night to see chickens do a mating dance. On a prairie. In twenty degrees.

Back in the city, I attended concerts, dance, or theater every week. There was always Maggie's newest Off-Off-Broadway show or one of Jae's modern dance performances to see and, at least once a month, I picked my way through the Times Square crowds to a Broadway theater. I had a secret skill at finagling free tickets from tourists who had bought one too many.

Attending the prairie chicken dance was also an opportunity for me to make my own connection with Chris's beloved outdoors. The outdoors in my former life had been a building-lined sidewalk between where I had been and where I was going. Chris had shown me that the outdoors could be the source of deep, almost spiritual, connection. I wanted to experience the outdoors in that way for myself.

I moved in the dark, feeling my way around the bedframe hand over hand. I squinted my eyes shut at the brightness of bathroom light. Behind the miasma of my eyelids was an imaginary poster: SHOWS AT DAWN, TWO WEEKS ONLY. A prairie chicken posed coyly against the dates.

My yawn was so big it hurt my jaw.

Feet cold on the bathroom floor, I clad myself in layers of wool, the costume of a very cold audience member. I tried to keep my feet quiet as I walked down the hall, past my studio, and down the stairs. In the foyer, I gathered the rest of my supplies: sleeping bag, down coat, wool hat, wool gloves, and snacks. The kettle whistled, and I poured hot water into the thermos I'd readied with a tea bag.

Car wheels made gravel ping like bullets down the driveway. A shiver ran down my spine as I passed the inky blackness I knew was Robin's cemetery plot.

I met Jamie and four others in the eerie middle-of-the-night quiet of downtown New York Mills. In New York City, there was always something to hear, even at 3:00 a.m.—a car alarm, the slam of a door, footsteps. Here, I heard only the snuffles of lungs trying to pull oxygen from icy air.

One hour's silent drive west, we arrived at the Bluestem Prairie. There were no posters, no ticket takers, and no signs directing us to the stage. "This way," Jamie indicated. His flashlight illuminated grass gone white with frost. Blades snapped audibly with each step. We walked for a mile along a grassy, wheel-grooved path, air sharp with cold, ground hard beneath my feet.

Two narrow sheds appeared out of the darkness. "This is the booming area," Jamie whispered. "And these are the blinds we'll be watching from." The six of us stood on the edge of a mowed section of prairie where prairie chickens would perform their mating dance. I bounced on my toes.

Jamie motioned me toward the first blind. "Once we go in, it's best if we stop talking until the end of the mating dance so we don't scare the birds away." My lips pressed together in silent acquiescence as I entered a tight space, six feet high, six feet long, and three feet deep. A plank bench ran its length. The front half-wall went up to my waist and left the top open like a picture window without glass.

I slid along the bench to make room for Jamie and another person, and it pressed a cold bar through the insulation of my ankle-length down coat. There was barely enough room for three of us, girths large with winter clothing. I stuffed my bag under my legs and sidled against the left wall. I tucked my elbows into my sides and held my binoculars ready like opera glasses. In the light from Jamie's flashlight, I could see my breath collecting in steam puffs in front of my mouth.

Jamie assembled his camera on a tripod and flicked off his flashlight. The woman beside him lifted her arm in a low shriek of nylon. I twisted awkwardly in the tight space to pull my thermos from my backpack. I wished Chris had come.

"No way," he had said the week before. "No way am I waking up that early to watch birds dance. I don't even wake up that early to go fishing."

The confined space was silent as a darkened theater, but instead of the pre-show unwrapping of candies and last-minute fits of throat clearing, there was the soft rustle of coat sleeves and the gentle crackle of Saran Wrap. I couldn't hear birds or animals. It was as if everything was asleep on the prairie except us.

My nose started to run. My sniffle roared in the hush. I wiped my nose on my sleeve.

The sky shifted from midnight black to soft gray. I could smell a swamp nearby. A duck quacked in the distance—the first sound of an animal. A goose honked. A songbird trilled. And then it all happened at once—there was no transition from Nature's overture to show. One moment I was listening to a smattering of bird sounds and then, cacophony. A smooth undulating swell of sound erupted over the prairie. It was music. It was song. It was like nothing I had ever heard before.

I held my breath, trying to make sense of the music flowing through my ears. The dim pre-dawn kept me from seeing what I was hearing. That sound! It was mesmerizing. Like the flutter-hoot-whine of air across the top of a glass bottle. Melodic and lofty with a deep and resonant undercurrent of vibration. The blowing was pitched somewhere between bassoon and oboe.

The sound throbbed up and down three plaintive notes. Each prairie chicken's melody was slightly offset, so the effect was that of an entire choir of bottle-blowers. Chicken hum layered on top of chicken hum, notes blending in a gorgeous bath of song resonating in a cathedral. I was swimming in music: glorious, ethereal, like nothing I had ever heard.

The prairie chickens' song continued without pause, without even an instant's rest for breath. Each chicken picked up the notes to fill in when a brother chicken stopped. Above the continuous swell were soft cackles and calls and something like cock-a-doodle-doos.

I had been lifted out of the Minnesota prairie and into a cathedral made from open sky. Divinity sounded in the chickens' voices.

The sky lightened, and I began to see what I was hearing. A full chorus of chickens—dozens of them—strutted through the shortened frost-faded prairie grass. My breath caught in my chest. Fifty roosters and twenty-odd hens flocked in an area of about an acre. They swaggered in circles and tore off in straight lines across the field. Chickens beckoned and taunted their rivals with clucks and chicken yells. They faced off in flurries of feathers and color, miniature dramas across the stage.

A rooster strutted toward center stage looking like he was readying for his solo. He puffed up white tail feathers and turned in a slow circle. He lifted a matched set of long brown neck feathers behind his ears so they stuck up in the air like a pair of horns. Behind the feathers, a matched pair of tangerine balloon sacs inflated on each side of his neck. The rooster puffed them up into two orange fruits trimmed with scarlet and hooted passionately toward the blinds.

My empty thermos cup tipped from my fingers, forgotten. I leaned as far out of the blind as I could. My eardrums vibrated with sound. My hands tried to shape the notes like a conductor.

A second prairie rooster strutted from stage left to the center. The first rooster hopped two feet straight up into the air and then dropped. The second rooster hopped two feet into the air and dropped. The first rooster jumped again. Then the second. Back to the first. My eyes flicked back and forth.

After a few rounds, the roosters stopped, bodies taut, breasts touching, chests rising and falling. Below the sound of the booming, I thought I could hear them panting. The roosters rustled their tail feathers at one another, their orange sacs twinkling like stars on their necks.

With as little warning as when it began, the match was over. The two roosters returned to their corners and vanished among the other roosters.

The sun was up now. A clutch of prairie hens pecked the ground and ambled placidly along the ridge, unconcerned with the roosters' drama. When the occasional rooster-Lothario dared to visit the ladies' camp, he was ignored. Universal romantic behavior, consistent among species. I laughed silently to myself, remembering how I had pushed Chris away at first.

A loud creak came from the other blind. All at once—as if on conductor's cue—the chickens stopped. The sound spilled away. Birds disappeared into the grass. The music was gone. I was slammed into present time and space, ears straining for more of the glorious sound, feeling loose and emptied in the silence.

"I couldn't hold it anymore," a man said defensively.

My flesh ached from the press of the bench. My toes stung with cold. I pushed up my sleeve to see my watch. Almost three hours had slipped by without my noticing. The tea in my thermos was lukewarm on my lips.

I emerged from my box into the sunshine, blinking away brightness. My body creaked as I stretched. My down coat regained its loft and floated up around me like the wings of an angel. I yearned for more of the beauty I had seen and heard.

Finally, I realized, I had had a taste of what Chris saw in the outdoors. I could share Chris's love for it, on my own terms.

The sun had warmed the grass, and the taller blades glistened with dew. I picked up my pace and jumped on the remaining sections of frozen grass to fill my newly empty ears with satisfying crunching sounds.

The next day, I was the one who insisted Chris go outside for a walk with me.

We left the columns behind us, and I almost skipped ahead. Though I knew better, a childlike part of me still hoped to find prairie chickens frolicking in the grasslands along 475th Avenue. "They were hopping up and down, like this." I demonstrated for Chris—again—raising dust and making neck sacks with my hands. "And they sounded like this." I tried to make the hooting sound that had so captivated me. Chris beamed with a combination of amusement and pride. He took my hand, and we strolled north on 475th with matched steps. We heard a motor increase in volume as we crested the small hill.

At the entrance to a field, Vernon rode astride an all-terrain vehicle. He shut off the motor when he saw us and waved us toward him. Chris veered off the road with enthusiastic greetings. I trudged over spiky winter-dried stumps of wild grass after him, standing a bit back.

"So this is where you live." I said, projecting voice and smile toward him.

"Sure is." Vernon's smoke-pocked baritone was creaky from lack of use. "Thought you oughta know I heard some prowlers the other night." He gestured toward a driveway that led to a structure hidden by trees. "If they had come any closer I would have shot them."

"Shot them?" I repeated. The breeze blew a sour fungal scent off the soil.

Vernon patted the rear of the vehicle. "This gun's always loaded. You never know what kind of crazy people might come around." He pursed his lips and inhaled through his veined nose. "Lots of crazy folks around these days. Armageddon is coming any time. Gotta prepare yourself." Vernon leaned back in his seat. "I won't willingly put myself in the hands Satan or his followers." He looked south toward our house. "A few years back some prowlers tried to get in your house. You better be careful down there."

A chill oozed between my ribs. Chris filled in my silence. "Thanks for telling us. Great weather we're having, isn't it?"

Vernon nodded at Chris. "You got that right."

"And those thistles," Chris chuckled at plants just starting to shoot up. "They sure like to grow, don't they?"

Vernon slapped his thigh. "They sure do. A man's gotta work hard to keep them down. So, you still going to the Masons meetings?"

"Well, we better get going," I interrupted.

Chris glared at me, and answered. "Not much these days. Heard you were still there. Well, I think Elisa is telling me it's time to leave. Good seeing you!"

"You too. Say hi to your dad for me." Vernon said.

"Sure will," Chris answered. I was already on the road, heading back to our house. Vernon revved his four-wheeler into motion.

When he reached me, Chris started to say something. I imagined it was something about how I shouldn't be so rude, about how—despite what I was used to in New York—in the country one lingered to talk to one's neighbors and didn't end conversations abruptly. I forestalled him with a look, my fear of guns and prowlers written in the creases of my forehead. He closed his mouth and squeezed my hand. The sun dimmed behind a wisp of gray-purple cloud, the torn-off corner of a storm.

32

The Minnesota Horah

You're a phrase full of blanks
A novel in shorthand
I understand
I could fill in your blanks

I'm an outline in pen
Nothing colored within
I'm a barely sketched hint
You could color me in

You be my missing colors
I'll be your missing words
If you color me, I'll color you, too
I'll fill you in, if you fill me in, too
– "Color Me In"

May–July

Our engagement had blown a storm into my relations with my family. The day after Chris and I were engaged, I had called my parents to tell them the news. Silence rang across the phone line. There was a quick intake of breath, and then something that sounded like a sob from my mother. I fingered the cigar paper ring still on my finger from the night before. My father—sober and intelligent, until now my barometer for the quality of my decisions—broke across the line, his voice hitched with disappointment. "Are you sure about this?"

The black couch pulled at the tender skin under my thigh. My voice came out strained. "Yes." The conversation ended quickly, and my tears started as I put down the phone.

Chris moved closer to me, his skin shrieking across the leather, our combined weight dipping the cushions. "It's okay, sweetie," he said. "This is very new for them. Your parents are scared of losing their daughter. Of having you so far away."

"But, why can't they be happy for me? For us?" I curled into Chris's arms. My sobs jarred his body so hard that the whole world seemed to be shaking around me. He put his cheek against my hair. One hand stroked my back, and the other pulled me as close to his wide chest as our bodies would allow. He couldn't fix this, but he could hold me.

My parents had needled me about getting married since I graduated college. Eleven years later, I was finally fulfilling their dream for me, with one glaring exception: Chris wasn't Jewish. He had grown up in a family as deeply Catholic as mine was Jewish. They went to church every week. They had the priest over to bless their house. They said grace before every meal, crossing themselves in a communal mumble, "In the name of the Father, the Son, and the Holy Spirit."

My parents were the Israeli children of Holocaust survivors. Through my childhood, I visited Israel annually to see grandparents and other relatives, many of whom kept kosher. At my aunt's house, I learned to be careful not to let meat touch the dairy dishes. My parents didn't have any friends who weren't Jewish. Everyone they lived near, spent time with, knew, or respected was Jewish. Most of my grandparents' generation were killed in Germany and Poland just for being Jewish, and those who hadn't been killed escaped with luck, cunning, and misery. This was all normal to me.

My connection to a Midwestern Catholic man was not normal to them, but over the course of the year between our engagement and the wedding, my parents thawed. Chris was at his amiable best with them, and by the time of the wedding, they were enamored with the unassuming, supportive, loving man I had chosen as my life mate. During some of Chris's less appealing moods, I wished he would be that amiable with me.

Wedding planning went less smoothly. I endured numerous cross-country hang-ups from my mother and the classic Minnesotan rebuke of Chris's parents' brow-tightening silence as we negotiated wedding plans between two factions. Who would officiate: rabbi or priest? How would my kosher-keeping aunt and uncle respond to hearing the name "Jesus" spoken at my wedding? Where did you find a rabbi in rural central Minnesota, anyway?

A month into the wedding planning process, I was ready to elope. Chris refused. "I want a ceremony, and someone religious to officiate, and all our family and friends to be there."

We agreed to have a wedding that would respect both traditions, and I collected worries like pennies in a jar. We searched for officiants: rabbis and priests would not co-officiate weddings. We searched for a location: the priest required the wedding take place in a Catholic Church. A rabbi wouldn't officiate in a church. My mother absolutely refused to entertain the idea of holding the wedding at a campground by the Crow Wing River. Partly because the Israeli and New York factions complained more loudly than the Minnesotans, we settled on hiring a rabbi. There were no rabbis within eighty miles of New York Mills. A rabbi would have to be imported.

Chris took me to the jewelry store in Fargo to distract me from the stresses of wedding planning. For my engagement ring, I chose a six-prong platinum circlet for the heirloom diamond that my Holocaust-survivor grandmother wore on her ring finger for as long as I knew her.

When we finally decided where to have our ceremony, we couldn't believe we had considered other options. The only place for our wedding was the tall-ceilinged gallery of the organization that had brought us together: the New York Mills Cultural Center.

The one rabbi in Fargo—who led a congregation that referred to themselves as the "Frozen Chosen"—agreed to travel the hour and a half to New York Mills, and Betty and Ken's beloved priest, Father Joe, agreed to make a Catholic blessing palatable for Jewish attendees by removing the words "Jesus" and "Christ." Every week, I fielded calls from both mothers, checking in on the wedding in their distinctly different styles.

My mother, voice loud, tight, and insistent over the long-distance phone line: "Have you talked to the rabbi yet? Don't you think you should have a contract from the Cultural Center? Are the seats comfortable? Who will be doing the flowers?"

Chris's mother, gentle and hesitant: "Is there anything I can do to help?"

By the end of spring, I couldn't think about the wedding without heart palpitations. Chris began to hyperventilate every time he heard the word "wedding." I couldn't eat, I couldn't sleep, and all I could do was pray I'd make it to a time after the wedding.

Two days before the ceremony, my parents arrived in a rental SUV the size of my Brooklyn apartment, its purpose to shuttle wedding decorations and guests to and from the house. My mother swept into the Cultural Center like a Greek Fury, raising her voice to redo things that had already been done. I struggled to keep my volume from rising to meet hers. If I were a guitar, my strings would have snapped.

The morning of our wedding dawned gold and turquoise. The sounds of birds and crickets pealed like bells in the tree-ringed chapel of Oak Hollow. Minnesota had dressed up for our wedding. I leaned on the white banister of the upstairs veranda to watch family and close friends arrive up the curved driveway. Vehicles collected on our lawn like matchbox cars, and beloved friends and relatives emerged dressed for photographs, shined and coiffed. The different sides of the family, Jewish and Catholic, greeted one another with polite handshakes. My New York City friends Maggie, Jae, and Michelle all showed up wearing the same shade of green without having planned it.

A friend put on my make-up in Chris's and my bathroom. Chris dressed in my studio, his wedding tux brushing my guitars. My mother came upstairs to see me, the lace-lined skirts of my off-white dress floating around me. Her black-lined green eyes softened under a shiny cap of dyed-blonde hair. "You look beautiful," she said, uncharacteristically gentle. A wave of Amerige perfume swelled around us as she circled me with her arms, careful not to muss my artfully curled and pinned hair.

I descended the stairs and exited the front door to a wave of greetings, hugs, and kisses. Chris took my hands in his and squeezed, our only moment of interaction before the photographer posed us with family and friends across the veranda. My jaws ached from smiling through multiple clicks. Finally, everyone piled into a parade of cars to drive the ten minutes to the Cultural Center for the ceremony.

Upstairs in the Center's wood-floored dance studio, we signed the *ketuba*, the Jewish marriage contract. My mother adjusted the circlet of flowers in my hair as we waited for guests to file into the gallery. "You take deep breaths and everything will be fine," she said, speaking more to herself than to me.

Strains of piano and violin transitioned into the wedding march. I clenched the muscles under my tight bodice for the moment when one faction of the family—Jewish or Catholic—walked out. Chris's parents led Chris out to the rabbi, while my parents and I waited at the bottom of the steep, narrow stairwell, out of sight of the guests. My father leaned in to kiss my cheek. His smooth, freshly shaved cheek rustled against mine, and I smelled a hint of his aftershave. He beamed at me. "My girl," he said, using his Yiddish pet name for me. The stairs behind him seemed to stretch and expand in a blur. My heart leaped and bucked.

It was our turn. In the Jewish tradition of both parents walking the bride down the aisle, we took our first steps to the altar as a threesome. The gallery was swathed in white taffeta. The landscape paintings on display that month had been removed to create a makeshift wedding chapel. Calla lilies, daisies, stephanotis, and roses arranged by Chris's sisters filled every corner. The scent of flowers, perfume, and cologne replaced the everyday smell of paint and clay. On one hundred and twenty plastic folding chairs sat our family and friends: one hundred Minnesotan Catholics and Lutherans and twenty mostly Jewish east coasters.

Trained as an artist in her youth, my mother created a *chuppah*—the Jewish wedding canopy—from a balsa-wood garden arbor by stringing it with silk flowers and hanging it from the rails of the mezzanine. It hovered under the skylights and the rays of sun unexpectedly projected the *chuppah*'s filigree shadow on the wall, creating a magical shadow-line drawing of branches and flowers behind the wedding party.

Chris waited for me by the rabbi. His feet were placed wide apart as if to steady himself, his face frozen, almost stunned.

I placed one foot in front of the other, trying not to be distracted by the many upturned faces beside me. Some of the faces jumped out at me. Lina smiled over the electric piano where she was playing Pachelbel's "Canon." My grandmother's sister—a woman who had eluded Nazi death squads by pretending to be Catholic and saved her family by hiding them in a closet with a false back—sat in the second row, with royal bearing and calm, rheumy eyes. She pointed at me and I heard her lilting accent as she spoke to her daughter. Lynn Kasma sat in the third row, corsage pinned to her jacket with a tag that read #1 MATCHMAKER. Chris's sisters and parents stood to one side of the rabbi at the front of the room, their husbands and children piled into the first row. My brother, Dan, stood to the other side of the rabbi.

We reached Chris, and my parents lifted my veil from my face to kiss my cheeks. They beamed at me and took their places beside my brother.

Now it was just Chris and me between our combined communities and the rabbi.

Rabbi Janeen had driven in with her guitar from the tiny synagogue in Fargo. Her shoulder-length blonde hair brushed her white rabbinical robe, and her voice was rich like Joni Mitchell's. Rabbi Janeen's voice rose and filled the gallery with Hebrew melodies never before heard in New York Mills.

She incanted the prayers Chris and I had helped choose. Our parents and siblings each said one of the traditional seven Jewish marriage blessings in English. The room swam around me. The rabbi directed Chris and me to walk seven circles around each other. First, Chris walked seven circles around me. Then it was my turn. I counted to myself in my head. *One, two, three.* My aunt Ruthie and uncle Jerry beamed in the third row. What number was I on? Four or five? The filigree shadow painting on the wall was hypnotizing. I did a couple more circles, then slowed to a stop. I looked at Chris, trying to make my gaze say *Help!* "One more," Chris mouthed. A chuckle started in the front row and migrated through the room. My cheeks burned. I looked at the guests and cocked my head in a performer's self-deprecating pout. The room laughed harder. I circled one more time, and my pout swelled into a grin.

Father Joe had been sitting in full black robes in the back of the room. He was in his thirties, grew his hair long like Jesus, drove a Harley motorcycle, and liked to look at the stars through his telescope. He rose to offer the one Catholic departure from the Jewish ceremony, his white priest's collar flickering against his robes, and walked up the center aisle. He put his hands on our foreheads, and we were blessed like Joseph in the Bible. Then he started his prayer, "In the name of the Father, His son Jesus Christ, and the Holy Spirit . . ." My stomach rose into my throat. He had said "Jesus" and "Christ," as he probably did multiple times a day. An honest mistake, but how would my family react? I stole a glance at the room. My mother's face was tense, my great-aunt's smile had slipped, and my aunt and uncle were a little paler. I held my breath. No one got up to leave. Maybe this was going to be okay.

The rabbi asked my brother to bring the wine glass covered in a cloth napkin. Dan placed it at Chris's feet. "We're not exactly sure why it is Jewish tradition for the groom to break a glass; some suggest it represents the destruction of the first temple, others suggest it is to show the challenges that lie ahead of the married couple. In any case, it is the sign the marriage is complete and the ceremony is over." Chris lifted his leg and stomped down. The floor resounded with a thump and the glass skittered, still intact, across the first row. Later, Chris would ask my father whether this was a bad omen. My father would respond, "No, just bad aim."

In the moment, Chris blushed and gulped. My brother rescued and rewrapped the glass, placing it again at Chris's feet. Chris concentrated, and aimed carefully. The glass shattered with a satisfying series of cracks. The Jewish crowd erupted with shouts of "*Mazel Tov*" and began to clap and sing the Jewish song of joy and congratulations, "*Simi tov u mazel tov.*" The rabbi led Chris and me down the center of the aisle and gestured up the stairs to the dance studio, where in Jewish tradition we would have our first few married moments alone together.

We reached the top of the stairs and looked at each other. "We did it." He kissed my lips with a loud smack and pulled me up and around into a twirl, our feet shuffling and catching in one another's on the wood dance floor.

I started giggling. "No one walked out!" My feet stilled. "We're married," I whispered, eyebrows high, reaching for Chris.

"Yes, we are," he said, smiling into my eyes. The stress of wedding planning slipped away and all that was left was Chris and me, bound together, in this unlikely place.

*T*he reception was held at the Perham golf course. White tablecloths and more of Chris's sisters' flowers adorned an elegant brown room with a wall-sized mural of golden branches.

Of all things for a musician to forget, the complex wedding negotiations had made me leave the music for our wedding to the last minute. We chose the DJ because he was available on short notice. Since we had forgotten to designate a song for our first dance, he chose one for us. The country ballad I didn't recognize twanged my teeth like a bite of aluminum foil. The floor seemed to reach up and slap at the soles of my feet. All the guests watched us sway amateurishly, dance lessons forgotten. I blushed, more embarrassed about the music than our dancing. "This is terrible," Chris whispered to me through gritted teeth. The slide guitar sliced into my temples. "Mmm-hmm," I said through a wilting smile.

When the dance was finally over, I collapsed into my chair. My mother asked the Minnesota DJ if he could play the song "Sunrise, Sunset" from *Fiddler on the Roof*, and the DJ looked at my mom blankly. Josh, my high school friend with an outsize personality who was acting as emcee at my request, pushed himself between them and handed his iPod to the DJ. "I've got 'Sunrise, Sunset' on my iPod. It's all ready to play." My mother settled her face into an aristocratic smile and gave Josh two air kisses. My uncle stood over the *challah* and said the *motzi*—Jewish prayer over bread—and my mother and great Aunt Stasia lit two tall white celebratory candles with another Hebrew prayer.

Josh took the mic. "Ladies and gentlemen," his voice boomed off the mural on the wall. "Now we have a sacred Jewish tradition."

I wondered how our guests would respond to what was coming next. All the good Minnesotan Catholics and Lutherans—already knocked sideways by the visitation of a rabbi and the recitation of Hebrew prayers—sat up straighter in their seats. Sacred traditions of any faith were to be respected.

"Please stand."

At most Jewish weddings on the East Coast, guests do not follow directions. The Minnesotans all stood on command. Not one Minnesotan bottom remained on a chair. The New Yorkers straggled upwards in fits and starts.

"You've heard the Hebrew prayers and seen the Jewish marriage ceremony. Now, everyone, please come to the dance floor for the most important tradition of a Jewish wedding."

The Jews led the way and the Minnesotans disentangled themselves from chairs and tablecloths. They weaved between circular tables and shuffled around chairs gone askew. They made a ring around the dance floor, straightening ties and patting down dresses, brave faces full of duty and doubt. The east coasters tamped down knowing smiles.

"Please hold hands."

One hundred touch-averse Minnesotans reached out their hands to the people next to them. My great-aunt Stasia held hands with the U.S. Air-Force lieutenant colonel who was now my brother-in-law. Father Joe held hands with my aunt Ruthie, who ran a Jewish high school in Philadelphia. Anticipation girdled my middle. This was my favorite part of a Jewish wedding, but how would the guests respond?

"It is now time for the dancing of the Horah and lifting of the chairs!" Josh announced with brio. "Chris, Elisa, parents of bride and groom, please come to the center." Off mic, Josh directed a few of the larger men to gather six chairs and bring them to the center of the circle.

I knew what was coming. The Jews and east coasters knew what was coming. Chris had been prepped. The Minnesotans looked like rabbits trying to stand really still so they blended into the background.

Josh reached for his iPod at the stereo and pressed play on "Hava Nagila."

Hav-a nagila, hav-a, nagila, hav-a, nagila, Ve' nismicha.

"Ladies and gentleman," Josh called over the music, "we will now all dance the Horah in a circle."

The Minnesotans looked at each other and then the floor.

"The Horah is like the grapevine dance. Move your feet like this." Josh demonstrated. He flung the wire of the mic out of his way and stepped one leg in front of the other, then one leg behind.

My aunt Ruthie and my friend Michelle pulled the large group of Minnesotans into motion around the circle. Ruthie led a line of smiling and tripping people toward Chris and grabbed his hand, pulling him into the train. Guests linked into her chain imitated how she lifted clasped hands up to the music. Michelle kicked her high-heeled shoes toward the tables, grabbed the nearest Minnesotan, took my arm with her free arm and pulled us behind her, dancing in stockinged feet. Soon we had two circles of dancers, one around the other, each moving in a different direction. Everyone bobbed and stepped and beamed. After a few stumbles, the Minnesotan guests got the hang of it. The entire room was dancing—Minnesotans and New Yorkers, Jews and Catholics—all faces glowing.

Josh's voice rose above music, claps and laughter. "Now, in the center of the circle, we lift the bride and groom and their parents in chairs. Everyone else dances the Horah around them. May I please have some strong men in the center of the circle to lift the chairs." A giggle fought with a gasp in my throat. I had warned Chris about this, and the dancing flush on his cheeks paled. His parents, also warned, stopped dancing and stood, frozen.

The larger men in the room—my uncle, Chris's high school friends, Father Joe—came to the center of the circle. "Eva, Shay, you know what to do! Betty and Ken, take a seat on the chairs in the center and relax. Elisa, Chris, let's go!" The event hall chair was hard under the layers of my tulle underskirts. Four men lifted me up toward the ceiling. I caught a glimpse of Chris, and the four large men grunting to lift his chair. Josh settled my parents and Chris's parents into chairs, and more guests lifted them into the air by their chair legs. Father Joe was at my father-in-law's chair, lifting it and dancing along with everyone else.

The inexperienced Minnesotan chair lifters, new to Jewish tradition, didn't know to keep the chairs straight as they danced. My chair bucked forward and the seat tilted. I clung to the chair back, abdomen muscles straining with effort. Chris laughed uncontrollably, stifling guffaws to keep himself still enough to stay in his chair. Betty held onto her chair bottom with white knuckles, blushing modestly while trying to nod to the people around her. Ken's round face was flushed, and he tried to keep from looking down. My father held himself straight, proud and elegant and uncomfortably large on the small chair, all six feet of him trying to shrink down so he could weigh less for the chair lifters. My mother waved from her chair like the queen of England.

My aunt handed Chris and me two corners of a white napkin. We bobbed in the air, linked by a flexing and twisting white handkerchief and the one hundred Minnesotan Lutherans and Catholics and twenty Jewish east coasters who danced the Horah around us.

33

Property Lines

Didn't think the world would leave her alone
Couldn't remember where she called home
– "About"

July

Through the scrim of sleep, brightness lit up gold behind my eyelids. I woke to a sense of peaceful recognition: *I am home.* Oak Hollow cradled me in its walls. Chris's breath shirred in the thick quiet of bedroom air. I had found a sanctum in husband, house, and creative purpose.

A hand turned my face toward sunlight. A shadow dimmed across the glow behind my eyes. Moist breath warmed my mouth. Softness fluttered against my lips.

"Time to get up," Chris's shout was an explosion reverberating in my skull.

I shrunk away from the sound, eyelids crushing themselves closed so hard I saw crimson. Chris held my body against my attempt to retreat under the covers. I groaned and pulled weakly against his grip.

"Honey. You don't want to miss how pretty it is outside right now."

I cracked open an eyelid.

Chris's face filled my view, brown stubble glinting in the morning light that twinkled through the white railings of the veranda, the apples of his cheeks full and puffed into a wicked grin. Fine, thin strands of brown hair fluffed upward into an impish halo. "Gotcha," he growled, spraying kisses across my cheeks and forehead.

We had just returned from a week-long honeymoon at a friend's cabin in Glacier National Park. The events of our wedding weekend were already a fast-moving blur from which seminal moments blazed large. The filagree shadow of *chuppah* behind the guitar-playing rabbi. My aunts and uncles gripping vinyl seats when the Kleins took my extended family on a pontoon ride on Big Pine Lake. (This event would be reminisced about by my side of the family for years.) My brother and father abashed and dripping in the Crow Wing River, calling for Chris's help when their canoe overturned during a daytrip the day after the wedding. (My brother would from then on insist that Chris was the person he most wanted to have with him on a desert island.) My family and friends had been delighted by the vibrant slice of country life we had selected to show them. Now that the wedding was over, daily life in the country was slowly adapting back to its normal, smoother, slower pace.

Chris hopped off the bed to a stand and his tone became matter-of fact. "It's time to look for wild raspberries in the front forty." It was common for owners of large land claims to call the half-section of forty acres behind their houses "the back forty." The extra four acres of our property were in front of our house, so Chris and I had started referring to it as our "front forty."

I unwrapped myself from blankets and tried to sound enthusiastic, "Raspberries? I love raspberries." The cotton sheets were smooth as I swung my legs to dangle off the side of our bed. A warm breeze floated through the French doors with the heady scent of basswood flowers. Birds sang to each other in the trees.

Chris took my arms and pulled me off the lip of the bed. I overbalanced, windmilling my arms for the second before my feet landed with a thump on the carpet. "Get dressed, and let's go." He marched toward the door. I was becoming accustomed to his emotional about-faces, how he liked to keep me off-balance by transforming from teddy bear to master-sergeant and back in an instant. By the time I'd pulled on clothes, Chris was already outside.

I trotted down the hall, hand running along the banister, and bounded into the turn in front of my studio. I opened the front door to a sea of green grass undulating under a turquoise sky. Warm air met bare skin in a dizzy rush of pleasure. The honeyed-mint of sweet clover filled my lungs. From the row of maples, a grouse beat his wings in a mating call that sounded like a twig stuck in the spokes of an accelerating bicycle. Once Chris finally got me outside, it was easy to share his love for the outdoors, especially in our beautiful private park that was Oak Hollow.

Chris handed me a plastic grocery sack for raspberry collection. I looped the handles around my wrist and the empty bag floated upward in the breeze. Chris led me away from our colonnaded porch, past the big oak, and across the open lawn. Our plastic bags flapped as we picked our way along a makeshift path between the hawthorns and plums.

Chris stopped at a small clearing blanketed with the thorny stems of raspberry plants, and I peered into a green tangle. "You have to look carefully . . ." Chris spoke in short bursts. "They like to hide under leaves . . ."

A mote of crimson peeked at me from under a green canopy. "I found one!" I squealed and thrust my arm into the plant. A thorny branch pricked my hand. I jerked up with a berry smaller than my pinky nail, still bitten down from the stress of the wedding. I put the hard red ball into my mouth and it exploded in a too-tiny burst of sweet redness.

I rooted through plants in a six-foot circle. Only one more raspberry. My plastic bag crinkled against my waist. I clicked my tongue against the roof of my mouth. "This is it?" I called through the hawthorn to Chris, where he was bent over double picking through plants.

His voice was muffled inside the teepee of his body. "You have to fight the bugs and birds and other critters for them. I like to save them up until I have a mouthful. Then I eat them all at once." He demonstrated, pouring a palmful in his mouth and making an exaggerated expression of delight. "Mmmmm . . ."

I expanded my search to the next clearing. A rose-breasted grosbeak beat its wings from a tree branch in complaint. A fox sparrow rushed from the woods in a chittering flurry. I was infiltrating their homes in my raspberry hunt. I apologized to them silently.

A half-hour's hunt yielded me a handful of tiny, red berries. My lower back creaked and pulled as I straightened to consider my crop. The miniature fruits filled the small depression at the center of my cupped palm. I tipped my head and funneled beads into my mouth. Small roundnesses rolled on my tongue. My mouth filled with the tangy-sweetness of bursting planets. Then they were gone, tartness trailing from my tongue.

I pulled the empty plastic sack off my wrist and crumpled it in my pocket. I headed west through the brushy mass of bushes and grass to my favorite tree, a pine tree of such grandeur I had named it the Great Tree. Its long branches trailed to the ground like welcoming arms. Underneath, deer left their bodies' impressions in soft mounds of dried pine needles.

Twenty yards before my tree, I almost tripped over a shiny metal surveying pole in the middle of knee-high grasses.

That hadn't been there the last time I walked here. "Chris, check this out," I called through the brush. From the direction of the Great Tree, metal thudded against wood. I took a step toward it. More thuds. It sounded like a hammer. Or an axe. I left Chris to find the pole himself and ran toward my tree.

I stopped short.

Beyond the leafy arms of a stand of willow, Robin hacked at the brush around the Great Tree with an axe. Toppled plum trees were scattered like corpses on a battlefield. A half-acre opening had been carved into the thatch of wild raspberries and hawthorne. A blue jay screeched.

I didn't understand. Wasn't this our property? Robin was cutting down trees right in the middle of our front forty, a good twenty yards closer than the barbed-wire fence we had thought was our property boundary.

I had to get away before he saw me. My feet wouldn't cooperate, rooted to the dirt in shock.

Robin's leonine face lifted to show his chiseled features and ice-blue eyes.

"Hi, Robin." My voice was twisted and warped.

Robin dropped the axe to his side. His arms hung long and feline from his shoulders. He moved a hand from his side and swiped the air in front of him. "I've been meaning to tell you. I bought this piece of land from Erlund." His gesture took in my favorite section of the front forty. "I'm building my new home here." He pointed at a site abutting the Great Tree.

The wind moaned through the hawthorn behind me, sweeping loose strands of hair in front of my eyes. I hadn't realized how attached I had become to what I thought was my land. "You're moving here?"

Chris's voice, only a touch less incredulous than mine, came from behind me. "You bought this property from Erlund?"

"Yes. I wanted to be near my mom and son." Robin gestured to the graves near the foot of our driveway. The wind blew the sharp ends of my hair into my eyes. "I'm building this house to be off-grid."

"Off-grid?" I parroted.

The axe handle made a line from Robin's arm to the ground. The pile of hacked-off branches beside him shifted in the wind. "My house will be self-sufficient. I'm going to dig a well. I'm going to build a windmill and make my own electricity. I'm going to build a large shed and garage for storage right over there." Robin pointed to the part of the front forty where I had envisioned a forest garden and bench for when I wanted to write outside.

A chilly trickle of loss crawled its way into my veins. "Where does our property begin?" I asked.

"Beyond that line of trees there."

Chris's eyes darted from Robin to the cleared land and back. The property line was much closer to the house than the realtor had led us to believe. Chris's body stilled, like a fish at the bottom of a boat who finally gives in to the inevitable and stops flopping. A mourning dove lamented with coos from the buckthorn bush. Chris stumbled. "We didn't realize where our property ended."

I felt sick. "Gotta get back to the house," I mumbled to the space behind Robin. I pushed aside a thick branch and sidled underneath to the driveway—a mere fifty feet from where Robin was building his new house. I held the branch up for Chris to follow. When I turned, thorny branches slapped me stingingly in the face.

"Did you see where he is building his new house?" Chris's voice was pitched high and frantic.

I nodded, unable to speak.

After years of living mere feet away from my neighbors, hearing them cough and clear their throats through the thin walls of my apartment, I was now furious that Robin was building his new house along my driveway. Minnesota had changed me. I now cherished the vast space around me. The privacy. The padding between me and the rest of the world. And here, now, in Robin's destruction of my fantasy garden, the space I hadn't even realized I had started to love was being taken from me.

"I know I didn't like the isolation when we first looked at this house," Chris admitted, "but I finally discovered how great it is to have privacy, and now he's building a house on our driveway."

I kept walking, the small cuts on my face and arms smarting. Chris's disappointment made mine more real, and Robin's slight against my property made me question the progress I had made in adjusting to my new life. I thought I had finally found my home. I had accepted Minnesota's idiosyncrasies. I had married the man who brought me here. I had found a house with him that could be my sanctuary. I thought I was learning how to be the artist I had hoped I could be. This balance of person, place, and purpose had given me the hope I could survive here, that I was making a life I could sustain.

Suddenly, it felt like my hard-wrought tapestry of home was being eaten away, one chopped-down tree at a time.

Part III

Oak Savanna

September 2008–June 2009

An oak savanna is a type of savanna, or lightly forested grassland, where oaks are the dominant trees.

– Wikipedia

34

Landing

Stripped bark and broken wing
No voice left for the song to sing
– "Sandy Lake"

September

Songwriting distracted me from my dejection over our newest, nearest neighbor. Under Chris's daily influence, the great outdoors was beginning to call to me, and this evening I was hoping it would inspire a new song. I sat cross-legged on the grass in the middle of our football field–sized front yard, notebook on my knee, humming a snippet of melody that I was trying to fit to the handwritten lyrics on the page. The sky was the silvered iron of a hidden sun setting. There was the gentle promise of coming rain and the hard scent of earth in damp air. The trees hung limply, thirsty for the succor the clouds might soon deliver.

I tried the tune again, this time adding words to it. The air was so dense it was as if the sky, dressed in pearly veils, had come down to kiss the land. I sang into the thick of it, my legs still rooted in the earth. Oak Hollow seemed to join in. A goldfinch chirrupped from the woods. Three bats with sculpted wings skittered above me. A buck huffed behind brambles of ash and wild plum.

My song hung in the dense air, and I was spellbound by the heady concoction of songwriting and outdoors, as moved as I had been in those prophetic first moments on the Crow Wing River, when the symphony of nature soothed me into a calm I had never felt before, a calm that had led me to fall in love with the man paddling behind me. The ease I had felt with Chris, the tantalizing serenity that brought me to Minnesota, that was what Oak Hollow had promised me, and for this moment it felt like it had delivered.

I closed my eyes and surrendered to earth and sky. I laid my head on the ground, dry crinkly blades of grass tickling my ears and cheek. The twilight was warm and easy. The sky inched ever closer to me as it darkened, caressing my skin with its breath. I sang my snippet of song into the grass, and this time the words and the melody fitted together like the two halves of a shell.

A chainsaw screeched to life, tearing my song into sharp, jagged edges that carved words away from melody. I heard a shout. It was Robin's voice, directing his brothers in the construction of his house. A swarm of flying bugs spun up around me—a hundred insects buzzing frantically in place. The sky shot upward to the unreachable heavens. The earth was no longer mine. The promise of Oak Hollow—of Minnesota—was broken again.

I ran to the protection of the big red house and shut the door on the construction.

35

Dogs

Forget that I forgot you
And remember me instead
– "Instead"

October

Down, Meadow." Chris opened the front door, shielding his body ineffectually with one hand as he tried to put on his fleece jacket. Our yellow labrador retriever puppy scraped herself up Chris's legs. Chris pulled his other arm into the sleeve and, with two arms, managed to wrestle Meadow out of the house in a tumult.

I followed, grinning. If we had to pass Robin's cabin while walking down our driveway, then at least I would have comic relief while we did it.

Meadow was now chewing on the hem of Chris's jeans. He picked up a large branch that had fallen off the oak tree and fended her off like a swordsman. "Hi-yah!" Meadow's puppy face broke into a puppy smile, furry cheeks wrinkling with glee.

I was the one who had insisted on getting a puppy. Though I had arrived in New York Mills as a cat person, my transition to dog lover had been thorough. It had started right after I moved to Minnesota, when Chris's ex-girlfriend bequeathed him a geriatric yellow labrador retriever named Scout.

"For how long?" I asked.

"I don't know. A few months. A year. Maybe forever."

"But I don't like dogs."

"Scout is the mellowest dog," he cajoled, desperate to convince me. "All he wants is to be loved. He'll spend all day following you around the house."

"I don't know how to take care of a dog."

"There's nothing to it. I promise. It's like taking care of cats, but better. Just feed him and walk him. You'll love him."

"Please, Chris, I'd really rather not get a dog."

Scout arrived a week later. He weighed eighty pounds, and his head came up to my waist. He had a collection of soft pink warts on his muzzle that made him look like an outcast character actor. His eyes were wet and brown and big and always looking at me longingly.

After we got into bed that first night, Scout stood by the edge of the bed and huffed. "He wants to come up," Chris said.

"Absolutely not."

"But—"

"I took him in. I don't want him on my bed."

Scout slept on a dog mat on the floor.

The next day, Chris left for an ill-timed business trip. I watched Scout warily. He watched me. I went to the kitchen. He followed me and panted. I didn't know what he wanted; I didn't speak dog. That night, Scout huffed by the edge of the bed again. "No," I told him, voice firm.

The next day, Scout followed me to the makeshift studio space I had created under the eaves of the gray cottage and lay on the carpet next to me. The cats vacated their normal spots on my desk to hide in high corners with eyes wary and fur puffed. I tentatively stroked Scout's flank with my foot. His fur was smooth and sleek under my arch, and he relaxed with a satisfied grunt.

By the time we moved to Oak Hollow, Scout's rhythms were a soft backdrop to mine. He lay on his mat in my studio as I wrote or practiced music. He followed me down the stairs when I got a snack in the kitchen. He snored gently on his dog mat at night next to our bed. Without realizing it, I had become accustomed to him. To the soft off-kilter *gallump* of his crippled legs on the wooden stairs. To the gentle huffing sound around 5:00 p.m. when Scout reminded me it was dinner time. Even to his pungent doggy scent.

I still loved my cats, but it was Scout who was usually by my side.

One snowy April morning after Chris had left for work, Scout huffed at me from his dog mat next to the bed. The pink warts on his yellow muzzle had gone dull and gray. His legs trembled and almost buckled. Two weeks before, the vet had found fluid around his lungs. "I don't know how long he has."

Scout's tail was usually a live thing, wagging with the force of a pick-up truck. Today it hung, limp. Maybe he needed to go out, I hoped. I got out of bed and went downstairs. Scout hobbled stair by stair behind me. He could barely make it off the porch and couldn't squat to relieve himself. Oh, so slowly, he made his way up the porch stairs and into the house. His breath came in heaves. As soon as Scout cleared the front door, he collapsed on the hall rug, his half-closed eyes rolling with panic.

I kneeled next to him. I stroked his back and a sob racked through me. I called Chris from Scout's side. "Come home now. It's Scout."

Tires squealed as he turned the car around. "I'm on my way. Call the vet."

Scout looked at me, his eyes pleading for aid. I didn't know what to do. I lay down on the carpet and curled my body around his. I couldn't believe how soft he was. Why hadn't I ever noticed it before? I regretted every night I hadn't let Scout sleep on the bed.

I knew it was the end without knowing how I knew. I called the vet's office and sobbed while I told them we were coming in. Scout lay on the ground, chest heaving. I petted his soft fur. He gave a small tail flop of appreciation and I praised him through my tears, trying to calm myself so I wouldn't scare him.

Chris returned and lifted eighty pounds of Scout into the car in one motion. Scout's head lolled to the side as Chris carried him into the vet's office.

We walked out with an unmoving Scout-sized bundle wrapped in blankets. Chris placed Scout's remains gently in the back of the car. Our faces were bunched and wet with tears. It was hard to breathe. I kept looking at Scout's blanketed body, unable to believe he was gone.

At home, Chris and I pulled a spade and shovel out of the garage and walked our property for a spot Scout would have liked. We chose a place in the trees where Scout liked to lounge, put our grief into our muscles and strained and pulled and dug into hard, cold ground. We didn't speak. The sound of our breathing melded with the sound of the breeze through the bare branches. Grief became a physical thing I could feel with each hard pull of the shovel.

The smell of clay and dirt wafted up from the freshly dug ground, and a pile collected next to the hole. When the trench was five feet deep, Chris retrieved Scout's body from the car. We unwrapped him from the blankets and there he was, almost as he was in life, but too stiff, too still. Chris lowered Scout into the grave, and Scout fell the last foot, landing splay-footed on his back. "I can't leave him like that," Chris said, and climbed into the trench to arrange Scout in a more comfortable position.

We made up a funeral service. I said the Hebrew Mourner's Kaddish, Chris said the Lord's Prayer, and each of us thanked Scout for what he had meant to us. We shoveled dirt down over his body. With each shovelful, the blow of our irrevocable separation deepened.

Once he was gone, there was no Scout to huff me awake in the morning. There was no Scout to keep me company as I worked on a song in my studio. There was no Scout to talk to when Chris was gone.

I tried to console myself: I could write without stopping for Scout's food and potty breaks. I stopped anyway, programmed to Scout's schedule. I wished I could reach out with a bare foot to pet Scout's warm yellow fur. I yearned to hear the *galumph* he made when he went down the stairs on his bad legs.

The truth was, I was lonely. I still had few close friends in Minnesota, and when Chris was busy with work and civic commitments—more and more it seemed these days—Scout had been my friend, my confidant, my community. Without him, I felt truly alone. I needed a loyal friend, even if that friend was four-legged.

"I want to get a puppy," I told Chris two weeks after we buried Scout.

He almost dropped the knife he was using to chop onions. "You do?"

"I miss having a dog around." I leaned against the counter, hands in my pockets.

"You know puppies are a lot of work, right?"

"Sure," I said, standing up again. I didn't know anything about puppies. But I didn't much care. "I've been looking at the most adorable dogs online."

"So that's what you do all day," he smirked. I batted his arm. Over dinner, Chris agreed to get a puppy, with the caveat that it be a yellow labrador retriever, in the hope it might be as loving as Scout had been.

A month later, a small yellow fluffball whined from the new puppy-sized kennel in the passenger seat next to me. I made it half a mile before—against the advice of every puppy book I had taken out of the library—I let her out of her kennel and placed her on my lap for the long drive home.

Meadow was now five months old and had managed to destroy enough household objects to fill four sheets of notebook paper posted on our fridge. With each new loss, Chris or I would shout "No" in exaggerated, elongated tones, until we looked into her shiny puppy face, and our anger dissipated in the light of her endless glee. My ankles were constantly scabbed from love bites from her sharp puppy teeth. Chris liked to play rough with her, punching and shoving, Meadow always bouncing right back, his growls matching hers in pitch till both of them were rolling together on the bed, giddy with play.

We were halfway down the driveway now. I tried to keep my eyes on Meadow. My eyes ached to shift to the right and glare at the house on the land I had thought was ours.

"Acres and acres of empty land, and Robin has to buy the property off our driveway," Chris said.

Meadow dropped the stick she had been toting and trotted ahead of us, nose to the air. Chris shifted and my eyes jerked right, out of my control.

The leaf cover that had camouflaged Robin's place over the summer had decayed into a patchy tangle of vegetation, a skeletal filagree, as see-through as a veil. The structure was half-built, a black crayon drawing of a house, a narrow door hanging open in the center, a window to each side, no siding over the black paper that covered the walls. The Great Tree stood next to it, its pointed tip towering above the brush, mocking me with its proximity and inaccessibility. A primitive, territorial anger rose in me, at this tarpaper shack, and the man who had infiltrated my property.

Meadow emerged from the marsh blackened with mud, carrying a piece of dead animal. I tried to take it from her and she leaped ahead of me, staying just far enough away I couldn't reach her. I gave up and we followed her up the driveway, a rotten-sweet miasma of dead things scenting the air in her wake.

36

Hunting Season

Prey needs its hunter like the hunter needs its prey
Ignoring your need won't make it go away
– "Hunger"

November

The first Saturday of November, I awoke too early, adrift in a half-awake daze. It was barely dawn; the strip of sky between curtain and wall painted a pale line of light onto the carpet. *Pop pop pop.* My chest convulsed before I registered the sound. It sounded like . . .

Bullets.

My body stiffened. "What's that?" I shoved myself upwards into a sitting position, wrestling sheets.

"Whhhuh?" Chris answered. Another flurry of gunshots rattled the panes in the French doors.

"The gunshots. Why are people shooting?" My voice rose; my mind filled with images of television news stories about gun violence. I remembered late-night walks to the subway in bad neighborhoods when cars backfired and I ran. Ironically, the sounds I heard in New York City had never been guns, but here in the country there was no doubt I was hearing real bullets careening past my house.

Chris groaned and blinked. His voice was a patient mumble. "It's people hunting deer. It's the first day of deer season. Shooting starts as soon as it's light enough to see." He punched his pillow into shape. "Don't worry, honey. This is normal here."

Everyone in the Creamery had been talking about deer season for a month, but to me, it was another local country event I had no part in. Until the shooting started outside my window. Suddenly, deer season was on my doorstep. I leaned against my pillow and pulled my pajama shirt tight against me. "It sounds close."

"Of course it's close. We live in the deer-hunting capital of Minnesota. Didn't you see the deer stand Robin built behind his cabin?" He turned over, giving me a glimpse of his bare torso under the lighter blanket on his side of the bed. His arm reached behind him to pat mine. "It's okay, honey. There's nothing to be afraid of. I'm going back to sleep." He burrowed under the covers. Meadow, taking up most of the bed near my feet, rolled onto her back for her morning scratch.

"How do I walk Meadow if Robin and his brothers are shooting?"

Chris sat straight up in bed, bare shoulders jutting forward. "You are not to go outside with or without Meadow unless both of you are wearing blaze orange. In fact, I would recommend you don't go outside at all, if you can help it, for the next two weeks."

But Meadow had to go outside, and she wouldn't do her business unless one of us—usually me—went out with her. That morning I drove twenty miles to Perham to pick up a blaze-orange doggie vest from the sports store. I sped down my driveway, looking left and right, as if I could catch sight of and avoid a bullet before it pierced the metal shell of my vehicle.

When I returned, I pulled Chris's orange vest over my shoulders, and spread out Meadow's. I laid the canvas over her back and she wriggled. I struggled to fasten the straps around her. She twisted and tugged at the canvas with her teeth. "I know how you feel," I said to her. "Come on." I held the door open. She sidestepped and shortened her pace against the constriction of the vest. I wrapped my own orange vest closer around me. I could almost smell the metal of the guns on the breeze. I stood ten feet away from the porch, skin prickling. Thin orange cloth would stop a bullet no better than deer hide. I felt like a target.

I yelled for Meadow to finish her business, and we sprinted inside. She nibbled at her vest and tried to help me pull it off of her. Freed, she ran to her food bowl. I removed my own vest, but couldn't shake off the burden of danger that surrounded my once-beloved new home.

Ten days later, sunset had closed the final day of hunting season. The next morning, I ached to be outside again, without the threat of bullets mowing me down. I planned to take a long walk with Meadow on my beautiful country road. After ten days of what felt like house arrest, I would not be cowed by the across-the-street neighbor's murderous dogs. Inspired by deer season, I decided to enlist a gun—a water gun, that is—to my aid. I planned to fill it with ammonia, hoping it would have enough sting to keep the dogs away from me and Meadow.

I overestimated how much liquid the plastic weapon could hold, and ammonia bubbled up from the water-gun's bladder into the cracks of flesh between nails and broken cuticles. I rinsed my hands in the kitchen sink. Fingers still stinging, I put on my coat, called to Meadow, and started down the half mile of gravel, water gun ready in my hand.

The barking started as soon as I reached the last stretch of driveway before the road. Meadow slowed and cocked her head. I aimed my ammonia-filled gun and pressed the trigger. A stream of liquid made a short, weak arc that faded and fell ten feet short. Molly rushed at me, her newest batch of mongrel puppies barking and snapping behind her. Closer now, I tried again, and the thin stream barely wet her flank. This wasn't working. The dogs were getting too close.

"Come, Meadow!" I yelled over my shoulder and sprinted up my driveway. The dogs chased us, and we only lost them at the bend.

My front door shut with a hollow thud. The best part of living on six acres of land in the country was supposed to be the country, but I couldn't get to it. First Robin, then hunting season, now my neighbor's dogs again. I couldn't walk to the end of my driveway without being accosted.

At least there was something I could do about the dogs. I found the phone book and flipped the blue government pages until I reached the number for the county sheriff. The hold Muzak was tuned to a local radio station. I sucked at my torn cuticles.

A deputy came on the line, and I summarized my predicament. He sounded weary as he answered by rote. "The county can issue citations to owners of wayward animals but, beyond that, there's nothing we can do until the animals cause harm."

The silence hung. A broken cuticle snagged on my sweater and searing pain ran up my finger as far as my wrist. "Let me get this straight. I need to get bitten and *injured* before you can do anything about the dogs who are chasing me up my own driveway?"

"That is correct."

That night, I told Chris the dogs had chased me, the ammonia gun hadn't worked, and the sheriff couldn't do anything until the dogs had caused harm. I laughed bitterly and waited for Chris to join in. He didn't.

"An ammonia gun is a clever idea, but not very effective. We need a real gun." He leafed through the stack of mail.

"You're not serious."

"Sure I am."

"Where would we get a gun?"

"I have one," he said casually, prying an envelope open with his finger.

The warmth bleached out of the room. "You do?"

"Of course."

"But . . . but I thought you stopped hunting as a teenager. After you shot a buck who stared you down while he was dying."

The envelope ripped. "Sure. But I didn't give up my guns. They're at my parents' house."

The blood left my cheeks. "You still own guns, plural?"

"You own guns, too. Community property, remember? What's mine is yours; what's yours is mine . . ."

My breath came in a shallow gasp. Deep inside my core, some part of my identity cracked, struck down by this seemingly small fact. I wasn't supposed to own a gun. It was beyond thought, part of who I had always been. I was a person who would never own a gun. And yet, now I did.

I laid my hands flat against the wood of the kitchen table, letting its smooth surface hold my weight. In New York City, people like me didn't own guns. Guns were for killing people, for criminals, law enforcement, the military. Not normal people. Not me. And yet, now, through marriage to Chris, I owned guns, plural.

The tang of the onion Chris was chopping stung my nostrils. I was a gun owner.

"Hey, sweetie," Chris put down the letter and stepped toward me. "It's okay. They're just guns. Everyone out here has them. There's less to worry about with guns around here than where you come from, because everyone around here knows how to use them, and how to respect them."

My eyes began to tear. I blamed the onions. I lived in the country now. Country guns had a purpose. They were not the handguns of city streets. They were rifles and shotguns, the legacy of homesteaders, for hunting food and protecting against wildlife. I owned the good kind of guns, not the bad kind.

I blinked my eyes clear of onion. I could be this kind of gun owner. Maybe I could even learn how to shoot, take a gun safety course, hunt. Maybe these guns I now owned could protect me.

I pushed myself upward and smirked. "Can we use them on the neighbor's dogs?"

Chris grinned.

With the guns, neighbors, and dogs, I was desperate to get out of the country. I made plans to visit my new friend Annie, a puppeteer, who had come to New York Mills as an artist in residence.

The clouds seemed to clear as I drove south to Minneapolis. Turning into Annie's cozy neighborhood of apartment buildings and townhouses, a black Mazda darted from a side street like a stray bullet. I cursed lustily at him. It felt great to be back in traffic, sparking with the electricity of interaction.

Over sushi, I relayed the stories of my new home, the demon dogs, my neighbors, and the fact I was now a gun owner. The umami flavor of soy melded with the smooth texture of salmon, and Annie squinted and winced in all the right places. I wasn't losing my mind: to another city dweller, my new life was as odd as I thought it was. No wonder I couldn't find a way to feel at home in it.

Annie spread mismatched sheets on an air mattress on her living room floor. Books and puppet parts were jumbled every which way on plank-and-concrete-block shelves. This was the closest I'd felt to my Brooklyn apartment since I'd left New York.

I woke early to once-familiar city sounds. I leaned against the bottom of Annie's couch, butt balanced on an unstable hump of air mattress. I wrapped blankets around me and stared at the corner of sky in the window. Silhouettes of crows flew across a rectangle-shaped view of buildings. A parade of cars rumbled past the front windows. A horn honked down the block. A plane took off with a roar from the airport, a few miles away. An alarm clock beeped a digital rhythm from somewhere in the apartment building.

I felt relieved here, comforted by the mildew-and-incense scent of urban artist apartment. The city energized me like a battery. This was a world I understood. Country life wore me down like water on a rockface. Its quiet, its slow pace, everything shutting down by 5:00 p.m.

When I lived in New York, I daydreamed about visiting nature. I yearned for the peace and quiet of forest, the slow pace of mountains.

I craved fresh air and the smell of trees and grass. Now that I was surrounded every day by country, all I wanted was traffic and crowds, theaters, shopping, museums. To be in a place where I fit in. A place where no one stared at me as the outsider.

A three-hour drive later, I returned to Oak Hollow. Its red siding was the color of dried blood. The oak tree's branches hung empty of leaves, dejected, naked, exposed.

The clutter in the den blinded me to the charm of quarter-sawn oak. Chris had let the dishes pile up in the kitchen sink. Footsteps resonated on the ceiling, heading down to greet me. "This house is a mess," I called bitterly, before I even said hello. The footsteps slowed.

I opened the hall closet to hang up my coat. Between vacuum cleaner and hiking boots, a rifle leaned against the closet wall, all wood and metal, line and curve.

My hand recoiled from the door handle.

37

Tullibee Fishing

Is she lost or found?
Will she fall down or bounce?
Smile turns to a scowl
About face
– "About"

November

Know what I'm doing right now?" Chris leaned against the kitchen doorframe by what I now referred to as the gun closet and swirled a mug of coffee.

"Drinking coffee?" I muttered while scrubbing at a serving bowl Chris had left so long it was dried and crusty.

"I'm fishing."

"What's new?"

"No! You don't get it. What I mean is I'm fishing right now." Chris crossed an arm behind his head.

"What are you talking about?" The bowl slipped from my soapy fingers with a splash.

"My dad and I put tullibee nets in the other day. We're going to check them this afternoon."

I tried to get purchase on the bowl and it slipped and clattered at the bottom of the sink. "I thought we were going to spend the afternoon together."

"Honey, I told you. Tullibees spawn only once a year, and now's the time to fish them. It's important to me. My dad and I do this every year." Tullibees, Chris had explained, were herring-like freshwater fish that required him and his dad to wade into a frigid lake with a fifty-foot fishing net. He thought that was fun.

I put my hands on my waist, remembering too late they were full of suds. "I wish you'd told me."

"I didn't know until this morning."

Chris went upstairs to get ready, and I scrubbed at the bowl even harder. There was a time when Chris wanted to spend all his time with me. Now, I rated below wading in a sub-zero lake. I wondered if this is what everyone meant about marriage changing a relationship.

Chris returned from the lake crestfallen because the nets were empty. I couldn't help but harbor a sense of bitter satisfaction.

The next Saturday, Chris stuck his head into my upstairs studio where I was working on the lyrics of a song. "We need to stop at Rice Lake today."

"Why?" I put my pen down and wrinkled my nose.

"I need to put the nets in."

"Can't you do that with your dad?" My finger traced circles around the spiral ring of my notebook.

"No, my dad's out of town." Chris paused. He seemed nervous. "So I'll need you to help me."

I turned toward him. My journal tilted and the pen rolled. "What?"

"I need you to help me with the nets. It's a two-person job." So, now he *needed* my company.

"It's freezing outside!" The weather was the bitterest of the year: windy, cold, dark. Snow hadn't come to stay yet, so the landscape was the crunchy tan of dried grasses and the dreary charcoal of leafless trees. Everything had a hard coating of frost, and the sky had been cloaked and heavy for a week. "Can't you wait for your dad?"

"Nope. I need to get the nets in this weekend. Won't it be great to have smoked fish for Thanksgiving?" Chris batted his eyelashes at me from my studio door. "Pretty please?"

I hated smoked fish. I leaned back. The chair groaned on my behalf. "Do I have to go in the water?"

"Probably not. But put on waterproof boots anyway."

I left my song half finished and padded to my closet to excavate the frigid-weather gear I had shoved behind the sweaters.

At Rice Lake, we parked Chris's father's pick-up on the side of the road. Meadow bounded out from the cab, all legs and energy. The wind made an eerie whistle across the water. The tang of winter—cold, woodsmoke, rotting ice—stung my nostrils. My nose started to run.

Everything within three feet of the lake was sheathed in thick ice. A hard wind must have blown, spraying the shore with lake water and then freezing it into a massive undulating ice sculpture. My foot slipped out from under me and I barely kept myself from falling. "I can't stand here, the rocks are too slippery." My front teeth ached with cold when I opened my mouth.

Chris said, "How about we try from the mudbank?"

I backtracked and stepped on hardened mud. Frozen grass crackled underfoot and poked into the sides of my boots. The edges of the lake were starting to crystalize; a shelf of ice had formed on the shallow water at the shore. I wiped snot on my coat sleeve and turned my face from the sting of the wind.

Chris cracked through the foot of ice shelf and waded into dark water a few degrees from solid. The lake slurped up the sides of his waders. I doled out net from shore, unrolling it from a forked branch. Meadow whined, water up to her knees. She wanted to follow Chris. "No," I told her.

Thick tubes of ice snaked across the shore where, a few months before, long grasses had rippled in the warm breeze. The icy pipes thickened the bent angles of grass and twigs into a pile of intestinal squiggles.

The lake was up to Chris's chest, an inch from the top of his waders. One false move and he'd be soaked. I held the branch up to keep the net taut. The slate sky pressed down, and the leaden water went on and on into the horizon. The mud under my feet was covered with the hardened memory of shoe treads made before the freeze. Ice filled the tiny inlet next to me.

Meadow leaped onto the ice shelf and started digging. A plate of ice broke off. Water bubbled up over it. Meadow lapped at it, then galloped across the shore in front of me and through the net, taking part of the net with her. "No!" I yelled. "Hold up!" I yelled to Chris as I untangled Meadow from the net. The fingers of my glove dipped into the water, and the insulation wicked icy wetness upward. "Okay. You can keep going."

Wind snuck through the spaces between the threads of my fleece pants. The tips of my fingers tingled with wet cold. The last of the net came off the forked branch. "All done!" I yelled. Chris secured his end of the net to the lake bottom then snake-walked through the water while pulling the loose end of the net toward him. Water poured off his waders. He walked the net parallel to the shore until it was stretched taut and secured the second end to the bottom.

"Am I done?" I called over the water, letting my branch droop.

"Yep."

Meadow waded into the water chest-high. I called her back to land, but she whined and shivered. She wanted to be with Chris. He called soothingly for Meadow to stay on shore. They were already each other's favorite. He couldn't get enough of her, and she wouldn't listen to me when he was around.

Is that what Chris would have me do, I wondered: stand in cold water up to my chest until he came back to me? Is this what the rest of my life in Minnesota would be like?

I circled on my heel, foot pressing for traction into frozen divots of mud. Leaving Meadow in the water, I trudged to the truck. I reached across the center console from the passenger seat to start up the engine and cranked up the heat as high as it would go.

When Chris returned to shore, I watched Meadow greet him from the rectangle of windshield, jumping and leaping, paws scrabbling at his chest. He tousled her ears, making cooing sounds, and led a shivering Meadow into the heated cab. Chris pulled off his wet waders with the door open, letting cold in. "Close the door," I snapped.

Chris leaped into the driver's seat grinning. My face had stiffened with the cold into a grimace of dissatisfaction. "That was great!" Chris said as he pulled out toward the road. Pique was coming off me in ripples large as waves. Chris didn't seem to notice. "Now we can fish in front of the fire," he said, turning left. Home was to the right.

"Where are you going?"

"I thought we'd stop to pick something up from my dad."

I made a sigh sound like a swear word. "I thought he was out of town, and that's why I was doing this with you."

"He was. He's back now."

The ice dam inside me finally broke, and waves of frustration poured out of me. "Do we have to do this now? I don't want to visit your parents today."

"It's just for a few minutes."

"It's never just for a few minutes. We'll go there, and you'll get caught up in something with your dad, and then we'll be there for dinner. I'm not in the mood for that."

Chris's foot eased off the gas pedal. "Why are you being so mean?"

"I'm not being mean," I yelled, then tried to tone my voice down. "I want to go home. I didn't want to come out in the first place. And I have a ton of work to do." I could hear the *clompety-clomp-whirr* of the heating fan, each revolution interrupted by a flicker of sound, a strand of dust caught in the vent, hitting the fan blades again and again.

"I don't understand you. You're always complaining we don't do anything fun, so I suggested we go outside and have an outdoor adventure. I know you never fished for tullibees in New York." Chris drummed his fingers on the dash.

I stared out at the empty fields, seeing for miles through the bare branches of the windbreaks. I willed myself not to cry. "This was not the kind of thing I meant." I flicked my head away from the window, my voice rising in pitch, speed, and volume. "This was fishing. For you. I don't want to go fishing. I have no interest in fishing. I want to go to the theater, to a good restaurant, to hear live music."

"We went to a concert at the Cultural Center last weekend," Chris said in tones of put-on calm.

"That's not enough!" My voice reverberated against the windshield, now showing a flat gray view of another flat gray lake.

Chris's chin lowered. "You are really cranky."

"No, I'm not cranky. I'm upset."

"You're always upset."

"That's not true! It's that I'm not getting what I need." I stared outside the window, looking for an exit in the gray-brown blahness of November landscape. The naked branches of the trees looked as vulnerable as I felt, arms reaching out in every direction for solace, finding nothing but cold wind.

Chris's shoulders moved up, then down, silencing his first thought and letting a better one emerge. "Well, what can I do to help?"

I whipped my head toward him. My voice was perched precariously on the edge between whine and yell. "Help me get what I need."

"I'm trying."

"Not hard enough."

Chris turned toward me, holding my gaze until I worried he would miss the curve ahead. "Honey, you visit the Cities all the time to get your city fix, and I don't complain about it. There isn't a lot of what you want around here. But we do what we can." Chris's voice took on the high tones of an adult trying to cheer up a child. "We attend concerts at the Cultural Center. We went out to eat yesterday."

"At the Eagles Cafe! That's not what I mean." The heat welled up around me, but my cold was bone-deep. "It's not enough. I don't know if I can keep this up." I tasted bile, felt mucous fill my throat. The bitter truth I had been trying to ignore bubbled into words. "I want to go back to New York."

The sobs I'd held hostage in my chest erupted. I was sobbing so hard I could hear my cries reverberate. Chris inhaled, then exhaled. His face drew shut, curtains across his eyes. My heart leaped like a caged thing trying to force its way out through the bars. By alienating Chris, I was pushing away the only comfort I had in this place.

"I hate it here." More sobs spilled out between words and I convulsed, vibrating like a frightened rabbit, air stuck in my lungs. I couldn't take a breath. I felt the deceleration in my belly as Chris pulled to the side of the road. Adjusting his body toward mine, he took my hand. His hand around mine was firm; he was holding me here, steady. I took strength from his grasp and looked up. Chris's brow was furrowed; taut and worried eyes stared into mine.

"I'm here because of you," I said between gasps of mouth breathing and snorts from my stuffy nose. Spittle spurted from my mouth. "I am willing to stay in this place I hate because I love you. But I need you to help me get a little more of what I need, or I'm not going to make it here." I wiped my nose with the back of my hand.

His face was a wasteland. He didn't know how to fix this, how to fix me. Neither did I. I dipped my head and stared at the muddy laces on my left boot.

"I love you, too," he said, his voice holding a gruffness I hadn't heard before. "I don't want you to be unhappy. I want you to stay here with me, and I'm willing to do what you need, okay?"

My sobs subsided from storm to flurry as Chris's words soaked through the pain in my temples. I nodded through my sniffles and looked up, expecting to see his distress eased. Instead, two stormy pools stared back at me.

He was scared. He thought was going to lose me.

38

Jerome's Death

I shall suffer
I shall weep
But your soul is no longer
Mine to keep . . .
When you go you take a piece of me
In the shape of you,
I give it freely . . .

– "It's Okay to Go,"
written for Lina and Jerome

November

I had lost touch with Lina and Jerome for a few months because Jerome was laid up with a lingering cold. Then the VA hospital diagnosed the cold as cancer. In the space of two months, Jerome went from under the weather to terminal.

I was in the kitchen preparing a sandwich when the phone rang. Lina's voice wavered, cutting in and out, phone cold against my cheek. Jerome wasn't going to make it to the six-month prognosis: the pancreatic cancer was killing him, now. I told her I was on my way. I ran up to my studio, slippers sliding on stairs, and grabbed my guitar.

I entered Lina's house through the unlocked back door, maneuvering my guitar case through the galley kitchen. The air felt heavy.

Floorboards whined under my feet. A rush of whispers and footsteps spilled from upstairs.

No one was downstairs. I waited for someone to come and get me, someone to tell me what to do. I sat down in the dining room and ran my fingers over the carvings on the large table. I took small, quick breaths. The house smelled old and stuffy. My eyes traced the slanted stripes of the dining room's wallpaper-reproduction fabric. Up and down and up and down, every direction askew.

Lina's cracked leather seat was empty. Jerome's fish platter was gathering dust on the sideboard. The hushed voice of the hospice nurse startled me. "You can come up now," she said. I unzipped my guitar case and went upstairs with her, holding my guitar by its neck.

The smell of sickness filled the dark hallway. Hobbled by shortened steps, I followed the nurse into a room I had never been in before. An oxygen tank whirred, inhaling and exhaling mechanically. Five sets of red-rimmed eyes turned toward me. Jerome's five sisters, whom I had never met, stared from mismatched chairs dragged from other parts of the house. Lina hunched by the headboard, forehead bowed against the mattress.

A mewling sound came from the bed. A body lay under sweat-creased sheets, twitching and jerking, naked, skeleton pushed up and visible through skin. Jerome's once joyful face had withered into a fright mask. Wide planes of cheekbone stretched yellow marks into his gray skin. His buoyant nimbus of hair had flattened into a greasy gray slick. His eyes were partially open, only the whites peaking through eyelids split like beetles' shells. A tube hung like a thread of spider's web from an I.V. to a portal cut into the bare skin of a clavicle.

My ears began to buzz. This couldn't be Jerome, that sweet, smiling presence of a man, the person I had come to love. This couldn't be the man who had found me an antique suitcase so I could carry my CDs from gig to gig, who helped me laugh at my experience of crawling into a ladybug nest in Chris's waders. My face buckled. Three weeks before, Jerome had looked weak, but he had looked human. Today, he was a twitching, moaning mass. I squirmed my facial muscles under control. I had the privilege of standing at Jerome's death bed. I was sharing one of Jerome's last moments before his metamorphosis.

My lungs were rigid. My voice caught. What was there to say that had any meaning, here, now? I couldn't find words, but I had songs.

I drew deep into my experience of countless hours on a stage to fake a sense of calm, and five sisters relaxed infinitesimally in my aura of control. Lina held Jerome's twitching fingers to her cheek. I strummed my guitar.

Jerome moaned.

My fingers staggered, and the guitar chirped to a stop. I looked around to see what the sisters would do.

No one moved.

Why didn't anyone help him? My head swerved around the room, to the sisters, to the nurse, to Lina still doubled over. Why did no one react to his sound of agony?

And it began to sink in: if no one was reacting, this must be the new normal. They had done everything they could.

I took another breath and vowed to give Jerome the best performance I had ever given in my life. My voice floated over finger-picked arpeggios. I sang, pouring every bit of myself into each note, each word, each musical flourish. Jerome moaned under my melody. But as I sang, his moans changed, at first subtly, then clearly.

Jerome was answering me. Every time I sang a line, he whimpered in response. He was talking to me in the only way he still could.

My music swirled in the shadows. Lina and Jerome's sisters sobbed in concert with my strums. Tears made snail trails down shirtfronts. Lina leaned toward my guitar. Jerome spasmed and mewled in time to the music.

I held out the final D-chord. A strip of light shone through a crack in the curtain and made motes of dust glow. Jerome's body quivered and eased as all the women beamed through their tears. I bowed to Jerome and left the house so the family could be alone with him. I called Chris to tell him what was happening.

A few hours later, a friend of Lina's called to say Jerome was worse—"He's not likely to make it through the night,"—and Lina had requested I come and play the same song again. I waited for Chris to return from work, and we drove to Perham together.

The dining room chairs were taken. I maneuvered my guitar past the cat fur-covered armchair where Jerome sat to watch his tiny television. People only spoke in brief murmurs. Chris and I perched on the large antique couch, holding tightly to each other's hands. I drew strength from him. Who would sit next to Lina now?

The nurse descended the stairs on light feet and signaled for Chris and me to come upstairs. The room was warmer now and smelled of feces. The top sheet was twisted in angry creases around Jerome's waist. Under the artificial light of nighttime, the skin on Jerome's bare chest was ashen. Jerome fussed, moaning, his body a collection of tics that were faster and more intense than I had seen a few hours before. Chris gazed at Jerome with love in his multicolored eyes. I waited stiff-armed with my guitar in front of me.

I knew the song that Lina requested might be the last music Jerome ever heard.

I was lost
I was alone
Blinded by the sunlight in my eyes
What I'd do for a night sky
If I could navigate by stars
I might see how far away I was
If the heavens could describe
What I can't see with my own eyes

Broken stars fall down
Pieces scatter to the ground
Closer to me now

They light my way
Maybe lost is on the way

I was scared
I felt abandoned
The map didn't match the road
All I could do was keep on going
Tried to remember what I passed
Rubbed the glare from the window glass
The compass led me astray
You gotta know where you are for it to guide your way

Broken stars fall down
Pieces scatter to the ground
Closer to me now
They light my way
Sometimes lost is on the way

I held out the final note and let it fade into the walls. Jerome's right cheek lifted. His mouth went crooked, the closest thing to a smile he could muster. Chris sat down on the side of the bed as close to Jerome as he could and, without hesitating, took Jerome's jerking hand firmly in both of his. "Don't worry, Jerome," he said. "We'll take care of Lina for you."

I blinked tears from my eyes and followed Chris to the living room. There were only four of us left now besides immediate family—Chris, myself, and two old friends, Rich and Tom. Minutes passed. A cuckoo clock rang the quarter hour. Then the hospice nurse barked urgently, "Girls!" Feet thumped on wood. Women's voices thrummed through walls. The four of us sat wide-eyed in the living room, not daring to speak, not daring to look at each other.

"The oxygen tank stopped," Chris said, voice strained.

For a moment, the house was utterly silent. No machines, no voices, no thoughts. Then the keening began. A wail, like the sound of a thousand locusts. Lina had finally come apart. The ever-competent Lina had finally bowed to the grief she had held at bay. Her lament was a siren pulsing into my bones. It went on and on, stopping only briefly when Lina gulped for air.

One of Jerome's sisters came down the stairs, face crumpled, to tell us Lina wanted us to come up and view the body. The four of us trailed her up the stairs, the sound of footsteps drowned out by Lina's howl. She was clutching Jerome's nearest hand in both of hers. Her body vibrated and pulsed. We scrunched together in the doorway, facing the bed.

The body was motionless. Its long limbs were bent and misdirected, its mouth open in a rictus of agony, eyes rolled upward toward the wall behind the bed. Jerome was gone.

Lina's wail stuttered as she noticed us. Rubbing Jerome's hand against her cheek, she whimpered, "He's gone. And he's taken a piece of me with him."

I put my arm around Lina, hoping the press of my strength into her shoulder would do what I had no words for. I stepped aside for Chris. He took Lina's hands in his, looked straight into her eyes, and spoke over her sobs.

"He was a great man," he said, pouring his voice into her like water. "He loved you so much. We will all miss him. We will take care of you for him."

Chris pulled Lina into his arms, and she fell against his wide shoulders, howl breaking into sobs. Together they rocked back and forth, Lina's shiny black bob against Chris's cheek. Her fingers clawed in his sweater. Her snot and tears leaked, unnoticed, into the curve of his shoulder.

A river emptied into my belly. Grief, and awe, and overwhelming love for Chris.

39

Hundred Miles to Nowhere

It's a hundred miles to nowhere
I feel the fatigue of the road
Sleep's always a few miles further
I can never lighten my load
– "100 Miles to Nowhere"

November

Four hundred and fifty people flowed through the streets of Perham to Jerome's funeral, and even more to the community benefit that followed at the firehouse. Jerome was supposed to be there—the event had been scheduled when Jerome was still alive to raise money for his medical bills. Instead, the benefit became a community-wide wake.

The volunteer fire department parked fire trucks on the street to make room. The supermarket and local restaurants donated food. Volunteers came by the dozens to barbecue hamburgers, warm the pulled turkey in chafing dishes, and serve stacked paper plates to lines of townspeople.

At 5:30 p.m., the cavernous building was packed. Sounds reverberated between corrugated tin walls and concrete floor, bouncing eddies of disembodied voices around the room. People balanced plates on their hands, waiting for space to free up at twenty extra-long picnic tables. A movie screen behind the lectern showed videos of Jerome when he had been vital and alive—parts of his life I hadn't had a chance to get to know. Jerome hosting his antique show for the local cable television channel. Jerome toddling around the stage in the local ballet school performance of the *Nutcracker*, gangly as a fawn. Jerome, smiling shyly behind large glasses, rings of reflection on the lenses hiding his eyes.

I filled a Dixie cup from a vat of too-sweet, too-yellow lemonade. Another industrial-sized plastic bottle had a handwritten sign: PLEASE DONATE TO HELP COVER JEROME'S MEDICAL BILLS. The bottle was already half-filled with ones and fives and twenties and motley checks.

The taste of musk filled my mouth. Until this moment, I had known without a doubt that a life in New York City was plain better than a life in rural, small-town Minnesota. But how many people would have shown up to my funeral if I had died in New York City? My head filled with the sound of rushing water, blocking out the voices in the room around me. I sipped the lemonade to clear my mouth and felt thirstier.

The town lawyer signaled to me from the lectern. I put down my sandwich and unzipped the guitar case I had stashed under the lemonade table. I pulled out a lyric sheet and walked around tables and people to the front of the room. Adjusting the microphone, I looked out. Hundreds of people looked back at me. Volunteer firefighters, city council members, mothers, children, teenagers, local business owners, antique aficionados, artists, plumbers, gardeners. An entire town full of lives Jerome had influenced.

I sang a new song, one I had just written, partially for Jerome, partially for Lina, and partially as the only way I could process what had happened.

When the song was over, I bowed awkwardly toward the image of Jerome on the screen behind me and left the lectern. The mayor told a story about Jerome's bashfulness at city council meetings, and I slunk to the table where I had stowed my guitar case. I loped outside with my guitar, swerving to avoid the few people I knew in the crowd. I huddled in the driver's seat of my car to grieve alone.

The clouds were heavy against the desolate brown landscape as I drove home. The whirr of the engine numbed me against feelings I didn't want to feel. I turned into 475th, and the two graves at the foot of my driveway jarred me back to the present. Jerome was now buried under his own headstone. I would never see him again.

The garage door had barely closed by the time I had hefted my guitar case through the oak-paneled den, past the library, and up the stairs to my studio. I dropped the guitar on the green couch and turned on my electric piano, barely understanding what I was doing. I plunked two hands on the piano in the shapes of chords. The notes rang out bell-clear, then faded. The harmonies disappeared into the stuffy quiet of empty house. I paused, hands hovering. I smelled the ozone of the piano's electric charge.

I forced my fingers onto the keys in random shapes. Chords surged around me, filling the desert of my room with rivulets of melodic life, gentle watery tendrils of sound eroding my hard shell. Without thinking, my voice picked up the stray end of a melodic thread. I could barely sense the note in the blankness of my insides, but I held on and pulled. My voice wavered and strained, and the words came out, birthed like Venus from the froth of sound. "*It's a hundred miles to nowhere, and nowhere's where I've been.*"

I started to tingle, and the wave of sensation moved up from my sacrum to the crown of my head, then back down to toes. The familiar thrill of songwriting soothed me, enlivened me. The glum ache in my gut quivered and released. "*It's a hundred miles to nowhere, and nowhere's where I've been.*" I sang the phrase over and over. My fingers surfed a progression of four chords that rang with mournfulness, sorrow, desire. I sang the words over top of the music, repeating the phrase that had come from nowhere to convey my pain. "*It's a hundred miles to nowhere . . .*"

The music pulled filaments of emotion from me like fine wisps of fluff from a milkweed pod. I let Jerome's memory grow into song. I let my fear of rural life flutter away with the feathery seeds. I teased out a stem of melody and wove. It was delicate work. I didn't want the melody to break off in my hands. I needed to tease the song out gently. I kept repeating the words, lyrics growing from my grief like shoots from seeds.

40

Hanukkah Party

From house of justice to house of worship
Secular to Jewish, civic to sacred
– "Courthouse Synagogue"

December

Poinsettias were blooming in a pot in front of the kitchen windows, a precious flash of color in the neutral white and brown that defined Minnesota at the end of autumn. "Hanukkah is starting on Thursday," I said to Chris over dinner. "Would you be willing to light the candles with me?"

"I'd love to." Chris grinned at me, then jumped up from the kitchen table and ducked into the dining room. The sideboard cabinet rustled, and Chris reappeared. The silver-embroidered dark-blue yarmulke he had worn at our wedding roosted atop the thinning center of his brown fluff of hair. He bent one arm in front of his chest and the other behind him and posed like a knight, waiting for his tribute. "Do I look Jewish enough?"

I laughed. "You look fabulous."

He relaxed his pose and patted the skull-cap more firmly on his head. "What do you think about having a Hanukkah party? Wouldn't it be fun to have our friends over to help us celebrate?"

"A party?" I hadn't considered inviting anyone else into my Jewish celebrations. It hadn't occurred to me anyone would be interested.

In New York City, I wore my Jewishness casually, without thought. Jewish people and culture were such a part of life that I could feel Jewish without expending any effort. Even my non-Jewish New York friends sprinkled their conversation with Yiddish words. Jewish-themed events were everywhere, so I didn't need to go to synagogue to feel Jewish, though when I wanted to there were synagogues of every flavor in every neighborhood.

In Minnesota, on the other hand, the nearest synagogue was ninety miles away. Judaism here was not ready-to-wear. I had to design the cut of my Jewishness, and then weave its cloth from bare thread.

"Sure," Chris said enthusiastically. "This house is made for entertaining, and we haven't had a party yet. What a great excuse! You could explain the holiday to everyone and they can watch us light the menorah."

Pleasure flickered like candle flame. I could create a Minnesota version of being Jewish by hosting my own Jewish-themed event and sharing it with my new friends, even if they weren't Jewish. "That's a great idea."

"Make sure you invite my parents," Chris said, still wearing his yarmulke as he started to eat. "They'd love to come."

"Are you going to take that off?" I asked.

He mimed confusion, then let his hand rise to the top of his head. "This?" He stroked the blue velvet. "Maybe not. I like it."

I called Chris's parents first. "I'm having a Hanukkah party on Saturday," I told my mother-in-law, Betty, who was in charge of the Christmas decorations for St. Henry's Catholic Church. "I'd love it if you and Ken can come."

"Gosh, that sounds like a nice idea. Do you need any help?"

"Thanks, but you don't have to help."

"It's not a problem." She laughed musically. "I'm happy to help. What can I do?"

I weighed the awkwardness of teaming up with my church-lady mother-in-law for a Hanukkah party against the benefit of her assistance. Her assistance won. "Do you want to help me make Hanukkah cookies?"

"That would be fun! How about I come over tomorrow?"

"Great. Um . . ." I tapped my fingers on the counter. "I've actually never made Hanukkah cookies before. I have these Hanukkah cookie-cutters I got last month when I was visiting my parents . . ." I had been overwhelmed by the mesmerizing number of cookie recipes in the *Good Housekeeping* cookbook. "Do you have any Christmas cookie recipes we could use?"

On Friday, I was bouncing along to Hanukkah music and setting out the dreidel-shaped cookie-cutters when Betty knocked. I opened the front door to a bracing chill, and Betty stood on the white veranda, which now blended into the white expanse of yard behind her. From her purse, she handed me a rectangular envelope and a sheaf of pages. I opened the envelope to find a Happy Hanukkah greeting card, one that must have required her to travel as far as Minneapolis to find. The sheaf of papers was a photocopy of her entire collection of Christmas cookie recipes. On top was a copy of a handwritten recipe card. "This one is the recipe my mother always made. We used to make it into little Santa Clauses and candy canes. It should work as well for dreidels."

Warmth rushed to my cheeks, balancing out the cold from the outdoor air. My culture and Chris's culture were finding a balance, too—we were going to use a Klein family Christmas recipe to make Hanukkah cookies.

Betty unburdened herself from coat and boots, and I fetched slippers for her. I bustled into the bright kitchen, lit up by a double abundance—the morning sun and its reflection off the snowscape. I gathered flour, sugar, and eggs and placed thrift-store ceramic bowls on the kitchen counter. Betty pulled a flowered apron from her cavernous handbag and set to work mixing and rolling and cutting dough into dreidel shapes. The smell of caramelized sugar started wafting out of the oven, and Betty showed me how to make cookie frosting with powdered sugar and milk.

"So what else are you making?" Betty asked. "What else do people eat for Hanukkah?"

I was mixing blue food coloring into the frosting. "Let's see . . . potato *latkes* with apple sauce . . ." My fingers were now sticky and blue. "Jelly doughnuts . . ." My chin itched, and I rubbed the back of my hand against my face. "Actually, pretty much anything greasy and sweet. The foods are supposed to help celebrate the miracle of light, representing the lamp oil for the eternal light that lasted eight days instead of one."

The timer rang and Betty pulled a cookie sheet out of the oven. The dreidels and Stars of David had turned golden-brown. She placed the pan on a trivet to cool. "You know, Ken was asking me what he might be able to help with. I think he might enjoy being in charge of cooking the la- . . . la- . . . What do you call them?"

"Lah-tkes." I tried to scrape the excess frosting off my turquoise fingers.

"Lah-tkes," Betty repeated. "Yes. I'll check with Ken, but I think he'd like to help with them."

"Seriously?'

She laughed at my surprise and continued rolling and cutting and baking. I kept poking at the cookies to see if they were ready to be frosted. A few minutes later, I gave up waiting and tried to frost a warm cookie. The frosting started at a consistency that was too thick to squeeze out of a pastry tube, but when it touched warm cookie, it went liquid. I gave up on the knife and spatula and used my fingers. Soon, sticky turquoise icing covered everything: my hands, the kitchen table, my apron. I even got some on Betty.

By the time she left, my kitchen was spotless, and I had two platters full of brightly colored dreidels and stars.

The next day, the phone rang. It was my father-in-law.

"E-lisa?" My parents-in-law always turned the first letter of my name, pronounced "Uh" by New Yorkers, to a long E. "It's Ken. I want to let you know I will be happy to help you make *latkes* tomorrow."

"Thanks, Ken."

"Are they like potato pancakes?"

"Um, well, they're a bit different. They have a lot of shredded onions and egg all fried up with the potato in a pancake."

"Potato pancakes," he insisted.

"Well, sort of. But they have a lot of grease and onions and eggs."

"They're potato pancakes."

I paused, phone pressing against my ear. "I guess so."

I prepared a vat of *latke* batter from onions and eggs and shredded potatoes. On the day of the party, I was almost done with preparations. I spent the morning designing a Happy Hanukkah sign with a Lite-Brite set I had bought at a garage sale. It took four hours to stick all the shiny little plastic pegs into the television-shaped receptacle—two hours to discover I could only fit up to the first "K" in Hanukkah, and two hours to pull out the pegs and reinsert them so the words fit.

At five o'clock, Ken arrived in his pick-up truck. He poked his head in my front door. "Can you open the garage?"

I went through the family room to the garage and pressed the door opener on the wall. Icy air flowed inside, and a ledge of snow fell from the roof into the garage. Ken backed his pick-up into the garage until its bed reached halfway in, then he got out of the truck and unloaded two sawhorses, a plank of wood, and an electric skillet. He pulled an apron out of the cab.

"What are those?"

"Things I need for frying." Ken tied the apron around his waist.

"Are you planning to fry the *latkes* out here?"

"Yep. This way it won't smell up the house."

"But it's okay, you're welcome to fry inside."

"No. This is better."

"Won't you be cold?"

Ken pulled a propane heater out of the bed of the truck. "Nope. Where's your electrical outlet?"

I pointed, and Ken plugged in the heater. In New York City, if the galley apartment kitchen didn't work, I would have ordered in. My handy, do-it-all Minnesotan father-in-law was setting up a portable kitchen in my garage.

"Can I get you anything else?" I asked as Ken pulled a stool out of the bed of the truck and placed it in front of his makeshift sawhorse-and-plank table.

"No, I'm fine."

When I returned to the garage twenty minutes later, Ken had removed the pick-up and closed the garage door. The propane heater glowed orange, and some of the chill had gone out of the air in the garage. Ken took a chef's hat out of his pocket and placed it on his head. He posed impishly in chef-readiness, doing a bit of business with his hands and the spatula. He was his son's father. "All right, I'm ready. Where's the oil?"

I handed him the Wesson, and the rich scent of fried potatoes and onions soon seeped into the house. Chris was chopping hot peppers at the kitchen counter for a mango salsa he decided to make at the last minute. I ran upstairs to shower and dress. As soon as my hair was coiffed into messy tendrils and my lips dressed up with lipstick, there was a knock, then the whine of screen door opening.

"Yoo-hoo!" called Sonja's voice.

I trotted down the stairs, to see Sonja's head inside the open door, her body still on the porch. She wore a blue floor-length sweater she had knitted like a royal cloak. David, her tall and taciturn husband, stood behind her.

"Come in, come in!" I met Sonja halfway into the house and gave her a hug that landed awkwardly while she tried to balance a rotund white ceramic jar with one hand and remove a black ankle boot with the other. A gold ring in the shape of a Jewish star glinted from her right index finger. I had become acquainted with Sonja through my writer's group and because she had been a friend of Jerome's. Sonja was also the only other Jew I knew of in west-central Minnesota. Her white-blonde hair, sky-blue eyes, and fair complexion gave away her origins as a Norwegian Catholic who had converted.

"Here." Sonja handed me the jar. "Homemade apple sauce. For the *latkes*."

I stood silent for a second, the jar round and substantial in my hand. Sonja was one of the few people in the area who would know what to bring to a Hanukkah party. I beamed widely and led Sonja and David toward the kitchen.

More people arrived, and the main floor of our house filled with friends. Ken popped out of the garage, chef's cap jaunty on his head, with another tray of completed *latkes*. I was brimming over with joy. "Ken, you're like a *latke* gnome who lives in the garage and brings out fresh hot *latkes* as needed." I stopped and played back what I had said: I had called my father-in-law a gnome. I steeled myself for reprisal—a dirty look, indignation, or worse.

Instead, my father-in-law grinned the wide gap-toothed smile his son had inherited. "I'm the *latke* gnome, eh?" He picked up the empty tray of latkes that had been picked clean of steaming, grease-glistening potato pancakes. "The *latke* gnome . . ." he muttered as he carried the tray into the now-warm garage to fill it up with fresh *latkes*.

Pam's shrill voice came from the open door and cut through the crowd in the foyer. "I made you a giant menorah out of one of the logs we cut down from our woods." Leaving Gary in her wake, Pam pushed through people removing their shoes and lifted up a large piece of wood, still covered with bark, into which she had drilled nine holes—eight for the days of Hanukkah and one for the leader candle that lights all the rest. Into each hole, Pam had stuck giant multicolored taper candles in the bright rainbow palette she favored for all of her artwork.

Pam waved away my thanks. "Mmmm . . . I smell potato pancakes," she said as she pushed past me toward the kitchen.

Lina knocked on the door. Her face was still pale and drawn, as it had been since Jerome had died, but her eyes held a hint of their old sparkle. "Happy Hanukkah," she said.

"To you, too," I said back. "I'm so glad you came."

"I wouldn't miss it," she answered.

Ken made three more trips out of the garage with *latke* trays. The guests devoured each tray-full as soon as it arrived. Betty was arm-deep at the kitchen sink. I found Chris talking to Lina and asked, "Do you think it's a good time to light the candles?"

"It's a fine time."

Ken arrived from the garage, bringing with him a blast of *latke* scent. I raised my voice to performance volume and called out in the center of the kitchen, "It's time to light the candles. Will everyone please join me in the dining room?" Chairs squeaked, and sock-covered feet shuffled on tile toward the dining room.

I took my place at the table, noticing the woven Jewish stars on the blue tablecloth Betty had traveled three hours to Minneapolis to get for me the year before. The menorah my mother had given me rested on top. Four candles stood tall in the menorah, three lined up from right to left and the leader candle on a pedestal in the center.

I raised my voice to carry through into the living room. "Thank you all for coming to help me celebrate Hanukkah." Everyone was paying attention, even the children, faces raised.

"Hanukkah is the festival of lights . . ." I told the story about the blotting out of the eternal light in the great temple in Jerusalem, and how a miracle caused one day of lamp oil to last eight days, long enough for new oil to be brought.

When the story was over, I handed out a sheaf of stapled papers. "I've printed out the Hanukkah prayers and some songs in transliteration. Please join in."

I lit the *shamash*, the leader candle, and began to sing. "*Baruch atah adonai.*" Voices joined me in Hebrew. I looked up. I knew Sonja knew the prayers, but Chris was also singing—he had been practicing. I touched the tip of the *shamash* to the tip of the first candle. "*Elohenu melech ha'olam.*" The two wicks kissed flames. "*Asher kidishanu b'mitzvotav.*" I lit the next two candles. "*Vetzivanu, l'hadlik ner, shel chanukah.*" My voice traced the flourishes on the last word, and I placed the *shamash* back in its slot.

Everyone joined in on the *Amen*, their voices swelling around me.

41

Shoot 'Em, Shovel 'Em, and Shut Up about It

(It's coming up too) fast
Can't turn back
Too late to break
Can't even fake it
Heading straight
Now it's too late
Wanna go home
Gotta stay on the road
– "Lean ito the Curve"

January 2009

The cold of the kitchen tile bled through the soles of my slippers. The Hanukkah party had been a delightful bright spot during the darkest, shortest days of the year, but the holidays were over now. Though I had managed to make my first winter into an artistic retreat, this winter, the novelty of my new life had worn out. It was just me in a too-big house echoing with Chris's absence and spiting me with the clutter and grime I couldn't keep up with.

These days, I sat at the breakfast table for as long as I could, soaking up every ounce of weak morning sunlight through the kitchen windows, trying to stretch the margins of my day wide enough to meet in the middle and shrink the stretches of time that weighed on me like shovels full of earth. I wasn't writing or composing much—everything seemed to take too much energy. I wondered offhandedly if I was depressed.

My studio faced west, and with the extended roof over the veranda, little light seemed to penetrate the French doors. Much of the day, it felt like a cave. I tried to brighten it with floor lamps and candles. I spent the day in sloppy clothes, uninspired to dress properly, balancing my laptop on a lap-blanket, reaching out to Minnesota venues to cobble together some future gigs for myself. It was hard to sell my music when I didn't feel very confident.

I returned to the kitchen to make myself tea, hoping caffeine might jolt me into productivity. The movement of a horse's head caught my eye out of the kitchen window. The big chestnut that should have been locked in the paddock across the street was digging a hoof into the snow, foraging for dried weeds on the side of our patio. The bay was doing the same by the remains of the day lilies. He lifted his long, fine tail in the air and relieved himself in steaming green clumps on my patio.

For a moment, I sat there. Incredulous. First Robin's infiltration onto my property, now the horses. I stormed to the back door. "Go home!"

The bay flicked an ear in my direction. The chestnut lifted his head and snorted derisively.

I ran at the two horses. They sauntered away from the patio and bent down pawing for grass. I ran at them again. They loped to the front yard and grouped at the fence line. I waved my arms, screaming. They looped behind me and grazed.

The sound of barking pulled my attention to the driveway. Two of the neighbor's dogs were running toward me—one was Molly, the Rottweiler, and the other was her stray German shepherd mate, father of her newest litter of puppies. I backed away.

I didn't care about being "Minnesota nice" any longer. I couldn't make Robin unbuild his house, or Vernon stop carrying loaded guns, but I could say something about the horses and the dogs. It was time to confront these neighbors, as "Minnesota nicely" as I could.

My car skidded on the ice at the curve in the driveway and careened forward. I hit the gas pedal and barreled past Robin's place, past the two tombstones, across the gravel road. The two dogs snarled and barked behind me. In the neighbors' driveway, Molly and her mate melted into the pack of their offspring—smaller pups from this season, larger teenage pups from last season—barking all the more viciously in their own territory, sound rattling my windshield.

Fury fueled me into the pack. I had to push the door hard to open it against the weight of dogs. I heard individual barks now, each with a frenzied edge. I smelled the musty funk of dirty dog. The air held the threat of something else, dank and rotten, but my attention was consumed by the dogs around me. They took turns lunging, jaws snapping inches from my legs. "Stop. Get back!"

They blocked my route to the front door. More dogs moved in behind me. Torn whiskers pricked through my pants. My world shrank into a small patch of mouths and teeth.

A small girl ran out of the house. "Stop," she said weakly. "Molly, stop."

I stood as still as I could. My voice was taut. "Could you get your mom?"

"She's inside." The girl didn't move.

"Get your mom." Dogs pressed into my legs. My voice sounded strangled. "I need to speak with your mom."

The girl stared at me.

I took a step toward the porch. A dog lunged, teeth bared. I tried to back up. Sharp teeth dug into my skin. I shrieked, "Get your mom!" Cold seared tears to my eyes.

The front door opened. A woman I had never seen walked onto the porch in a faded robe.

The barking stopped. The dog that bit me backed away. A couple of dogs sat down. Molly eyed me suspiciously, placing herself between my neighbor and me.

The woman clutched her robe shut at her neck.

"Hello." I tried for calm and friendly, feeling ludicrous in the midst of frenzy. I took a step closer to the porch. Molly growled. "Shut up!" the woman yelled. Dog sounds petered out. Half the dogs started playing with something behind the porch. A boy, older than the girl, came out of the house and stood behind his mother.

I checked my leg. No blood. I exhaled a sour breath.

I had never been close enough to the house to notice its details. The porch was sagging. Decaying cardboard boxes spilled their contents onto its pockmarked concrete. The torn-up sections of plastic house wrap made *thwapping* sounds against the side of the house. The yard had no grass, just dirt and mud puddles covered with empty potato-chip bags and plastic wrappers.

I forced my tone into a neighborly good humor. "Hi, I'm Elisa from across the street."

The lady spoke too slowly, wide-set blue eyes only half focused on me. "I'm Kelly."

"Pleased to meet you." I stepped over a black banana peel that had been ground into the dirt near an empty beer can.

The girl started talking. "The dogs are playing with the cats. They like to run and play. I like to play with them. I feed them sometimes. Yesterday the dogs went—"

In a dreamy voice, Kelly interrupted her daughter. "When we finally finish this house, we'd love to invite you over for dinner."

"You know one of your dogs bit me." I rubbed my leg, bringing the sting to the surface again.

Kelly let a beat pass, then waved her hand, pushing the subject away. "Oh, those puppies. They're such trouble." She pointed to her feet, clad in faded slippers. "I can't walk very well. I had to have my big toe removed in the fall. Diabetes."

Sympathy began to outstrip my frustration. "I'm so sorry," I sighed deeply, then continued with less force than I had intended. "I came over to let you know your horses are at our place again."

"Oh, dear. Those horses keep getting out!" She nodded her head as if to say that was how it was, and she wasn't planning to do a thing about it. "You tell them to go when you see them."

My adrenaline began to wane, the hint of a headache in its wake. "That didn't seem to work."

"Oh, just holler and chase them."

"How about I get your phone number in case this happens again?"

"I guess that works, too." She recited her number. "Roger," she yelled toward the door. She lowered her voice to speak to me. "Roger's getting dressed so he can bring back the horses."

A man opened the door behind Kelly. He walked around her and leaped down the three front stairs without meeting my eye. I thrust my hand out to him as he passed. "Hi, I'm Elisa."

"Hello," he muttered, shifting his eyes without making eye contact. Carrying a couple of halters, he headed across the gravel road and up my driveway.

One of the overgrown puppies was chewing on a fur toy. Another puppy took the other side of the toy and pulled with a playful puppy growl. A bone-white grill caught my eye in the midst of fur. It looked like a tiny ribcage. I blinked and looked again. I wanted to believe the puppies were playing with a slipper. The rancid-sweet smell wafting up with the light breeze registered. The cold had tamped it down but, this close, I couldn't miss the scent of death.

Kelly tracked my gaze. "What are they chewing on?"

The boy snickered. "A dead cat." The children moved closer to the puppies fighting over the carcass.

I was through the Looking Glass, where all the colors had faded to dirty-snow gray and the Red Queen really would cut off my head. I breathed shallowly through my mouth and tried to keep the horror off my face.

"Yeah, our cats died," the girl said softly. She pointed behind the porch, toward the sprawling swampy backyard acreage. A few more piles of fur were lying on the mud alongside empty cookie packages.

Ginger and white. Gray tabby. I pulled my eyes away. My cats would not be going outside in this neighborhood. Ever.

"I love this place." Kelly's words floated at me. "We have fifteen acres."

Behind the house, dozens, maybe hundreds, of full trash bags rested in messy piles. I hadn't seen them before because a slight rise in the land hid them from the road. From here, I could see that the bag mounds were at least six feet high and went left and right across the length of the yard. Trash spilled out through ragged tears and fluttered in the wind. Shredded black plastic blew and snapped. A soda can skittered across the yard and rammed into the broken fence.

My head began to throb. I swiveled away. "Oh, I almost forgot. Two of your dogs were at our place, too."

"Mmm-hmmm," Kelly hummed. "They've been stuck together. We have to wait till they're not stuck together to get them."

"Yeah, they're stuck together," the children echoed.

"Stuck together?"

"You know, stuck together . . ." Kelly's eyes widened with insinuation.

I stifled a shudder. "So, you'll have some more puppies."

"Oh, no, don't say that," sighed Kelly. "These puppies are so much trouble."

The boy said, "This one time, we had ten puppies, but eight of them died."

I imagined a trash bag full of puppy carcasses somewhere in the mountains of trash.

My mind spun as if I was trying for too long to speak a language I barely knew. "I have a meeting I have to get to. Nice to meet you."

"You too," Kelly called, as I navigated my way to the car through the now-docile dog pack.

I couldn't listen to music on my way to Perham. My mind was too full, my heart too confused over the contradictions that lived across the street from me, contradictions that were so much easier to ignore in a city. Compassion battled resentment.

I arrived at my writer's group meeting, nerves still jangling. Five local writers, including Sonja, ranged in age from thirteen to sixty-five and met in the library's community room every week. I started the story of meeting my neighbors and their dogs before I even sat down.

"You gotta shoot 'em," one of the writers said.

Sonja, added, "I'm a pacifist. But there's a reason people have shotguns around here."

"Yes, but I can't imagine actually shooting someone's pet . . ."

"They'd shoot your dog if it came on their property," the first writer said.

Another writer added, "I called the sheriff once about a dog run wild on our property. The sheriff came by and told me to abide by the rule of three Ss."

"What's that?" I asked.

"Shoot 'em. Shovel 'em. And Shut up about it."

42

Losing Home

Doors hang off hinges, keys got lost
Welcome mat faded and then got tossed
No one's there, just a note on the stair
"I've gone," but there's no one to care
– "No Vacancy"

March

I had been so buried in songwriting, performing, and—most of all—trying to find my way in Minnesota that I hadn't been back to New York City since my gigs two Junes before. I invited Chris, but he hemmed and hawed about a business trip he had to take, and by the time I bought my plane tickets, I was glad he wasn't coming.

"You know, it would be really nice if you didn't sound so pleased to be going without me," his voice bounced sharply against the bathroom mirror.

"You know, it would be really nice if you picked your clothes up off the floor sometimes," I responded.

He slammed the bedroom door and his footsteps thudded into the bowels of the basement.

I was desperate to return to the familiarity of the place where I felt most at home.

My pulse began to race at the roundabout that led to the toll booths for the Lincoln Tunnel. The bus coughed as it crawled downhill to the tunnel-entrance no-man's land near Teaneck, New Jersey. The skyline of Manhattan twinkled above the Hudson River. I leaned my forehead against the cool window to fill as much of my vision with New York as I could. Acrid exhaust fumes filtered into the bus. I inhaled sour air and closed my eyes in pleasure.

This was the reek of city. *My* city.

The bus sputtered through toll booths and entered the tunnel. The sunlight dimmed, then disappeared. Concrete walls surrounded us in the blackout before the show. The bus window pressed cool flatness into my forehead. I craned my neck to look beyond every curve for sunlight. I was aching to be in my city already.

As we drove out of the yawn of tunnel, the shadows of tall buildings on Eighth Avenue split the sunlight into parade streamers. My body rippled like the stretch of flags in front of the United Nations.

I was back. I couldn't take in enough. Look at all those cars. And the people on the street—all kinds of them, all colors, all different types of clothing and styles. I looked left and right. My body canted forward and back while the bus jerked with the traffic. The bus stopped at the corner of Eighth Avenue and Thirty-Fourth Street. The doors opened with a series of musical chimes. I shuffled into the aisle, moving with what seemed like speed, but people crushed me, pushing past on their way to the exit. I wasn't fast enough anymore.

I stepped onto the chewing gum-pocked sidewalk. I inhaled New York City: sharp scent of car exhaust, yeasty whiff of freshly baked pizza, ugly-sweet funk of rotting garbage. I had made it.

I was sideswiped by a fast-moving pedestrian with headphones. I turned to look, and I was jostled from the other side by a businessman in an Italian suit. *Oh, no.* I had become the hated tourist, standing still to gawk from the middle of the sidewalk while the real New Yorkers tried to go about their everyday lives. I moved to a clear area of sidewalk in the shade of a building. A hard line of sunlight cut across me, and the little man on the pedestrian traffic light glowed green. I entered the flow of pedestrians, stepped onto the asphalt, and was immediately overcome with confusion.

From the middle of the street—if I ignored the cars coming at me from every direction—I could see city, going left and right for miles, but I couldn't make sense of the commotion within inches of me. A bus exploded in a noisy burst of acceleration. A baby cried. A passerby rustled my sleeve. Horns were honking. People were talking and banging into me. Cars were trying to turn. I couldn't choose what to focus on, which sensation was the most important. I had lost my filter, the invisible city membrane I didn't know I had that used to keep out all the sensations I didn't need to pay attention to.

I looked down and followed the black-and-white zebra crossing like a map to the other side. I lifted my leg onto the curb and panted with relief. I shuffled to the subway entrance and grabbed onto the railing with both hands. There was too much noise, too much motion, too many people too close to me. All my senses competed for my attention. Everything blurred together. My city hadn't felt this unfamiliar and dangerous to me since the Twin Towers collapsed. I searched the horizon for the place where the Twin Towers used to dominate the skyline, the immutable landmark that oriented me to my city. Now it was just empty sky.

Once, on a road trip to Wisconsin, Chris and I had passed what looked like a dead bobcat on the road. We slowed to look at it more closely, and the bobcat rose uncertainly to its feet. It wandered in endless, aimless circles on the asphalt, unable to find its way off the road and into the forest, a few yards away.

I felt as disoriented as that bobcat as crowds of New York City pedestrians rushed around me, in and out of the maw of subway. I reminded myself of all that was in front of me for the next three days: dinners with friends, theater, museums, a visit to my favorite second-hand clothing shop, all the things I once loved. Renewed, I let go of the subway railing and wedged myself into the stream of people flowing down the stairs.

Over my long weekend in New York, I met old friends, visited my favorite stores and restaurants, and attended as much theater as I could fit in. Everything seemed awry, a little off, like I was seeing it backwards through a mirror.

During meals with friends, there was always a point in the conversation, after we had caught up on our adventures, where I felt the chasm between our lives. The museums felt crowded and overlarge, daunting, with too much to see in one visit. The shows I had tickets for ended up being duds. And the clothes I tried on were too flashy to wear in Minnesota.

My New York City friends—Maggie, Jae, Michelle—had moved on to lives that were increasingly unfamiliar to me, and yet I hadn't built a shared history with anyone in Minnesota. I was in-between, stuck in the middle of before and after, here and there. My time with friends reminded me that most of the women my age in rural Minnesota already had three or four kids. I was an urban artist, and the only people who seemed to understand me were the local retirees who had left the city for the quiet of the countryside. My alienation was strangely akin to the way I felt when I went on stage. Not stage fright, exactly, more like the lonely, one-sided pressure to create connection with people who didn't yet know if they wanted to connect with me.

I returned to Minnesota, resentful I hadn't had enough time to center my needle into New York's groove, sure that if I had only had more time I would have been able to rediscover my urban self and reclaim the love I had once had for my city.

43

Moonshine on Tour

It was simple to make a still in a chop,
Get a wash boiler with a copper top
Stick a tube on it in the shop
And weld the top to the pot
– "Moonshine"

April–May

Back at Oak Hollow, the vestiges of winter were holding spring at bay. The French doors remained closed against the cold air. My studio felt tight and claustrophobic. Dust accumulated in forgotten corners, and neither Chris nor I had the time or inclination to clean. When I ventured outside, I heard the sounds of Robin building an addition down my driveway.

I was glad to be leaving for a tour, this one of Minnesotan venues. I dragged guitar, amp, and drum down to the foyer, and placed them on a carpet that hadn't been vacuumed in so long it was hard to see the pattern under the dog hair.

Chris and I were struggling to rediscover the intimacy we had once shared. We hadn't been camping in months. We could barely find time to spend together what with his work, social life, and fishing trips and my music and travel. My trip to New York had further pounded the wedge into the space between us.

"Don't go," he said with exaggerated sadness, lips in a pout.

"I have to." I was short with him. I was focused on packing for the string of spring performances of my song-and-story show about Minnesotan oddballs.

Chris's tone shifted from cajole to grumble. "Leaving me again."

I let the mic stand drop to the carpet with a thud. "Do we have to have this argument every time?"

He crashed his coffee mug into the sink and left for work without another word, or a kiss goodbye.

In a small town in northwestern Minnesota, I stood in the wings, shielded by an angled black curtain from the locals attending this library-sponsored concert. The audience chattered in a wordless hum, and seats clattered as people sat down. As usual, by the time I stood next to the stage, all my body parts had gotten mixed up. My lungs were in my throat. My stomach was in my legs. My heart was on a trip down through the planks of the stage.

The emcee spoke complimentary words from the bio on my website. I couldn't identify with the person she was talking about. She said my name. There was a splatter of applause. It was time for me to go on.

I pasted my show-smile on my face.

The next thing I knew I was center stage, not remembering how I got from the wings to the microphone. The stage lights reflected in twisting amoebas on my guitar's glossy sound board. Time, too, stretched and compressed like images in a funhouse mirror.

The audience shuffled in anticipation, waiting to learn who I was, and decide how much of themselves they would allow me to touch.

I was breathing too fast to sing. I forced myself to inhale slowly. Kahea hung by her strap off my left shoulder, familiar as underwear, shielding the empty chasm in my belly from the audience. I stomped on the tuner to unmute the guitar. I leaned into the mic.

"Hello." My voice boomed through the half-full hall. The lights were so bright I could only see some shadowy body shapes in the third row—Minnesotans didn't like to sit near the front. There were a couple of muted coughs. The warm, tender bodies of people behind the shadows breathed en masse.

I pulled away from the mic and projected my voice to make the volume sound right to my ears. I introduced my first song, speaking too fast. I only just remembered to play a chord to give the sound technician a chance to make last minute corrections to the balance between my voice and guitar.

I didn't know what words were coming out of my mouth; I could only hope I was making sense. This early in a performance, everything is autopilot. Every one of my neurons was attending to the overwhelming sensation of being in front of an audience. I had one goal: to win the audience over. I depended on muscle memory to get me through the first couple of songs.

I let vibrations fill up my throat and spill out of my body. My voice resonated through the bones in my skull and then, a split second later, bounced back to me, a million times louder, from the main speakers on the auditorium walls. *Please, please let them like me.* This feeling was more familiar to me in Minnesota, repeating itself everyday in my non-performing Minnesota life.

An audience member laughed at the right spot in the song. My feet could feel the stage again. I caught up to where my body had been for the last few minutes. The audience and I were in conversation. I spoke with voice and guitar; they spoke with their attention, laughter, and, hopefully, applause.

The song ended in a long, held-out G, and I let my voice fade in volume a bit before I stopped the sound, catching it in my throat. I lingered in that expectant moment between when I knew the song had ended and when the audience caught on. Time stretched, then settled. Did they want what I had to offer them?

The clapping began with one pair of hands and was picked up by others, then the entire audience was applauding. I had been accepted.

The blessed sound of appreciation filled the room and the empty space inside me.

My in-charge performer's voice was already starting the introduction to the next song. This time, when my right arm reached to my music stand to adjust the pages, my mind had told it to move first. I started my spiel about bootleggers, tilting my head comically on my line about the mob. The audience laughed, and I sailed from the intro into an upbeat drinking song called "Moonshine" about a Minnesota bootlegger.

For the rest of the show, there was nothing but the conversation between the audience and me.

When the final applause died down, I stood alone in the wings again, behind the thick black curtain. The house lights rose. The spotlight was gone, and with it the tentative bond I had created. The audience transformed back from one into many. Red-velvet seat bottoms clapped up against red-velvet seat backs.

I metamorphosed in reverse, from fluttering butterfly to earthbound caterpillar. I was myself again, empty, with pain in the shoulder of my strumming arm. I knew I would carry the emptiness with me to a lumpy bed in a sterile hotel room. I hoped checking in wouldn't take too long.

When the audience had gone, I returned to the stage to pack up my equipment. I was doubled over my guitar case when a tenor voice said, "Have you ever tried moonshine?"

I caught a whiff of Aqua Velva. I snapped my head up to see a man with faded hair and thin freckled skin standing by the stage.

"No, actually, I haven't." I grinned my automatic thousand-watt performer's smile. I flipped the switch in my head back from roadie to performer. "I'd love to try moonshine. I've never had the chance." Interacting with audience members after a show always involved walking the tightrope between too little intimacy and too much. I stuck my right hand out. This was my post-performance habit I'd developed to make myself more at ease and remind the audience member that, despite how well he thinks he knows me from the stage, I don't yet know him. "I'm Elisa."

"Richard," he said over a firm handshake.

I turned to close my guitar case, relieved that Richard didn't seem like one of the creepy audience types.

"That's too bad," Richard said. I finished latching the case. He was grinning mischievously. "My friend makes moonshine." His voice rose almost imperceptibly on the word "friend." "If I had known you wanted to taste moonshine, I could have arranged something."

"Oh no! That is too bad. I would have loved a taste. Maybe next time I'm in town, you could set me up with some."

Richard heard the flimsy promise behind my words. His face dimmed.

"Thanks for coming tonight." Richard's footsteps echoed down the aisle. I folded up my music stand and slipped it into its nylon sleeve. I considered whether the sting of loneliness after a performance—with no one to share the slide from star to regular person—was keener than the loneliness of building a life in an alien place.

I was still chewing on that question when I pulled the backpack straps of my guitar case over my shoulders. I collected my check from the house manager and rolled my gear out to my car. The night air was sharp. I pulled the ache of cold into my throat and lungs. I was alone again, a stranger in an unfamiliar place.

There were no stars; the sky was the deep dull charcoal of clouds. I pressed my key fob, and the *beep-beep* of my car's response sounded plaintive in the empty stillness. My arm muscles strained with the weight of my gear as I lifted it into the trunk. I sat down in the driver's seat feeling too weary to turn the key in the ignition. I yearned for my own bed and the comforting warmth of Chris beside me. I still needed to check into the hotel. I started the car and let the quiet rumble of it vibrate into my tired leg muscles. Pulling out of the parking lot, I said goodnight to Chris's voicemail.

Two days, three performances, and two hundred country miles later, I backtracked across northern Minnesota to do another show in another town. Another trial of winning another group of people over. The rollercoaster of alone, together, alone was rougher than the ongoing loneliness of my normal life.

This performance was in the public library in the relatively large town of Bemidji, population 13,000. I found a parking spot close to the front door and steeled myself for the blast of cold, damp air after the comfort of my heated vehicle. Sleet stung my cheeks as I pulled one guitar case strap over my shoulder and wrestled the rolling bag Chris had given me for our first Christmas out of the trunk. I jogged to the library's front door, tugging hard on the plastic pull handle to get the duffle up onto the curb. The guitar strap dug into my shoulder.

The papery smell of worn books washed over me, reminding me of reading in lazy recesses behind bookshelves in my elementary school library. Gentle voices at the check-out desk blended into the soothing hum of heaters.

"Where do I set up?" I asked the library director, who introduced himself as John. He pointed to a large space between bookshelves where a mismatched collection of library chairs were arranged in neat rows.

I lowered guitar to floor with a carpet-muted thud. I rolled my head around my neck. It was time to bury my nerves behind the familiar routine of setting up.

I stood in the center of the space and tried to sense where I'd have the most presence in the room. I took a couple of steps toward the rows of chairs and imagined singing from there. Not quite. I took a half step to the right. There. Centered, commanding, neither too close nor too far from the audience. I clicked the mic cable into my Shure SM58 mic. I was winding the cable around the mic stand when John came up to my makeshift stage with a dented cardboard box.

"This is for you." My name was handwritten on a shoe-sized box over the library's address, and both were split in half across the open box flaps. A wad of crumpled newspaper puffed out at the gap. "It came in the mail yesterday, and I opened it before I realized it was addressed to you."

My practiced pre-performance smile faltered. The box felt light but substantial in my hands. "Thanks," I said, double-checking it was my name on the box. "I have no idea why someone would send me something here. What is it?"

John shrugged. "Dunno." He gave a perfunctory grin, then strode with quiet, purposeful steps toward his office.

I pulled at the flap. Tape snapped, and clumps of newspaper swelled out of the box. I pulled them out one at a time.

Under the third clump, green glass glinted. I reached in and tilted the object. It was a Jagermeister bottle the size of a hip flask. *Jagermeister?* I lifted the smooth glass bottle from the box, and its rounded edges fitted comfortably in my palm. The bottle was only half full. The liquid inside sloshed, glittering green. *Who would send me a bottle of Jagermeister?* I wondered. *An already-opened, half-empty bottle of Jagermeister?*

Chairs shifted and conversation rose. Audience members had started to claim the more comfortable armchairs. I had to finish setting up, but I needed to figure out the package first. I turned the box over and shook it, dumping out the remaining wads of balled-up newspaper that skittered across the table. Nothing else came out. I righted the box. At the bottom, stuck to the adhesive of the outer tape through a gap in the cardboard, was a folded piece of notebook paper. The two-line message was handwritten in spindly pencil. There was no signature. "This isn't Jaegermeister. Hope you like it."

I flashed back to my conversation two nights before, when the freckled man named Richard had come up to me after the show. *Have you ever tried moonshine?* Blood rushed to my cheeks. I unscrewed the dented metal cap and sniffed at the top of the bottle. The strong, clean scent of spirits burned my nostrils and filled me with the thrill of connection.

Richard must have figured out where I was performing from my website, found the address, packaged the moonshine, and posted it. By reaching out, Richard had plucked me from the touring rote of drive, set-up, perform, put away, drive, sleep, start over.

A stroke of ink in the line drawing of my life shifted, but I didn't have time to figure out how. The show was about to start, and I hadn't finished setting up. I stashed the package—box, note, newspaper wads, bottle and all—into my bag. I hooked my guitar cable to the library's amplifier and readied myself to start the show.

Introducing the song "Moonshine" in the middle of my set, I couldn't help but tell the audience about the moonshine I had received in the mail. They laughed at the story in which their own library figured.

I drove the hours home along dark roads with only the occasional passing headlight making me dim my brights. As I drove I examined the image of my life to find the small change Richard's moonshine had wrought. By reaching out to me, he had demonstrated what it took to create a connection with another human being: take the risk and give of yourself first.

Two hours later, I reached downtown New York Mills, where the kitchen lights at the Creamery coffee shop were still glowing in the blue-blackness. The door sign was flipped to closed and the main lights were off, but through the glass door I could see Cheryl cleaning up. My foot lifted off the gas and the car slowed. If I could connect to a random person at a gig, maybe I could also connect to some of the people in my own community. It was time for me to take my own risk. I turned into the Creamery's parking lot.

When I knocked, Cheryl smiled and wiped her hands on her apron as she came to the door to let me in. The room was warm and smelled like almond cookies.

"Hi," I said. "I saw the light on and wanted to say hello." I looked at the Jaegermeister bottle in my hands and lifted it up. "Actually, I wanted to know whether you would like to try some moonshine with me."

"Moonshine?" Cheryl asked.

I told the story of Richard and the moonshine in the warm, bright Creamery kitchen as the cookies for tomorrow baked.

When I finished, Cheryl reached under the counter and pulled out two Dixie cups. I poured. Outside the green bottle, the liquid was clear as water.

"On three," she said. "One, two, three."

We drank.

44

Holding

Hold on
Though there's nothing left within you
Except for that voice that says "hold on"
– "Hold On"

June

A few weeks later, I was sipping my take-out cup of Creamery coffee in my car when Chris's name appeared on my cell phone. We were still circling one another, like two alpha dogs forced into the same kennel, but after my music tour we had started to find a measure of solace in one another again.

I tried to disentangle the purse strap that had wrapped around my arm when I reached for the phone. "Hi, honey, what's up?"

"Where are you?" Chris's voice was sharp and urgent.

"Mills. Why?" I balanced phone between ear and shoulder to close the window.

"Tornadoes are on their way. Go home and get into the basement. Now."

The sky was as clear and blue as rock candy, and the sun was bathing everything in a happy yellow light. I looked out the window at the wide-open, empty, shelterless land around me. "Tornadoes? Are you sure?"

"They're saying half an hour. Go home and get into the basement."

I veered the car into a U-turn and headed home. I popped on the radio. The speakers shrieked with three ear-piercing buzzes that normally preceded the phrase, "This is a test of the emergency broadcasting system."

The radio announcer said something else. "Tornadoes are expected in sections of Otter Tail County . . ."

This wasn't a test.

The seatbelt dug into my neck. I accelerated, wheels careening across asphalt. Wind whooshed past. The car squealed into the turn onto 475th Avenue. Gravel skittered, leaping into the car's undercarriage in a clatter of high pings. The two headstones at the end of my driveway squatted menacingly.

Brakes screeched to a halt in the garage, I torqued the key and the engine whined to a stop. Four muted steps on concrete floor, then six hollow knocks up wood stairs. The door creaked open. My sandals smacked tile.

The house was the kind of pillow-quiet where all sounds are absorbed as if surrounded by gauze. The hush was as quiet as breath, almost too quiet to hear.

I veered around the kitchen table, banging a chair to a slant out of my way. My temples were so taut my ears whistled. I thundered out the front door and clicked the catch on Meadow's collar, dropping her long leash in coils on the ground. Meadow greeted me in an explosion of happiness. I fended off her hullaballoo of panting and tail thumping and pulled her into the house. It was time to get to the basement. I grabbed the two cats, one under each arm. They struggled, claws embedding into the soft flesh of my underarms. "Meadow, come!" I raised my voice, high-pitched and tight, over Sander's meowing. Tree hissed when Meadow got too close.

The basement movie room smelled like mold covered with the residue of old cleaning products. Meadow snorted, and Tree hissed wetly in response.

I sat on the couch and Sander climbed into my lap. As I cranked the radio to charge it, Meadow climbed her front quarters up on the couch to nibble on Sander's leg. Sander meowed and swiped Meadow's nose. The radio speakers ticked and whirred, then the red power light started to glow and the radio gave a whoosh of static. I whirled the volume knob down and tweaked the tuning knob to find a station.

It had been thirty minutes since Chris had called. I wanted to hear the "all clear."

I kept fiddling with the radio's tuner. Nothing—the basement was too sheltered. I circled the room to find a spot with reception. *There.* I moved back a step and toggled the tuner dial. To make out voices from the radio hiss, I had to hold the radio at a slant with my left arm in just the right spot.

". . . tornado passed through Amor, causing damage. No news on injuries. Looks like that tornado is heading north. There are three tornadoes south of Wadena also heading north. All after-school activities have been canceled . . . The weather advisory is for a tornado warning; this means tornadoes have been spotted in the area. Please make sure you get off the roads and into a safe and secure building, preferably a basement, immediately. If you are in a vehicle when you spot a tornado, get out of the vehicle and lay down flat on the ground in a ditch . . ."

My eyes stretched wide with adrenaline. My arm was hurting from holding up the radio. I put it down and tried to read. The lights went out.

In the room without windows, the dark was thick. Meadow barked at the sudden change, and the cats meowed and hissed, but behind the dog and cat noises was an eerie silence: none of the normal sounds of leaves and birds.

I clicked my cell phone on, and its backlit screen hurt my eyes. I reached for the flashlight I had put on the coffee table.

Meadow nipped at Sander. Sander yowled a low, plaintive moan. Tree leaped out of reach of Meadow's mouth, claws making a ripping sound on fabric, fur poofed out in an aggressive halo. He started, spat, and hissed. Meadow panted with the excitement of oncoming conflict and barked back. *Bark! Meow! Hiss! Bark! Yowl!*

Suddenly, the animals went silent.

I flashed the light toward them. Each leaned forward, as if waiting for something to happen.

Then the outside sound began, loud and insistent.

45

Tornado

Take me hard, don't give me time to recover
Take me hard, don't give me room to breathe
Suffocate me, in an embrace that cancels me
– "Take Me Slowly"

June

Afterward, people likened the sound of a tornado to the roar of a locomotive.

All I heard was noise.

My ears ached. My body vibrated. I was in a lake and the water was sound. The uproar was inside me. Sound and pressure couldn't be separated. Harder and harder the air pressed. Louder and louder the air thundered. The space in my ears swelled. My eardrums flexed inside out. There was no separation between sound and pain. Even in the enclosed basement, air was rushing, rushing. My eardrums were on the verge of tearing apart, stretched as thin as a membrane, a balloon blown up too much. They were going to pop. Everything was going to—

BOOM.

The sound reached a crescendo and exploded. My eardrums rebounded hard in the other direction. The pressure of the room ruptured, a reverse explosion into emptiness. The watery substrate of sound and pressure was gone; I was again living in air. I inhaled tentatively, feeling air enter my lungs and withdraw in a wave. The last bit of sound receded like the final flow of air from a balloon. The cats and dog were frozen in place.

This silence was quieter than any I'd ever heard. It was as silent as loss.

I sat motionless, scared to move.

Suddenly the animals were making noise again. Meadow was panting across the room after Tree. Sander was yowling. My cell phone rang. Chris.

"I think it just passed over!" I yelled into the phone.

"Is everything okay?"

I modulated my voice. "I don't know. The basement seems intact."

"Go upstairs."

I latched the door behind me to keep the animals back. At the bottom of the basement stairs, I hesitated, stomach leaden. What would I find? Besides Chris and the animals, my house was the thing I most loved in Minnesota. I had to know. I pushed myself forward.

The wood stairs were smooth under my bare feet. I rounded the turn in the stairs and heard a *shhhhh* sound from outside. The walls were still vertical. I sighed with relief.

"Everything okay?"

"No blowing air. I think the house is still standing."

The tile of the kitchen floor felt clammy on my feet. The daylight that came through the kitchen window was greenish, dim and diffuse. The windows were blurry with curtains of water. Sheets and blankets of rain. An ocean crashing down.

I could smell wet greenery. I rushed to the living room. The windows weren't broken, but they weren't passing light as well as they should. I moved closer until the blur on the windows sharpened and took form. Each pane was polka-dotted with shreds of leaves and bits of branches and crumbs of unidentifiable vegetation. My eyes traced the French doors from bottom to top. Water had been propelled with so much force through the tiny crack between the French doors that it had stained a fan shape onto the living room ceiling six feet into the room.

"What's going on?" Chris's voice was small and tinny in my ear. I had forgotten I was talking to him. The phone was moist from being held so tightly. My ear stung, flattened by the phone against my skull.

"I'm in the living room. The windows aren't broken, but I can't see out."

"You can't see out? What happened?"

I went to the kitchen and put my nose against the glass. I peered beyond sheets of water. "Oh, my God."

The solid toothy grin of green trees behind our house had been replaced by a splinter-toothed smirk. One-hundred-and-fifty-year-old oaks and maples had broken in half, their proud, leafy heads brushing the ground.

"What?"

"I . . . I . . ."

I ran to the front of the house and peered out the living room window. Silhouetted on a dark gray sky, once-vertical trees lay horizontal. A one-hundred-year-old basswood had fallen over across the driveway, blocking passage. An ironwood had smashed through the roof of Chris's Vanagon camper.

My lungs heaved into a moan.

"Honey? . . . Honey!" Chris's muffled voice came to me from behind a curtain. "What happened?"

"It . . . they . . . the trees . . ." I hiccuped.

"What about the trees?"

"Broken . . . gone . . ."

"What do you mean?"

My hand had cramped around the phone. "I don't . . . I . . . Please come home." The air in the room felt dead, unmoving. It smelled wrong.

"I'm on my way."

He clicked off and I was alone. In my strangely deadened house.

Meadow began to bark her intruder warning from downstairs. Vernon's gray Buick was in my driveway. I scrambled into a pair of shoes and opened the door.

Heat hit me in a wave. The day had gone from late spring to monsoon to swamp in seconds. Sun reflected on the wide expanse of my yard. I blinked. My lawn had become a lake. I took the porch stairs carefully and stepped ankle deep in water. My shoes squelched as I walked to the Cadillac.

His window was wide open. "Are you okay?" Vernon asked, stubbled cheeks paled pink, hooded eyes intense with concern.

I was so stunned by the new terrain, both inside and outside me, that the surprise of seeing Vernon on my property didn't even register. "I'm okay . . . The trees are gone."

"You should see your neighbors. The Erlund farm is flattened. All the houses down on 490th are gone." The grassy tips of our lawn jutted up from the lake, glowing neon green in the new sun.

What did he say? "Gone?" My throat was so tight, my voice was a croak. I pictured the road a half mile behind my house, the gray strip of road I could see from the upstairs bathroom window when the leaves were off the trees. I pictured the handful of modest, neat clapboard houses that ran along it, separated by barns and fields.

"They're all gone. The mobile home behind your house was picked up in the air and crashed into pieces in the field behind you. No one was in it, praise God. The houses south of the farm have only a few feet of wall left near the ground. All the trees for two miles were pulled out of the ground. It missed you by a few feet. You're incredibly lucky."

"Lucky," I repeated.

Vernon's thick hand rubbed his blue-veined nose. "When I saw the Erlund farm, I had to come out and make sure you were okay. It's a miracle your house is still standing." I turned toward the farm behind my house. The two gray silos with the pointy white roofs, usually obscured by trees, were visible, the trees in front of them flattened. The once-tall cylinders now ended a third of the way up in serrated wooden strips. Where the pointy roofs of the silo used to be was now only sky.

My knees buckled, and I locked them straight. I was twisted awkwardly in space, feet facing front, torso turned back. I untwisted my body and caught up to myself. Gratitude swelled in me for Vernon, his compassion, that he had even thought to check on me. "Thank you so much for coming. Thank you for being here." I couldn't stop, I was a skipping record caught in a groove. "Thank you for coming."

Vernon sucked at his teeth and shook his head. "What a mess. Glad you're okay."

I remembered, finally, that his house was just beyond mine and could have been hit. "How's your house? How's Robin's cabin and the house across the street?"

"Oh, everyone's houses there are fine. The tornado didn't touch anything west of you."

I thanked him again for coming. "Glad you're okay," he said again. "I'm going to go check if anyone over on 490th needs my help." Vernon waved out the open window and turned the car around, making ripples in the water covering my lawn.

I stood alone in a six-acre puddle and took in the upside-down version of my life. The garden fence, once vertical, was canted thirty degrees, crushing my tomato plants. Car-sized pieces of crumpled, corrugated tin littered my property like wads of aluminum foil thrown by a giant who missed the bin. I couldn't tell what the metal had once been.

Strips of tan had appeared between the red cedar planks of siding on our house—two-by-fours ripped right off the walls. The rooftop had buckled where the wind had pulled off shingles. The round vent cover from above the garage was in pieces at my feet.

Our stacked verandas were now galleries of modernist sculpture. All the outdoor furniture had been pushed to one side. A chair perched upside down on top of a table; a fishing boot hung from the upturned chair leg by its laces. An empty iron frame once covered with a glass tabletop stood uncapped next to a neat table-length slice in the white pickets of the veranda railing.

One bounce to the side, and my house would have been destroyed.

Black, oily bile filled my lungs. I couldn't breathe. My home had almost been destroyed. My home.

The feeling was unfamiliar, new, unrecognizable. Like the numb rubbery skin gone white under a wet Band-Aid: this couldn't be *my skin*, this couldn't be *me*. Minnesota was never supposed to actually become home.

I felt ripped open, as if the tornado had rent me in half like it did the two-hundred-year-old oak to the side of the house. Until this moment, until the trees were sideways and the siding was off, I was only halfway living in Minnesota. I had spent my time in Minnesota being only half present, keeping half of myself on hold for the inevitable moment, I thought, when I'd give up on this life. I had only been halfway committed to my marriage, convinced I was acting a role I could leave behind. The rest of me, the half of me I was too scared to show anyone, that part I had held in trust. I kept it to myself waiting for this moment, the moment when I was faced with a betrayal. And here it was. The tornado had come. The moment had arrived.

I wanted to run as far away as I could, to rewind the tape of my life and correct it. To speed backwards to before the letter in my Brooklyn stairwell, to before I applied to the New York Mills Cultural Center.

Because I wasn't going to leave.

My home was here. In Minnesota. With Chris. And it was well past time for me to commit to it. It was time I stopped believing, in the deepest recesses of my mind, that running away was an option.

This home was the only home I had.

I doubled over as if I had been sucker-punched. I put my hand on a white column to steady myself. I struggled to fill my lungs with the thick, syrupy air.

I couldn't get up and leave and return to New York City anytime I wanted. I couldn't give up on Minnesota. I couldn't give up on Chris. I could no longer cling to the idea of another me who lived in New York, who lived a life I could return to whenever I got bored of Minnesota.

Like a shard of glass slicing through my hand, like the glass tabletop that had frisbeed through the railings, so smooth and sharp that pain was an afterthought, everything was finally, irrevocably clear: Minnesota was my home. And all I wanted was for Chris to come home so we could fix everything together.

Part IV

Prairie Fire

June 2009–April 2010

[Oak] savannas were maintained historically through wildfires set by lightning or humans.

– Wikipedia

46

Grace

Grace only comes
When the moon hides the sun
When the mooring's undone
When the end has begun
She comes in disguise
She's the blow that blacks eyes,
She's the boat that capsizes
She's the riptide
But she gives you the urge
To emerge
From underwater
– "Underwater"

June

The bombshell of comprehension had exploded and left me in shards. I was numb. I held myself very still on the porch. I hunched my shoulders, feeling as barren as the whistling of the wind.

A glitch broke into the white noise roaring in my head. An engine. I stepped forward, desperate to see Chris. A white pick-up rumbled into view. Not Chris.

My father-in-law, Ken, stopped where the basswood tree blocked the driveway. "Are you okay?" he asked, getting out of his truck.

"I'm okay . . . But, the trees."

"But you're okay."

"Yes."

"Good. Let's take a look at the house."

Ken splashed toward the backyard. A piece of siding had fallen straight across the mud, like a plank footpath across a swamp. Ken sloshed around it. "After seeing those trees, it's incredible how well the house stood up." He shook his head and gave a morose chuckle. "You're very lucky."

I nodded and felt the bite of danger catch up to me like the unexpected cold of a lake after jumping in.

"I'm gonna clear the driveway." Ken lifted a chainsaw from his pick-up bed. I traded my weight from leg to leg, and pivoted my head to take in the chaos around me. Trees were topsy-turvy, roots in the air, trunks gone diagonal.

I was as vacant as the eye of the storm, blank, empty, stripped, abandoned and left behind, stale as the scent of a house shut up for too long.

Ken aimed the chainsaw. I walked inside, hoping the house would provide me with direction, purpose.

The stillness of the indoors emphasized the blankness inside me. I went outside, then back in, always on the wrong side of the door. The buzz of the chainsaw cut through my skull, but couldn't penetrate the smog in my head. I punched my head with my fist a couple of times, hoping to bang something out of place enough to feel. It didn't work, but the pain of knuckle on skull was better than nothing.

My cell phone rang, and my mother-in-law's voice was chipper and no-nonsense. "I'm on my way. I'm bringing pizza."

Another car sounded on the driveway and I glued my eyes to the curve. *Please let it be Chris.* His sedan pulled into view. I heaved with relief and ran off the porch to the driveway, my feet splashing across the lake of lawn. I wanted to throw myself into him, curl up under the protective umbrella of his arms. I stopped short.

Chris was out of his car and staring at the Volkswagen Vanagon, his lips a tight line. Esmeralda—where I had first tasted home with Chris—was broken, split in two by the spine of a tree that bisected the roof.

Chris waded closer. "I think it's totaled." His face was pale. He was talking to his father, to me, to no one. I clutched his arm. He was as stunned as I was.

"Better the car than the house," Ken said, laying his chainsaw on the downed basswood.

"I can't believe how close it came," Chris said, talking just to talk, processing out loud. "Look at these trees. The tornado pulled them right out of the ground." He spoke in a rush, voice hovering between dullness and panic. He turned a slow 360 degrees until his eyes returned to the Vanagon and lingered on the crack in its white beanie of a roof. He had no spare comfort to offer me.

"It's a miracle the tornado didn't do more damage," Ken said.

"What did it do to the house?"

Ken led Chris to the backyard and pointed to ripped shingles and broken siding. Chris nodded. I stood aside, alone with my grief.

Another car rumbled up the driveway, I barely lifted my head, expecting Betty's Volkswagen. Instead, Robin's red Chevrolet pulled in. Robin exited the driver's side door. Kyle's small form emerged from the passenger side and scooted to catch up to his tall father.

Chris greeted them. "I'm glad you guys are okay. Can you believe this?"

Robin shook his head. "Quite a storm. Vernon told me the house was all right." He drew his eyes across the field of fallen trees. Kyle peeked out from behind Robin's leg, recognized me and took a step in my direction.

Chris said, "I can't believe how close it came. I mean, look at these trees. The tornado pulled them right out of the ground."

Robin repeated what Ken and Vernon had already said. "It's a miracle that the tornado didn't do more damage."

Chris nodded. I considered the state of the silos behind the house and noticed that the planks of siding that had been torn off the house were most obvious by how few they were.

Robin addressed his son. "Kyle, this is proof of the power of prayer." A breeze rustled the bunched-up leaves of downed trees, and Robin turned to us. "Kyle and I spent the last couple of hours on our knees in prayer. We were praying it would pass over." He turned his gaze to the blue, blue sky. "It did." Then he looked right into my eyes. "If you pray, God will listen."

I held eye contact, and my hand moved to my heart. I had been the subject of someone else's prayers, someone else whom I had started out resenting. "Thank you," I said, meaning it.

After Robin and Kyle had gone, Betty pulled up the drive. She hugged me and gathered me up in her wake, bustling around the kitchen, making order from chaos. Soon I was sitting at the table with a plate of pizza, inhaling the scent of oregano. The slice was warm and gooey in my mouth. Grease covered my hands in a sheen. After two slices, I put my hands under the kitchen faucet. It whined and a few drops rained onto ceramic, then no more. Facts moved into place with the speed of molasses. The water pump needed electricity to work. No electricity meant no water pump, meant no water. No water meant I couldn't wash my hands or flush the toilet. I wiped greasy hands on my jeans. "When will the electricity come back on?"

"I don't know," Betty said. "It might be a few days. Three tornadoes went through Wadena, and power is out across the county. You'll stay with us tonight."

Her words held the comfort of a blanket being tucked around me. We would stay with Chris's parents.

The afternoon was waning, and the light with it. I needed to pack before the sun set. I went up the stairs and into my closet. What did I need to pack for three days at the lake? I plucked clothes from hangers: a sparkly silk evening dress I hadn't worn for a couple of years, a formal velvet blazer that no longer fit. The thought, *underwear*, undulated through the mists in my head. I grabbed a handful from my bureau. *Will fifteen be enough for three days?* I couldn't do the math. I stuffed them all into the bag with a few more for good measure. The pile from the suitcase spilled onto the carpet. Evening dress. Velvet blazer. Underwear.

The absurdity hit me like the jolt of microphone feedback. The gears of my brain stuttered to life. The clothes were all wrong. I returned the finery to the closet and replaced them with T-shirts, shorts, and sweat-shirts. I kept adding more. Soon I had enough clothing for a month. I couldn't fit it all into the bag.

The daylight was dimming. I left whatever I couldn't stuff in, hoping I had something wearable. I lugged the bag downstairs by one strap.

A cat brushed my leg. I'd almost forgotten: the cats needed food and water. I piled dry food into the cat bowl till it overflowed. I stuck the water bowl under the tap, and the faucet moaned. *Oh, right: no water.* I raided the cupboards and pulled out the glass bottle of sparkling Pellegrino Chris had been saving. It fizzed and bubbled into the cats' water bowl.

At Ken and Betty's house, Meadow was relegated to the garage. I went upstairs to the guest room I had never stayed in because we lived so close. I lay down on the unfamiliar bed and stared at the ceiling, tracing imaginary lines across it.

"Why don't you take a hot bath before bed?" Betty's voice came from the doorway. She was an anchor, keeping me steady. I let her lead me to the bathroom, where I drew a bath.

Afterward, I curled up tightly against Chris's body. "Will it be okay?" My voice sounded small in the unfamiliar darkness.

"It's already okay," Chris answered, unconvinced.

We slept in a tumble of limbs.

On the third day after the tornado, I drove to Oak Hollow. A quarter mile past 475th Street the police had set up a barricade. A line of vehicles was parked along the gravel road, as out of place in our usually empty landscape as the fluorescent orange-and-white striped pylons blocking the road. Five cars idled near the blockade, spectators to the damage. The houses that nestled into copses of woods between corn and wheat fields were no longer there. Trees had been plucked up and dropped like discarded flowers.

Fear, dislocation, and submerged panic spilled out of the locker where I had stuffed them. I heaved a sob into my steering wheel. The sight of the lost houses had picked the scab of my protective numbness. Underneath was only sensitive pink flesh, not yet tough enough for air. I stifled my sobs and turned my car toward Oak Hollow. I reviewed the funhouse mirror of my memory of what had happened three days before. Facts and stray images warped and stretched. I couldn't recall what I'd find at my house.

The two graves at the end of my driveway were quiet today, cold and sober in the waning afternoon sun. I curved around the bend, gravel crunching, past the brambles and brush that blocked Oak Hollow from the road.

And then the house appeared. Underneath wind-pasted leaves and bits of branches, the remaining siding was red as licorice, the now-spotted white columns still tall and proud among the jumble of broken trees, crumpled hunks of tin, and fragments of buildings that littered the yard.

I inhaled and exhaled slowly. The black roof was polka-dotted with blank spaces where the shingles had been stripped off, but my house had survived.

We returned home the next day. I ran upstairs to my studio. It smelled like torn leaves and ozone, but it was waiting for me to pick up pen and raise my voice in song. I cradled my guitar in my arms and strummed a chord into the quiet of our absence.

At the kitchen table, I created a Tetris board of Post-its, each with a different post-tornado task. *Call the plumber. Find someone to fix the leak in the basement. Call the carpenter.*

On Saturday, a string of pick-up trucks rolled up our driveway and parked on the grass. There were neighbors I barely knew and friends

I hadn't seen in months. Every driver pulled a chainsaw and hardhat out of their vehicles. Meadow pranced from one visitor to another, welcoming everyone with licks and wags. Soon, twelve chainsaws buzzed in atonal symphony.

I assigned myself the task of clearing up the small branches and sawdust left on the lawn in the wake of the saws. I passed a rake again and again across a small section of grass, leaving stretches of litter and debris. An engine droned, and I looked up. Chris was driving an all-terrain vehicle, his legs spread-eagled around the seat, mouth stretched into a toothy grin. He whooped at me.

"What are you doing?" I yelled over the chorus of chainsaws.

"Bringing the wood to the woodpile. Isn't this great? Vernon brought it over to help us cart wood around."

"I thought you hated four-wheelers."

The hair that escaped his fishing cap was wind-mussed. His eyes opened wide enough to show whites. "I *might* need to change my mind about them." He revved the engine and whipped past with another whoop, trailer full of wood bouncing in his wake.

I picked up my rake and raised the scent of grass with my strokes. A strong arm stilled the rake handle. Gary Robinson said, "City girl's not so good with the rake, eh?" He chuckled and took it from my hands. He made sure, forceful strokes. In one pass, he cleared all the debris I had been raking at for a half an hour, and the grass sparkled like a cleaned emerald. He handed the rake to me. "Can't expect a city person to know these things, can we?" He cocked his head affectionately, letting me know I was the local pet city girl. I could live with that.

By the end of the day, the domino-fall of trees had been condensed into two cone-shaped heaps—twin pyres taller than the house, each with bright green leaves still fluttering on the branches.

After everyone left, Chris put his arm around me, and we stood together in front of the house that had survived. He kissed the top of my head. "When these piles dry out," he said, "we're going to have one hell of a bonfire party."

47

Isle Royale

I love to be loved as I love when I love
I'm gonna be loved as I love when I love
If you want to love as I love when I love
You gotta be loved as you love when you love
– "Love to Love"

September

By the time the roadside sumac had turned as red as Oak Hollow's newly repaired siding, the leaves on the twin woodpiles had dried into husks that crackled in the gusty wind. I paused along the driveway to imagine them ablaze and came to reflect on what had changed since the tornado.

I had finally committed to my new life and the man I had married. I could appreciate Minnesota for giving me the space to create the art I wanted to make. I had a home here with the man I had fallen in love with, but I still wasn't certain how to make my artistic life fit into my life with Chris. I was about to get some help.

Inside the kitchen, I pressed play on the answering machine. I was half listening when a man's voice said, "Congratulations." I pressed rewind.

I had been accepted to an artist residency in Isle Royale National Park, a remote, roadless wilderness island in the middle of Lake Superior where the only full-time residents were moose and wolves. I whooped out loud. Besides the isolated cabin on a mostly uninhabited island in the middle of a Great Lake, there was another unusual perk: Chris could come, too.

Chris was the person who had told me about Isle Royale—he had backpacked there years before and spoke about it in tones of awe. I couldn't wait to tell him he could go back.

He arrived home shortly after me, the back of his button-down shirt striped with car-seat creases like altostratus clouds. "What a day," he said.

"I know something that will make you feel better."

"Try me."

"I got a two-week artist residency on Isle Royale."

"Hey, that's great," he said, wilting into a kitchen chair. "You'll love it."

"So will you."

"Huh?"

"You're coming with me." I smiled impishly at him. "Only if you want to, of course."

Chris's mouth stopped half open. His inhale was an abbreviated gust. "I can come?"

"Uh-huh. And we get to stay in a cabin with no electricity and no running water and a pit toilet on a rocky point looking out on Lake Superior. And they give us a canoe."

Chris rose, his round face split wide by his gap-toothed grin. "I get to come?"

"Yup."

Chris rushed into the center of the kitchen and rocked me into a waltz. He sang a made-up song as our feet beat on kitchen tile. "*We're going to Isle Royale. We're going to Isle Royale. We're going to be artists on Isle Royale.*"

I giggled and tripped, my feet all a-tumble. "You're not an artist."

Chris didn't miss a beat. "*We're going to Isle Royale. We're going to Isle Royale. We're going to be an artist, and a fisherman, on Isle*

Royale." Chris pulled me into a fancy turn and dipped me over his leg, where I promptly overbalanced, pulling both of us down into a pile on the floor, laughing.

It took eight hours of driving and a six-hour cruise on Lake Superior to reach the ranger station, still two miles from the artist cabin on an island with no roads. A park volunteer took us on a thirty-minute motorboat ride over choppy seas to reach our retreat.

From the water, the island was magnificent. Jagged shores and cliffs were dramatic rock interruptions to a green expanse of forest.

At the far end of the island, on a thin spit of land, a hobbit house gazed at the boat out of rounded windows. We alighted from the boat at a dock. A narrow path traversed the rocky cliff into a circle of pine trees, where the small house waited. Inside, two willow-sapling chairs faced a stone hearth like a married couple.

The next day, we settled into a simple routine. Every morning one of us would walk two buckets down to the lake to collect water for the gravity filters in the kitchen. It became our daily waking argument.

"Your turn to get water," I nudged Chris. He rolled over and put his back toward me.

"Your turn," he mumbled into the pillows. Most days, I fetched the morning batch of water and then worked on my songs while Chris slept in and cooked lunch for us. Respecting my wishes, he didn't knock on the door of the room where I was writing until he had a steaming plate of lunch waiting for me on the wood table carved with decades of graffiti.

After lunch, we searched for adventures together on foot or by canoe. At dusk, I sat on a bench by the side of the house over a sheer cliff, watching Chris fish the mercury-colored water below me, the shadow silhouette of his body balanced on a sliver of canoe against a sky lit up with pink and orange fire. Some evenings, he convinced me to join him and paddle the canoe so he could concentrate on fishing. When he came back after dark with steelhead or lake trout for the next day's meals, we snuffed out the bouncy yellow flames in the propane lanterns and went to sleep in the double bed under the eaves.

On the first cold and windy afternoon of our stay, I fed logs to the fire I had built and read a thin, yellowed Agatha Christie mystery a previous artist had left in the cabin. Outside the windows, the trees flickered in the wind. Chris stepped out of the kitchen. Books rasped off the bookshelf and the weight of them dropped one at a time onto the mystery novel balanced in my lap. *The Elfin World of Mosses*, *Michigan Lichens*, and *The Mushroom Book*. Chris slid the Agatha Christie out from under the book pile.

"Time to stop reading," he said, closing the book.

"Chris!" I wailed, drawing his name out long and wriggling my arm out from the blanket I was using as a shawl. "Give it back!" I leaned the rocking chair forward and reached.

Chris placed the book, closed, on the table. "We're going on a field trip around the cabin to look for lichens, mosses, and mushrooms."

I groaned loudly. "I want to read. Give me my book. It's cold and wet and rainy. I've been looking forward to reading all day. I don't want to go outside. I want to sit here by the fire."

"You are always reading or writing. It's time to go out and do something. You complain now, but I know you'll like it."

I grunted and huddled deeper under the blankets, hip bones digging into the willow dowels of the seat. A gust of wind whistled into the cracks around the leaded glass windows.

Chris's tone hardened. "We're going to do this whether you like it or not." He added, as was his wont, "So, my advice is, you better start liking it."

I pulled the blanket off my shoulders and dumped it on the plank floor in defeat.

"Are you wearing your long underwear?" he asked.

I nodded begrudgingly.

"Good. Now put these on." Chris handed me a thick furry fleece pullover, a waterproof coat, and fleece gloves.

I rose with so much force the blades of the rockers clattered like a weather vane in a storm. I swiped the clothing out of Chris's hands and put them on, grumbling audibly. Doubled over to tie my hiking boots, I spoke to my feet. "For the record, I don't want to go outside."

"So noted," Chris said as he opened the rough-hewn wood door and held it for me. "But you'll be glad you did."

I made another multi-syllabic groan and pushed myself over the threshold and into the damp gray chill of the outdoors. The entire circle of pine trees was gilt in silver damp. Each plant, leaf and stem was covered with tiny globules of dew. Rivulets of water flowed along the footpaths. Chris held up the books. "Which one do you want?"

I took the lichens book and read from the introduction as we stepped along the narrow dirt path. "Lichens are a symbiotic relationship between fungi and algae." I skipped ahead. "Hey, did you know Isle Royale has more species of lichen than any other place in the United States?"

Chris didn't answer, but his bemused smile was light in the heavy air.

Once I started looking, lichens were everywhere, every version a new fantastical creature. Some carpeted rocks in swirls of orange, gray, and green. Some hung from tree branches like the beards of old men. Some jutted up from the ground. I knelt next to whimsically shaped Dr. Seuss lichen trees and brought my face as close as I could. I wished I could shrink us down so we could walk together through the elfin forest.

"Honey, look!" I yelled from farther down the path. "Reindeer lichen has fronds like antlers."

I had never stopped to pay attention to lichen before. I wondered how I might write a song about lichen. Chris knelt by a mushroom that looked like it came out of an Alice in Wonderland cartoon.

"*Amanita muscaria*," Chris announced, not even needing to consult the mushroom book under his arm. "Also known as the Yellow Fly Agaric."

We passed the outhouse and I held my breath to keep out the stench. I sprinted down the rocky path and sipped the cleaner air by the shore. It tasted of pine needles and rain-soaked leaves.

Our feet made satisfying clumping sounds and an occasional squelch and splash. The faint trail wound through dense wood, offering peek-a-boo views of big lake. We paused every few steps to name the lichens, mosses, and mushrooms we passed, giving our verdicts on which were the best examples of their species. The path ended in an old boarded-up cabin overlooking another bay, and we turned around to wind our way back to our cabin, our feet kicking large pebbles that tumbled into the lake.

Our cabin welcomed us like a warm bath, the embers of our depleted fire as orange as the lichen on the rocks. Chris stepped down to the kitchen to pour water from a bucket into the kettle, and I added wood to the fire from the pile by the door. When the flames were dancing again, Chris handed me a mug full of steaming hot chocolate. We sat together in the willow rocking chairs and let the heat of the fire lap over us.

The next day, it was storming, the wind so strong we could hear branches cracking and waves slamming into the point. The middle of the morning was dim as dusk, the sky dark as lead. Thunder shook the walls of the cabin. The park volunteer who had charge of us radioed to cancel the field trip we had planned for the afternoon. "Waves are forecast to rise to eighteen feet. You two ought to stay inside and sit tight till the storm passes."

I stuffed the fireplace full with wood and settled into my nest of blankets on the rocking chair to write. Flames spiraled around logs, surrounding them in yellow-blue light. Soon, orange flames licked the hearthstones.

Chris emerged from the bedroom dressed in fleece.

"Your turn to get water," I said.

"Didn't I do it yesterday?"

"Nope."

"How about the day before?"

"Nope again. I've done it for the last four days." I gave him a smug smile. "It's your turn."

Chris groaned. He pulled on a jacket, went into the kitchen, and hung one brown plastic water pail on each wrist. He minced out of the kitchen, holding the handles of the water pails up as daintily as a milkmaid. I kept my focus on my notebook. Chris detoured across the cabin to stop in front of me. In my peripheral vision he tilted his face to the side and pursed his lips like a princess. He posed with both buckets up in the air, right higher than left, one knee bent to show off an ankle. My eyes stayed focused on my notebook. Chris switched his buckets, so now left was higher than right. I stifled the giggles that wanted to bubble out of me and kept my head down. Finally, Chris skipped into motion, his feet prancing and lifting in a neat jig while he twirled the empty water pails in loops around his wrists.

I raised my head, smiling. Stifled laughter made my voice start with a snort. "Thanks for going to get water, honey. You're my hero."

Chris batted his long eyelashes at me, then leaped, with a leprechaun hop and heel-clicking kick, out the front door into the roaring wind.

A few minutes later Chris's footsteps sounded on the rocky path, now slower with the weight of the water. "Honey!" The screen door slammed. "It's incredible out there! You've got to come out and see."

"No. I'm writing."

"No, really, you have to come out."

I sighed exaggeratedly. "Honey, I went outside with you yesterday."

"And you loved it. But, really," his voice held awe. "I know you're working, but you're not going to regret this. You have to come see. This is something you can't miss."

Chris sloshed the water pails onto the kitchen floor and held my coat out to me. I lumbered out of the rocking chair and stuck my arms into it. Chris led me twenty feet down the rocky path to the small bay where we collected our daily water from Lake Superior.

Pine branches slashed through the air, but offered a modicum of protection against the storm. As soon as we left the cover of the pine tree circle, the storm surrounded us. Winds bellowed; waves crashed. The very earth vibrated. Sea spray whipped my cheeks to a chill and, before they could warm, spray-laden wind chilled my skin again. Waves piled into the small cove in attack formation, phalanxes of them driving toward shore. When the gray-green waves hit the rocks, they erupted in gushing columns of white spray.

Chris led me into a hollow between two boulders where we could hide from the bite of the wind. We had to yell to be heard. "It's amazing!" I screamed into the roar of air and water. Chris took my hand, and I turned to look at him. His eyes were as full as storm clouds, swirling with color.

I finally understood. As gale fused wind and water into a powerful, earth-shaping force, it was Chris who gave me the strength and stability I needed to reach higher and go deeper in my music.

The waters of the cove churned and boiled as if there were a giant flame underneath. Chris placed his hands on my cool cheeks and pulled me into his chest. He kissed me, the heat of his mouth like embers from the hearth. I kissed him back. An orchestra of elements buffeted our bodies. Waves crashed against rocks. We were artist and fisherman, and each of us was stronger when we were together.

48

Bonfire

Moose was a whale they say
Till the whale swam into
A shallow bay
And the ocean went away
– "Molly Spotted Elk"

October

After Isle Royale, Chris seemed better able to accept my artistic absences and respect my need for songwriting space.

Usually.

The door to my studio burst open. Chris erupted through it, eyes shining. "You won't believe it!" he said.

"Um, honey. I'm trying to write."

"No, you have to hear this! You won't believe what one of the kids from across the street told me when I was picking up our mail," Chris said.

"They're putting siding on their house?"

Chris snorted. "Not quite. But still good." His eyes twinkled. "Apparently, someone shot Molly."

"Seriously? That dog is gone?"

"Yep. And you know who I think did it?" Chris did a little skip. "Vernon."

I put down my pen.

"And because one of the dogs got shot, the neighbors have taken to tying up the remaining dogs out back." Chris closed notebook over pen, slipped it off my lap, and took both my hands in his. "And now," he said, pulling me up off the couch, "We are going to celebrate with a walk down the driveway."

I started to groan, and Chris gave me a look. I remembered the joy he had given me by leading me outside to see lichen and a wind-whipped cove in Isle Royale. I let him pull me up and followed him into the early evening.

The breeze carried the lush earthy scent of dried leaves and the promise of winter. Meadow trotted proudly ahead of us, balancing a six-foot branch in her mouth. I could hear the murmurs of the few deeply colored leaves that still hung on trees. Some of the trees that had been pitched sideways by the tornado had decided to continue growing despite their new diagonal trajectories.

In the dim light of the half moon, we stepped slowly down the driveway, keeping our footsteps quiet, listening to every nuance of night over the soft crunch of shoes on gravel. I could hear the gentle wheezing of my sleeves and the squeaking of bats that lived under our roof. A small creature made rustling noises in the grass. A train whistled over street crossings in town. It seemed like I could hear every sound in the night for miles, except barking.

The yellow glow of Robin's windows glimmered through the branches. His cabin seemed homey this evening, comforting, as if there was someone at the edge of our property who was looking out for us.

At the rock wall that signaled the beginning of the cemetery, I steeled myself for barks and the rush of dogs on gravel. Nothing happened.

"The dogs are cooped up." Chris whispered. He took my hand. We walked past the graves, silent and unseen in the dim and unearthly light of the stars, all the way to the end of our driveway. We turned back together, our pace slow, enjoying the renewed sanctity of our home.

A swathe of stars twinkled against a velvet sky. I could smell the dry clay of the road and the musk of drying leaves. Chris paused in front of the haystack-shaped pile on our front lawn full of tornado-felled trees. "We should have a bonfire party," he said. "It's getting cold. There won't be many more nights like this. How about Saturday?"

Saturday morning, we drove to the large supermarket in Perham for supplies. I opened the car door to a sweet perfume: lemon drops and licorice, fireballs and red vines. Perham had finally given me the scent of candy, the hidden prize at the bottom of the box. I closed my eyes and inhaled deeply.

We loaded our cart with groceries and went home to prepare for our guests. By evening, our house was full of friends and loved ones. Cheryl and Jack were there. Lynn, Pam, and Gary. Chris's parents. All the people who made up my new life. Guests stood around the counters and sat at the kitchen table. They piled on couches in the living room and the family room. They surrounded the barbecue and discussed the best ways to grill burgers. Kids played tag outside and swung on the tire swing. Even Robin and Vernon were there. I knew Chris had invited them as the neighborly thing to do, but I hadn't expected either of them to come.

Lina and Sonja arrived together. Sonja cradled a black, square plastic pot in her arms. In it was a small oak seedling. "To replace one of the trees you lost," she said as she handed it to me. A lump formed in my throat. I hugged her, long and hard.

When the sun set into a watercolor sky, Chris announced it was time to start the fires. Guests put on coats, pulled lawn chairs from vehicles, and set themselves up in a wide perimeter around the front wood pile. My fingers curled into my hands to fend off the chill of the October evening.

Robin stood talking to Vernon at the far side of the semi-circle of guests. I considered how much had changed in my life: once upon a time these men had scared me, had made me want to leave. Now they were guests, neighbors, people who watched out for us, prayed for us, and helped us when we needed help. People I never would have met in my old life were now essential parts of my new life. I waved at Robin and Vernon, and they waved back.

At the first woodpile, Chris lifted the gas torch, and it came to life in a stream of fire. He waved the blaze in the air and gestured maniacally over the front pile of debris. People laughed delightedly. He was a magician, maneuvering fire from hand to wood. Branches ignited in dancing orange fingers that turned into flame hands that shook and caressed each other. The whole pile caught, and fire towered above the roof of the house. It licked the sky and poured up from the ground like a geyser, scattering orange stars into dark-blue sky, melding into the orange remnants of sunset, until it seemed the entire sky was made up of our fire.

Later, in Sonja's photographs, I saw myself surrounded by fire, my body a black silhouette against heaving orange. My hands were on my hips, my hair blowing free behind me. I was standing tall, alive, flames glowing yellow-white through the Vs of my bent arms, lighting up my face to reveal a serene expression of homecoming.

After the party, Chris and I stood together around the remains of the fire that was still burning, a vivid red gem in a silver setting of ash. The Milky Way was the roof above us. We walked in quiet back to the house and went to bed, curled up together under the covers to watch the ruby glow from our bedroom window.

Two days later, the gray coals from the fires still smoked in the center of the perfect ash circle, twenty yards wide. I turned over the dust with a pitchfork and it rose into the air in a cloud, blowing on my pants and sweatshirt and into my lungs. I breathed in the powdery leftovers of my forest, and I imagined the gray circle transformed, surrounded by a white picket fence and full to bursting with native prairie flowers: pink butterfly weed, purple coneflower, yellow goatsbeard and yarrow, wild bergamont and trillium. My heart beat a waltz. Trees to fire, wood to ash, ash to soil.

Tornado to flowers.

49

Ice Sailing

If I jumped off the mountaintop
Gravity would make me drop
There wouldn't be any more to lose

When I get back to the mountaintop
I'll twirl around like a spinning top
Until my heart's been born anew
– "Mountaintop"

December

Cold bloomed under the insulation of my snow pants. I stood on top of a frozen lake, water solid as pavement beneath my feet.

"You first," Chris said. "Wind's not strong enough for the rest of us." Each of the three men next to Chris was football player-sized. It had sounded like an adventure when Chris told me his client, Randall, had invited us ice-sailing. "It's like sailing on water, but you do it on ice."

The surface of the lake was covered with thousands of delicately plumed crystalline formations, tiny ice feathers as dense as down. New York City was too built-up and too full of humanity to reveal Nature's whimsy like my new world did. Three shiny black tracks through the fairy ice garden led us to the iceboat, a surfboard on ice skates with a triangle of sail tacked to the top like the crest of a cockatoo.

"So you've never been ice sailing before, eh?" Randall's feet crunched ice feathers as he walked me to the cockpit.

"No," I answered. "But Chris promises me this is something too good to miss."

Randall chuckled. "That it is, that it is." One of Randall's sons steadied the boat. "Well, hop on."

My breath froze in a fog. A shiver started at the base of my spine and fluttered its way up to my teeth. I pulled up on the zipper of the long yellow down coat Chris had nicknamed "Big Bird." I wrapped my scarf up to cover my mouth and fastened my hood over my wool hat.

"Lie back on the cockpit, feet forward," Randall instructed, and handed me a coil of frayed rope that was attached to the rigging. The plank of the cockpit dug into my back, the sail flapped above me. I clutched the rope awkwardly between the padded thumbs and palms of my mittens. The men pushed the boat into the wind. Randall and one son ran on one side, Chris and the other son on the other. The boat soared forward. Feet thumped and crunched on the surface of the lake. Wind rushed past me. Cold slapped my cheeks. Skates hissed against the hard lake. The men let go. The sail caught the wind. I took wing.

As my skin tingled and sang, I inhaled the stannic scent of winter and tasted the metal of ice on my tongue. Cold made me numb and then set me on fire. I was flying. Weightless. Frictionless. I was pure and alive.

Whiteness was all around me: in the bright clear sky, in the solid water beneath me, in the ice feathers that covered the surface of the lake, in the hoarfrost that coated every branch and limb. The world was white, like a blank page, clear, empty, waiting to be filled. I was flying through possibility. Minnesota's winter was not my adversary, its cold not something to be overcome. Winter was a gift of time, of space, of clarity. I was flying across the lake, and winter gave me wings.

Too quickly, the breeze at my cheeks ebbed, and my momentum slowed. The boat eased to a stop. It was over.

I sat up on the wooden plank, panting with the thrill of flight. When the men caught up to me, Randall gripped my hand and helped me out of the cockpit. Chris led me a few steps away from the boat. "What'd you think?" he said.

My face was taut from smiling. My fingers tingled. "That was awesome." My teeth started to chatter, adding consonants to the word "awesome."

As I walked back to the shore on a cushion of ice feathers, each step left a perfectly shaped, feather-encrusted footprint on the hard surface of shiny black lake. I cast my eyes along the trail of footsteps I had made from the ice-boat. The mark was as vivid as graffiti. A black on white tag that read ELISA WAS HERE. Minnesota had made its impression on me from the day I arrived. Now, I was beginning to make my mark on Minnesota.

50

Finding Home

Concrete tempest on a rock-hard sea
Concrete cementing you and me
Concrete glistening from too much rain
Concrete leads me home again
– "Concrete"

April

The concrete of the Union Square subway platform was marked by the shoes and gum of millions of New Yorkers. I lingered by the subway wall map, its lines and contours as familiar as an old friend. When the train arrived, I slid myself into the spaces between riders.

A crowd soared past me through the jaws of subway stairs on the other side of the East River. I was half an hour early to meet Maggie in Brooklyn. My wheeled suitcase made a series of percussive *thwacks* over sidewalk cracks. As I sped up, it began to make the sound of a train, *chucka-chucka-chucka*. My suitcase blocked out the sounds of the city. I stopped walking, and my suitcase wheels fell silent. I closed my eyes to listen. Cars, trucks, people, conversation, music, banging dumpsters: the constant hum of my city—No, the constant hum of what *used* to be my city.

The spring air was warm, tempered to my skin. The sun made the back of my eyelids glow red. I opened my eyes and dropped my sun-glamoured gaze to the cement-scape, all color burnt white.

Young, fashion-forward urbanites strode by, their movements casual and quick. I started walking again and turned onto a side street. A chrome-lined coffee shop bordered a Korean corner grocery; a small black-box theater squatted next to a high-fashion boutique. I passed one of the venues I used to play when I lived in New York. I considered how hard it had always been to keep the attention of jaded New York City audiences. My Minnesota audiences, no matter how small, seemed so grateful to have me perform for them. Some of them even mailed me moonshine.

I confidently looked people in the eyes as they passed. Their eyes darted away from mine. I smiled to myself; I was turning country.

The air was filled with a mixture of scents: fresh bagels, the tang of Thai curry, the perfume of handmade soap. For a moment, it was all too much, and everything around me flickered like an illusion. I steadied myself against brick and concrete and decided to enjoy the overload: I was back in New York City.

I walked into an espresso bar and I was thrust back into life before Minnesota. The paint-muted walls were littered haphazardly with full-color postcards and posters of art events, plays, and concerts. The tables were full of artists and writers and technology workers staring into the screens of Apple MacBooks.

"Sixteen ounce, half caf, white chocolate mocha," I told the tattooed barista and wheeled my suitcase to an empty table. I sat down with a sigh of relief, my flatland-weakened leg muscles now buckling from eight stories of subway staircases.

I read table tents and people-watched until it was time to meet Maggie. My suitcase squeaked around chairs and rolled a *ratatatat* over sidewalk cracks until I arrived at the Brick Theater.

Maggie was waiting for me, yoga-sculpted arms outstretched, deep smile-creases in her cheeks. She enveloped me with taut limbs and tipped me backwards in a hug. She was six inches shorter than me, and twice as strong. Our greetings tumbled over each other in gleeful harmony. "Hello!" "Ohmygosh!" "It's so good to see you!" I followed

Maggie into the theater so she could give me a tour of the dressing rooms before her show started. We went out to eat a fusion dinner of Chinese and Cuban, then Maggie left me in the lobby of the theater to pick up my ticket. As I watched Maggie perform, I could see all the different Maggies I had known over the years—middle school Maggie, college Maggie, New York City Maggie—juxtaposed. I imagined I carried all my own layers in me too, the city Elisa and country Elisa right on top of each other.

After the show, we went to the cast party at a nearby bar with dark silk walls. A dozen actors and audience members traded philosophy and accomplishments over microbrews. This was the New York City I remembered: every moment an opportunity to meet someone new and engaging. Every moment ripe with possibility. But something was different for me now. I had never felt so free and easy here before.

I forced myself to remember how I used to feel. How I *really* used to feel. Sure, there had been flashes of brilliance, luminous moments, soaring escapades that would tower in my memory, but most of the time in New York City, I had felt left out of the flow of everyone else's lives. Now that this was no longer my life, I could finally enjoy it.

The next day I woke early to take the subway to Manhattan and visit my old friend Jae and her new baby. I tried to guess the stories of the mix-and-match people I passed—youths with multi-colored hair, a man wearing a black cape trailing two leashes attached to black Chihuahuas, a lithe woman with sparkles on her cheeks.

I buzzed up to Jae's new one-bedroom apartment in Midtown and we went for a walk on the Manhattan streets. She wheeled her baby in his stroller. This new version of my friend walked slowly and cooed nonsense to her baby. We'd both been changed. Life had moved on.

When we walked past the Flatiron building, Jae asked, "What do you want to do now that you are here? What have you been missing?"

"Hmmmm . . ." I made room for a pair of fast-walking men in suits and thought about all the things I had longed to do when I returned to New York City. I couldn't think of anything. I pushed harder into my memories. Still nothing. There was nothing I still wanted or needed to do. I had seen Maggie. I had seen Jae. I had gone out to eat. I had seen a show. What else was there? Once upon a time there was a world-class city full of things I wanted to do. Today, I was satisfied with catching up with Jae before I left for the airport. But Jae expected me to want something. Who wouldn't want something in New York City?

I dusted off my mental New York City map. I triangulated between the points of where we were at the moment, Jae's apartment, and the subway station I needed to get to. I had an idea. The memory of caramelized brown sugar and chocolate chips hit a millisecond before the name of the restaurant. "City Bakery. I would love a City Bakery chocolate chip cookie." The frisson of uncertainty between Jae and me disappeared now that we had a destination. We turned right, walked a block, and purchased cookies from a steel-and-glass counter.

I bit into gooey cookie and felt my body loosen with delight at the oozing chocolate and brown sugar. I opened my eyes. Somehow, leaving New York City behind had made it all the more satisfying. And now, I was ready to leave. New York City was my past. My present was elsewhere. Jae walked me to the subway. People swarmed around us. There were more people in Union Square at that moment than lived in my entire town.

"Do you miss this?" Jae asked, gesturing to the swirling masses.

I watched people move in random lines through the square, each vector representing a separate life with separate goals. A bus squealed to a halt in front of us and burped exhaust. I loved it, but I didn't need it anymore. "No."

Jae nodded. We hugged, and Jae wished me a safe trip home. I carried my suitcase down the subway stairs.

Boarding the plane to Minnesota, relief surged through me. The buzz of the engines lulled me into a waking half-sleep. Stray thoughts and sensations floated by like clouds. I drifted off.

The plane landed on a strip of black runway in the blue-white glow of a snow-covered Minnesota night. The plane doors opened onto icy tarmac. The passengers had to walk through the cold to get to the terminal.

I collected my luggage and located my car in the parking lot. My tires rumbled on the road. I had to will my eyelids to stay open. I steeled myself for the hour's drive home and picked up the cell phone to dial Chris.

"Sweetie!" he answered. Behind him, I could hear the clatter of dishes, and I pictured him in our warm kitchen with the turquoise countertops.

"I just arrived in Brainerd. I'll be home in an hour."

"I missed you." I could hear a note of fear creep into his voice, wondering if I would return from New York only to want to leave him again. "How was it?"

"It was good." I smiled into the phone. "I'm glad to be back."

"You are?" his voice squeaked.

"Yes, I really am."

"Oh." I heard the rustle of stubble against phone. "I didn't expect that."

"What do you mean?"

"Well, I guess I thought you might want to stay there."

The line crackled. I almost laughed out loud. He had actually worried I wouldn't want to come home. My laughter sputtered out before I gave it voice. I had once worried the same thing. "No, honey, I want to come home to you."

"Oh. Good!" His voice lifted in relief. "I can't wait to see you."

I turned onto the highway that would lead me home to the red-and-white sanctuary of Oak Hollow, and Chris. Between Pillager and Motley, I noticed the sky. It was velvet black, a midnight hue that skirted color and lack of color and played light off darkness. In a blue-blackness devoid of city lights, each cloud was outlined in moonglow. Rivulets of light ran through clouds like the braided waters of a river. The sky filled my windshield and every window around me. It was a canopy over me, welcoming me with its glow. It felt big and wide and American: vast with possibility, big enough to encompass all of me—my New York past and my Minnesota future. Chris and me, together.

This sky was my sky. And it held me in its embrace all the way home to Chris.

Reader's Guide

1. Is *Hundred Miles to Nowhere* more a story of finding yourself, choosing a path, having an adventure, or falling in love?
2. Every chapter opens with lyrics from one of Elisa's songs. Did the lyrics help set the stage for each chapter? How? Which lyrics resonated most with you?
3. How was Elisa prejudiced against Minnesota before she arrived? How did that change over time?
4. In chapter three, "Being the Artist," Elisa's first impressions of New York Mills include "modest clapboard houses," "a stop sign with a flashing yellow light," "a water tower . . . with the silhouette of Rodin's "Thinker" perched on a tractor," and "a tiny park nestled along the railroad tracks." She also notices the absence of things she expected: "no traffic lights," "no string of pretty little boutiques," "no pizza place." How would a visitor describe your hometown? What would stand out to them? What would seem to be missing?
5. Contrast Elisa's experience in New York Mills in chapter eight, "City Girl in the Country," with Chris's experience in New York City in chapter twelve, "Country Boy in the City." How is being a stranger different in New York City and New York Mills?
6. What advice would you give to someone considering a move from New York City to rural America? How about from rural America to New York City?
7. How does place shape identity? What about your hometown has influenced who you are or who you see yourself as?
8. How did Elisa maintain her identity while trying to fit into small-town life?

9. In chapter twenty-six, "Paper Ballots," conversation among the election monitors stops when unfamiliar newcomer Elisa walks in. How does your community interact with outsiders? Are there prejudices that could be overcome?

10. How does the theme of being a fish out of water play out in this book?

11. Name a situation when you felt like a fish out of water. How did you cope?

12. With which supporting character would you most want have lunch? Why?

13. In chapter twenty-eight, "Cursing," former New Yorker Lina says, "There's always more to do for the museum than I can get done," perhaps demonstrating more of an urban tendency than a rural one. Are you the same person no matter where you are? Or does where you live affect who you are?

14. Assume Chris and Elisa are asking you for relationship advice. How would your advice to them change from the beginning of the book to the end of the book?

15. In chapter thirty-two, "The Minnesota Horah," Chris and Elisa's wedding showcases the differences between the bride's guests and the groom's guests. What were the most significant differences between the two sets of guests? Did you notice any similarities?

16. Did your opinion of Elisa change from the beginning of the book to the end of the book? How and why?

17. In chapter thirty-six, "Hunting Season," Elisa writes, "The city energized me like a battery . . . Country life wore me down like water on a rockface." Which places and experiences energize you? Which wear you down?

18. In chapter thirty-eight, "Jerome's Death," Elisa poignantly describes being at the deathbed of her friend as a "privilege." Have you ever had a similarly terrible experience that was also a privilege?

19. In chapter forty-two, "Losing Home," Elisa writes fondly of her first sniff of some of the less-than-pleasant scents of New York City: "sharp scent of car exhaust, yeasty whiff of freshly baked pizza, ugly-sweet funk of rotting garbage. I had made it." What is it about the sense of home that transforms what might be annoying into something charming?

20. Elisa's first sense of home in the Midwest is her connection to Chris in chapter twenty, "Once Upon a Time in the Vanagon." When Elisa first returns to New York City it no longer feels like home, and it takes a tornado before Minnesota can begin to feel like home for her. What defines home for you? Can home be something other than a place? What needs to happen before your relationship to a place can change?

21. Which themes in *Hundred Miles to Nowhere* are universal to readers? Which themes would be most relevant to Minnesotans or New Yorkers?

Acknowledgements

I would like to thank the staff at North Star Press—Corinne Dwyer, Curtis Weinrich, and Anne Rasset—for giving me the opportunity to share my story. Corinne, I'm so glad you saw more in the story of my journey than I even knew was there.

Thank you, Krista Rolfzen Soukup, for being my literary publicist and cheerleader. Thank you, Chip Borkenhagen, for your beautiful cover image. Thank you, Corey Kretsinger, for your website design and music fellowship.

Thank you to writer and teacher Mary Carroll Moore, who edited two versions of this manuscript, and moreover, who took a songwriter with grand (and false) ideas about how well she could write prose and, through visionary instruction and hard truths gently shared, transformed me into a real writer.

Thank you to my fellow writers in Your Book Starts Here classes for reading, re-reading, and reading again to help me—sometimes painfully—learn how to write. Special thanks to Jan Child, Katherine Dering, Shelley Jerige, Ember Johnson, Mary Kipp, Laura Lively, Yvette Louis, Deb Nelson, Sharon Ornelas, Allyson Perling, Beth Rosenschein, and Linda Zlotnick for your suggestions, many of which made their way into the book.

Most keen gratitude to three fellow writers who started with me in MCM's classes and became dear friends and partners on this journey to book. Thank you, Leah Galle, for your sweetness and marketing prowess. Thank you, Welcome Jerde, for your straight talk, your compassion, your hospitality, your shared laughter, and your generosity of spirit and talent. And thank you, Ann Kempke, for sharing so many personal and writing adventures with me, for your family's hospitality, for endless conversation, and for reading more early versions and sections of my book, and more times, and fielding more desperate emails and phone calls, than anyone ought to have done.

Thanks to Gabe Robinson, who edited an early version of this manuscript.

Thanks to Sharon Harris, who copy-edited two versions of my book and who, with her words about the first, buoyed me enough to make a second.

Thank you to my beta readers Maureen Kenney, Amy Sobieski, Kelly Nelson, Mary Beth Baptiste, Maureen Hennessey, and Elizabeth Tannen.

Thank you, Jerry Mevissen, for trading writing at the Wadena McDonald's—it really does have great light—and all your encouragement and wisdom.

Thanks to all the members of the Jackpine Writers Bloc and the (sadly now defunct) Lakes Region Writers Network for being local stalwarts of writing skill.

Thank you, Sonja Kosler and Lina Belar, my first-and-always readers and dear friends, who fostered my first drafts, allowed their names and lives to be used to serve my art, continue to serve as my local writing group, and support me and my family by going well beyond the role of friends. You are family.

Thank you to the Cultural Center of New York Mills—all its staff and ,oard members, past and present, and the community members and grantmakers who support it—for bringing the arts to central Minnesota, for giving artists magical opportunities, and for changing my life.

Thank you, Annie Rollins, Wendy Deschene (both of whom allowed me to use them in this book), Kelly Nelson, and other Cultural Center artists in residence who helped me renew my connection to artists and reinvigorate my own creativity when I really needed it. Thank you to all the resident artists who come to New York Mills, for sharing your creativity with me and this community.

Thank you Jennifer Arno for embracing me as soon as I arrived, tucking me into your already full life, and being a patient and loving guide to rural Minnesota. Thank you Amy Sobieski for being my ever-loving confidant and cheerleader, and talking me through cultural dissonance. Thank you Vicki Chepulis for your never-flagging support in both my creative and personal life. I couldn't be a writer without you all.

Thank you, Maggie Cino, for being the companion of decades, who not only let herself be part of this book but also used her story-genius to help me understand how to build its stakes. Thank you, Michelle Solomon, Josh Kamensky, and Jae Gruenke, who will always be essential parts of my life, and who were willing to have some of their parts show up in this book. Thank you, Jodi Kantor, friend since infancy, for allowing yourself to appear in this book and for showing me through your beautiful relationship what could be possible in mine. Thank you, Jodi and Erika Meitner, for all your support and encouragement in my dual odysseys—one professional and one personal—these past few years.

Thank you to my Seriously Mysterious writing group for keeping me writing by fostering my mystery novel while I worked to get my memoir into the world. (Keep an eye out for my next book, a mystery, provisionally titled *Song of a Woodturner.*)

Thank you to the inhabitants of New York Mills and its environs—particularly Lynn Kasma, Pam and Gary Robinson, Cheryl Humbert, and Jack Monty—for accepting me as part of your community and inviting me into your lives. Thank you to the readers of local papers, for reading my fledgling writing efforts and using my columns as opportunities to start conversations with me. Thank you to my new neighbors and friends for allowing me to include you in this book.

Thank you to all my audiences and the listeners who support my music. You give me the chance to inhabit the world in the way I love most.

Thank you to Chris's family—the Kleins, the Pelkeys, and the Geronimes—who shepherded me into my new world with open arms, generosity, humor, and love.

Thank you to my family for your love, support, and for—without always understanding my choices—coming to accept them anyway

Thank you most of all to Chris, my fellow gallivanter, who understands that to be an artist's partner sometimes means sharing his life—and me—with the world. You make the world a better place. Your support for the arts, and most of all for my art, has allowed me to become who I am today. Thank you for continuing to reach across the cultural gap between us to help me be a better person—and artist—than I am without you. May we have many more adventures in life, family, and world.